CULTURE, PLACE, AND NATURE
Studies in Anthropology and Environment
K. Sivaramakrishnan, Series Editor

Centered in anthropology, the Culture, Place, and Nature series encompasses new interdisciplinary social science research on environmental issues, focusing on the intersection of culture, ecology, and politics in global, national, and local contexts. Contributors to the series view environmental knowledge and issues from the multiple and often conflicting perspectives of various cultural systems.

Upland Geopolitics

POSTWAR LAOS AND THE GLOBAL LAND RUSH

Michael B. Dwyer

POSTSOCIALISTS
UNiTE!!
11/22

UNIVERSITY OF WASHINGTON PRESS

Seattle

Upland Geopolitics was made possible in part by a grant from the Association for Asian Studies First Book Subvention Program.

This work was partially funded by the Indiana University Bloomington Office of the Vice Provost for Research and the Indiana University Libraries.

Publication of this open monograph was the result of Indiana University's participation in TOME (Toward an Open Monograph Ecosystem), a collaboration of the Association of American Universities, the Association of University Presses, and the Association of Research Libraries. TOME aims to expand the reach of long-form humanities and social science scholarship, including digital scholarship. Additionally, the program looks to ensure the sustainability of university press monograph publishing by supporting the highest quality scholarship and promoting a new ecology of scholarly publishing in which authors' institutions bear the publication costs.

Funding from Indiana University made it possible to open this publication to the world. www.openmonographs.org

UNIVERSITY OF WASHINGTON PRESS
uwapress.uw.edu

LIBRARY OF CONGRESS CONTROL NUMBER: 2021050722

ISBN 978-0-295-75048-4 (hardcover)
ISBN 978-0-295-75049-1 (paperback)
ISBN 978-0-295-75050-7 (ebook)

♾ This paper meets the requirements of ANSI/NISO z39.48-1992 (Permanence of Paper).

CONTENTS

FOREWORD

This historically grounded examination is situated in northwestern Laos, a region given recently to rubber plantations. Michael Dwyer argues that socialist and other successor states in postcolonial Southeast Asia played an active role in state consolidation of power over land. These activities across the latter part of the twentieth century have at times been discussed as "land grabs." Such land deals, and the consequent repurposing or sequestration of land, are better understood as a land rush that may or may not result in the kind of predictable outcomes that is indicated by the language of land grabs. This rush goes on, however, to generate wealth for national and regional political elites, influence over land-based economic activity for foreign powers and capital, and acute forms of dispossession for the rural poor. Thus, Dwyer offers a welcome focus on historical processes and regional particularity to shed light on these land-control projects, which are sometimes uniformly characterized around the world in the dramatic accents of land-grab analysis.

The politics of land control has long been a favored topic of study in environmental anthropology. Earlier work often examined the emergence of nineteenth-century and early twentieth-century colonial forms of exclusionary and monopolistic land zoning and use in parts of Asia, Africa, and South America, in the cases of forests, pastures, commercial agriculture, and floodplain development. Protected areas, biosphere reserves, and public-land designation became principal methods for nation-states to control vast stretches of land in the name of species conservation, natural heritage preservation, and promoting sustainable development in the later part of the twentieth century. However, the new land grabs of the twenty-first century, as they are referred to, seem to present a new configuration of both national and transnational forces, driven by land markets and food security scares, and they seem to have unleashed an intense wave of land dispossession for the rural poor and other marginalized communities in many parts of the world.

The initial spate of research on the global land rush, reported often in the pages of the *Journal of Peasant Studies*, focused most on the seizure of vast tracts of land and other natural resources by large corporations or sovereign wealth funds to provision a growing global extractive economy for minerals, metals, grain and fodder cultivation, and offshore industry.[1] Some more ethnographic work has led to finely observed accounts of the uncertain, often fitful, and locally variegated forms, cultural and economic, that emerge in struggles over land in the shadow of more global land commercialization.[2] Yet other studies have broadened the discussion to include land-control ventures responding to current environmental concerns, notably climate change.[3] In that sense, the politics of land control remains entangled in projects of environmental governance.

Through his study in Laos, Dwyer elucidates what he calls the social and spatial unevenness of dispossession from contemporary land deals. He finds that processes of enclosure operate on multiple time scales, perpetuating different waves of land alienation toward locally unsuitable and disadvantageous purposes—an approach well used also by Liza Grandia in her research on Guatemala.[4] Dwyer, in this context, situates the outcomes in Laos in legacies of the Cold War and in the tense relations between the United States and China as actors in Laos's economic development. Dwyer also pays attention to the role played by local government agents, illuminating the processes of population management and property formalization that variously facilitate or impede the realization of grand schemes that are posited on large-scale land control and conversion.

In addition to imperial and Cold War legacies and the role of different levels of government action, Dwyer also considers the variable ways Laotians are included as citizens, and the tenuous ways in which uplanders lay claim to social recognition and legal protection. Thus, the study distinguishes different layers of socio-spatial unevenness while revealing how the layers work across and through each other to produce multiscalar processes and understandings of land struggles and modes of expropriation. One of the signal achievements of the book, then, is to show how different levels of government work with and against each other to control the allocation of land to commercial and social development projects in service of different interpretations of the public good and local authority.

The Chinese-funded rubber boom in northwestern Laos is the initial field of inquiry for this study, which was conducted over a decade of place-based and broader research. Dwyer shows how the legacies of wartime resettlement, earlier forest management programs, and more recent state efforts to control local authorities shape current land policies in and around rubber cultivation. This work emerges then as a study in state formation, shifting strategies of land control by foreign and domestic actors, and the facilitation and obscuring of land transfers often too simply characterized as land grabs. As Dwyer observes, the apparent messy and arbitrary nature of the land deals is not a sign of chaos or anarchy, but part of the very process by which different agencies struggle to retain influence on outcomes that seem overdetermined by global capital or national governments. His approach is timely because this way of connecting land policy to state formation has emerged as a topic of renewed interest.[5]

Dwyer contributes an original, well-researched, clearly written case study of land politics, and thereby offers portable analytical frameworks for the study of land grabs—a growth industry, I might add—that include historical shifts in the constellation of geopolitical forces at work in any location and the imprint of these histories on contemporary land struggles. Along the way he offers some new conceptual tools, such as *the calibration of enclosure to citizenship*, the role of land deals in upland *population management work*, and the way that *formal geography* helps manage the legal optics of land control. In combining these, Dwyer stresses the importance of not simply discerning a process of enclosure getting underway but of studying how that process is legalized, managed, and presented as ostensibly imbued with some social purpose.

Tensions have often surrounded special economic zones where, too, large swaths of land are earmarked for foreign investment unencumbered by tariffs or social protections for local communities. Identifying similar frictions in Laos's upland hinterland, Dwyer reveals the fraught politics of shifting land out of local control and use without stoking widespread resentment and a legitimacy crisis in the government. In these parts of Asia, proximate to China, agribusiness—built around rubber plantations in this case—converges on mega-infrastructure projects. This amounts to the global integration of land and its productive potential as it combines with the influx of foreign capital and expertise. Ultimately new relations of dependence are forged in nations only recently released from the grip of European colonial domination and American imperial influence. Studies in the style Dwyer has devised will likely uncover such convergence and external influence on other continents. A similar pattern might unite these phenomena into what may be a global problem, but each case will require discovering the specific historical development of conditions that fomented and furthered a twenty-first-century land rush.

K. SIVARAMAKRISHNAN
YALE UNIVERSITY

ACKNOWLEDGMENTS

The bulk of the research for this book was conducted during a period of regulatory reform in Laos, when central-government institutions were taking a series of steps to address mounting concerns about large-scale land deals. Resource concessions had long featured in the socialist development arsenal, but the ramping up of land concessions in the boom years of the early 2000s created a set of distinctly new problems. The Lao government was pursuing numerous large-scale and often interacting hydropower, mining, and infrastructure projects, all of which demanded detailed and up-to-date knowledge of the rural social landscape. In such a context, worries about out-of-control concession-granting carried a mix of social, economic, environmental, and political dimensions. Numerous individuals and institutions—many connected directly or indirectly to Laos's newly created National Land Management Authority—welcomed me into this regulatory milieu. As my research interests overlapped with their work, they generously offered me unique access to study concession-making in practice, both on the ground in northern Laos and within the Lao capital of Vientiane.

For privacy reasons, I can only thank a handful by name of the many who helped me navigate this fieldwork setting. First and foremost, a few dozen anonymous key informants deserve my greatest thanks. Without them, the land deals, maps, and hinterland geographies that comprise the bulk of this book would have remained hopelessly beyond my reach. Jerome Whitington, who was himself in the field when I made my first trip to Laos, provided essential early help and inspiration. Numerous others, including Ian Baird, Andrew Bartlett, Khamouane Boupha, Charlie Carroll, Sean Foley, Yayoi Fujita Lagerqvist, Richard Hackman, Andreas Heinimann, Nick Hogarth, Chanthaviphone Inthavong, Melody Kemp, Souphab Khouangvichit, Stuart Ling, Chantha Luanglath, Pete Messerli, Garry Oughton, Khamla Phanvilay, Florian Rock, and Peter Vandergeest, opened key doors for me, both conceptual and practical. Fellow researchers Keith Barney, Antonella Diana, Glenn Hunt, and Weiyi Shi provided essential comradery and discussion in the field, while subsequent collaborations with Ian Baird, Naomi Basik Treanor, Cornelia Hett, Phil Hirsch, Micah Ingalls, Miles Kenney-Lazar, Juliet Lu, Vong Nanhthavong, Natalia Scurrah, Thoumthone Vongvisouk, Jerome Whitington, and Kevin Woods have improved my work in numerous ways.

The National University of Laos's Faculties of Environment and Forestry Sciences provided me with institutional homes away from home at key points, while a number of other institutions in Vientiane helped me contextualize and understand what I was seeing in the field through a mix of library materials and informal discussions with staff. These included the Asian Development Bank, CIDSE-Laos, German Technical Assistance, Helvetas, the International Union for the Conservation of Nature, the Japan Volunteer Center, the Land Issues Working Group, the Lao Department of Forestry, Laos's National Forestry Research Institute, the United Nations Development Program, the Wildlife Conservation Society, and WWF-Laos. Outside Laos, Texas Tech University's Vietnam Center provided a key source for archival materials from the 1980s.

At the University of California, Berkeley, the Energy and Resources Group provided an ideal home for the early stages of this project, allowing me the support and flexibility to learn slowly and deeply across multiple related disciplines. Nancy Peluso, Michael Watts, Jeff Romm, and Nathan Sayre provided an invaluable mix of guidance, inspiration, patience, and critique; I also learned so much along the way from Gillian Hart, Dan Kammen, Dick Norgaard, and Isha Ray. Nancy Peluso's Land Lab provided a forum to develop key ideas among a revolving cast of amazing scholars. Mez Baker-Médard, Catherine Corson, Dan Fahey, Derek Hall, Alice Kelly, Juliet Lu, Christian Lund, Johannes Stahl, Dan Suarez, Kevin Woods, and Megan Ybarra all read early versions of some of the material presented here, as did Sapana Doshi, Rozy Fredericks, Asher Ghertner, Tracey Osborne, and Malini Ranganathan. Thank you all!

The later stages of this project have benefited from my time as a researcher at the University of Bern's Center for Development and Environment (CDE) and the Center for International Forestry Research (CIFOR), as well as my time as a university faculty member in geography, first at the University of Colorado, Boulder, and currently at Indiana University, Bloomington. At these institutions, Rebecca Lave, Pete Messerli, Tim Oakes, Krystof Obidzinski, Scott Robeson, and Emily Yeh have each helped this project develop in crucial ways for which I remain deeply grateful.

I have also been lucky enough to workshop portions of this book in various stages of its development. The comments I have received, and in many cases the ongoing discussions I have had with the following colleagues, have been immensely valuable: Zach Anderson, Sarah Besky, Erin Collins, Jason Cons, Rodolphe De Koninck, Michael Eilenberg, Jamey Essex, Jennifer Fluri, Tyler Harlan, Cheryl Holzmeyer, Reece Jones, Julie Klinger, Jean Lave, Philippe Le Billon, Christian Lentz, Christian Lund, Ashwin Mathew, Duncan McDuie-Ra, Ellen Moore, Josh Muldavin, Galen Murton, Gustavo Oliveira, Jonathan Padwe, Nancy Peluso, Alessandro Rippa, Anu Sabhlok, Annie Shattuck, Melanie Somerville, Janaki Srinivasan, Yaffa Truelove, Yang Yang, Emily Yeh, and Wen Zhou. Special thanks go to Jun Borras, who read an early version of the text with graduate students in the Agrarian Studies Program at The Hague's International Institute of Social Studies; Jim Scott and K. Sivaramakrishnan, whose invitation and gracious hosting allowed me to present a version of what became chapter 5 at the Yale Agrarian Studies Colloquium; and Elizabeth Dunn, who generously read the full text as it was nearing completion.

At the University of Washington Press, Lorri Hagman and K. Sivaramakrishnan offered a wonderful combination of ongoing support and critical review. Likewise, two anonymous reviewers provided excellent feedback that has helped me sharpen the book's ideas as well as its execution. Ben Pease did an outstanding job with the book's cartography, which was often anything but straightforward, while John Crowley's photo editing worked miracles on images taken under less-than-ideal field conditions. Chad Attenborough and Joeth Zucco helped guide the manuscript through production, while David Hornik and Chris Dodge, respectively, expertly provided copyediting and indexing.

Funding for the research on which this book is based was generously provided by the Social Science Research Council (International Dissertation Research Fellowship, with funds from the Andrew W. Mellon Foundation), the National Science Foundation, the University of California, the University of Bern, Indiana University, and the Academy of Finland.

Portions of chapter 1 appeared in articles published in the journals *Political Geography* and *Territory, Politics, Governance*, while an earlier version of chapter 4 appeared in *Geopolitics*. Short sections of chapters 3 and the conclusion appeared, respectively, in the *Kyoto Review of Southeast Asia* and *Development and Change*.

For multiple reasons, my family will be happy that this book is done. My parents (all of them!) have been endlessly supportive of this project in its various stages, and in both my father Eugene Dwyer and my wife Annie Shattuck, I have models to emulate in disguising serious scholarship as good storytelling. With Annie and our son Rubin, I look forward to the next project, whatever that turns out to be.

This book is dedicated to the memory of Professor Khamla Phanvilay, *ajaan*, teacher, scholar, and mentor to so many at the Faculty of Forestry Sciences, National University of Laos.

NOTE ON LAO SPELLING
AND PRONUNCIATION

This book follows a relatively standard approach to rendering Lao-language names and terms into English. A few explanations are helpful up front, however, for readers not familiar with Lao- or Thai-language transliteration.

The word *Lao* can be used as a noun or adjective, but more often appears as the latter, as in "Lao territory" or "Lao people." If used as a noun, *Lao* refers to the language while *Laos* refers to the country.

A number of common place names (e.g., Vientiane and Luang Prabang) follow older French spellings rather than precise renderings of how they are pronounced in Lao (Vieng-chan, Luang Phabang). I use the conventional spellings throughout. I also split some longer place names into two words to help readers new to Lao geography; for example, Vieng Phoukha rather than Viengphoukha and Luang Namtha rather than Luangnamtha.

Lastly, a note on pronunciation. The letter *h* appears in many Lao words immediately after the letters *k*, *p*, and *t*. This stems from different but similar-sounding source letters in the Lao alphabet: the harder ກ (*k*) vs. the softer, aspirated ຄ (*kh*), for instance. For the present purposes, however, this *h* should be regarded as silent. For example, the words Phoukha and Namtha should be pronounced with hard *p* and *k* sounds (Pou-ka) and hard *t* sounds (Nam-ta), respectively.

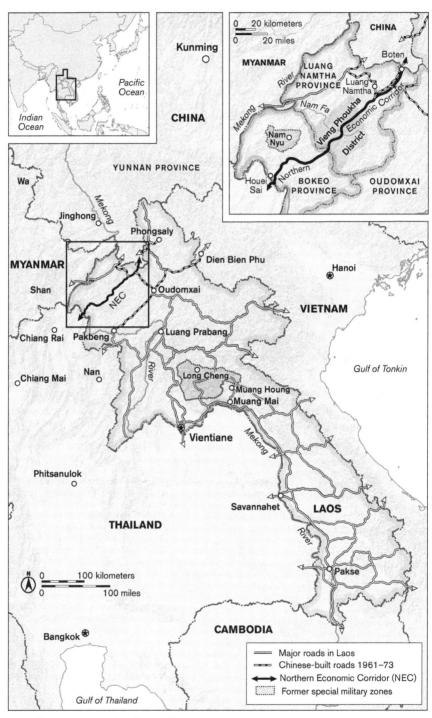

Key locations in the book. Map by Ben Pease.

UPLAND GEOPOLITICS

Introduction

Governing the Global Land Rush

A LARGE, hand-painted map greets visitors to the rubber-tree nursery just outside Vieng Phoukha, a rural district capital in northwestern Laos. Taking up much of the second-story wall of the nursery's main building, its title is long and formal: "Land-use map of the 3,000-hectare rubber planting promotion project, Vieng Phoukha District, of Bolisat Ltd., Yunnan Province, People's Republic of China."[1] Despite its size and prominent display, however, the map itself is easy to miss. Aside from its thickly painted title, little else is visible. Its thin black lines and faded yellow patches blend in with the weathered off-white background. The legend, lightly sketched out in the map's bottom-right corner, has yet to be filled in.

When my Lao colleagues and I first came across this map in 2007, it was barely legible. This was not simply because it was hard to see. Even when the image came into view, it was still impossible to *read*. Maps make sense because they contain symbols that tie or "index" them to the real world.[2] This map had no visible indices—at least none that our team, a research delegation from Laos's National Land Management Authority, could make out. The cartography itself gave few visual clues about what the various lines or patches might represent, and no obvious symbols for roads, rivers, villages, or prominent landmarks linked its faintly drawn polygons to the landscape around us. The missing legend didn't help either. It was as if the whole thing had been drawn to announce the project's presence without actually giving away anything about its operations.

Our confusion stemmed from the fact that we were seeing this formal geography of rubber plantation "promotion" for the first time. We were from Laos's national capital, Vientiane, and, for reasons I will get into later, we had few details about either this or other plantation development projects in the area. For us, the map thus lacked the meaning it carried for local officials and company representatives, who had seen the fleshed-out paper version in the local government Agriculture and Forestry office. They knew two things that we did not: first, that the map's lines represented the boundaries of local villages and land-use zones derived from an earlier generation of land-use planning maps (which we were not familiar with); and second, that the areas shown faintly in yellow corresponded to the roughly 8,400 hectares that, during this earlier process, had been zoned as agricultural land (*din kasikam*) in the map's twelve villages.

Because we knew none of this, we were limited to the sorts of inquiries reserved for unprepared visitors: What was the project doing? Where was it working, and with whom? How far along was it? When would the rubber trees mature? Had we understood the map, we might have asked why the project was targeting agriculturally zoned land for conversion to industrial tree crops, a violation of central-government food-security policy designed to prevent the replacement of food crops by industrial tree plantations. We might also have asked how the project was impacting local landholdings since, as we would later learn, the project's greatest conversions of food-production land to rubber plantations were in the district's poorest and most socially vulnerable villages. Finally, we might have pushed harder to find out exactly what project planners and local authorities meant by rubber plantation "promotion" (*songserm*), since later we would discover that this term meant different things in different places.

These were the questions that mattered. As it was, however, the map confronted us as an inscrutable black box.[3] Unable to open it, we could only ask the polite questions reserved for visitors.

REREADING TRANSNATIONAL LAND ACCESS

Over the last decade, the proliferation of transnational land deals like those my colleagues and I had been investigating has become increasingly recognized as a coherent, if complex, phenomenon. Sometimes termed a new "global land grab"—or more properly but less captivatingly, a new global land *rush* (since only some of the land targeted has actually been acquired)—the linking of individual land deals to a larger pattern of transnational land access entered public consciousness around the time of the 2008 global financial crisis.[4] Embodying a more explicitly interventionist, state-managed model of international cooperation, transnational land deals have generated concerns about land dispossession and foreign land access across the global

South, as well as more specific questions about the new geopolitics of development aid and infrastructure exemplified by China's rise.[5] As these concerns have remained current in the post-2008 landscape, they have helped re-center attention to geopolitics in the sense discussed by critical geographers and other scholars: as not just about geostrategic relations among states, but also about how land and the social relations that surround it shape the reconfiguration of political space, both sub- and transnationally.[6]

In the first decade of the 2000s, the economic and institutional linkages between agriculture, property, and finance deepened as sovereign and private wealth increasingly entered the global agribusiness arena.[7] This coincided and overlapped with the emergence of more explicitly state-managed approaches to development, taking different forms in different contexts but, in general, reacting to the social instability created by the dominant market-fundamentalist (or neoliberal) approach of the preceding decades. China figured centrally here, having embraced a more regulated form of state capitalism in the 1980s and 1990s and, with the turn of the millennium, having begun to mobilize its substantial economic power into state-backed foreign investment and development cooperation abroad.[8] This all came together in the buildup to the 2008 financial crisis, as private investors increasingly diversified into commodities as a way to hedge against stock market volatility, and a number of countries—worried about the effects of this hedging on their own commodity imports (both food and otherwise)—began to pursue direct land access abroad.[9] When GRAIN, an organization allied with the global peasant movement La Via Campesina, helped break the "global land grab" story in late 2008,[10] there was a sense among many people I knew in Southeast Asia that the rest of the world was finally starting to catch up with what had already been going on there for a few years.

Much of the initial urgency came from a public intervention by the director general of the UN Food and Agriculture Organization (FAO), Jacques Diouf, in late 2008. A few months earlier, in June, the FAO had hosted a Conference on World Food Security in Rome aimed at addressing the recent spike in global food prices and the associated wave of unrest across the global South.[11] At the time, Diouf had called for "innovative new solutions" to the chronic problem of agricultural underinvestment in the global South, including "partnership or joint-venture agreements" between, "on the one hand, those countries that have the financial resources and on the other, those that possess land, water and human resources."[12] Summer 2008 had seen the announcement of numerous transnational farmland deals across sub-Saharan Africa and Central, South, and Southeast Asia, mostly involving state-linked companies from across Asia, and often in the tens to hundreds of thousands of hectares each.[13] In October of the same year, in a widely quoted article on "The Food Crisis and the Wrong Solutions," Diouf used some very blunt language to clarify his earlier remarks. Criticizing these new land deals as "unequal international relations and short-term mercantilist agriculture," he worried publicly about the creation of "a neocolonial pact" for the provision of raw materials to the rest of the world.[14]

Diouf's comments circulated widely. It was one thing for the head of the FAO to advocate increased investment in agricultural development, and quite another to warn of an emerging neocolonial pact targeting poor countries across the global South. Lending official legitimacy to what might have been otherwise dismissed as activist concerns, his comments also helped cement an explicitly geopolitical framing onto the new land rush. Exemplified by headlines invoking "the new farms race" (Toronto *Globe and Mail*), "agricultural imperialism" (*New York Times Magazine*), and a "great land grab to safeguard [rich countries'] food supply" (the *Guardian*),[15] this discourse reflected the resonance of the new land deals with the land grabs of the late-colonial era. Decrying a new scramble for Africa and beyond,[16] many Western observers were particularly worried about the global rise of China and other emerging economies like India and Brazil; more than a few preferred to focus their concerns here rather than on the linkages to Wall Street and the 2008 financial crisis that also figured centrally in GRAIN's initial missive. *The Economist*, for instance, published a piece in May 2009 on "outsourcing's third wave" that wondered whether farmland might be the next logical step in globalization via comparative advantage. But in the same breath—and highlighting the tension between optimistic and more critical takes on the new land deals—the magazine readily rolled them into what it criticized as "Chinese neocolonialism" in Africa, described in a pointed example as "going down well with Mozambique's elite."[17]

Laos became caught up directly in this discourse. Barely a month after GRAIN's report and Diouf's article, the *Guardian* published a multipart feature with the headline, quoted above, about the "great land grab." This included a map based on GRAIN's data that purported to show over 7.5 million hectares that had been purchased by governments and private companies from South Korea (which had allegedly bought 2.3 m ha), China (2.1 m ha), Saudi Arabia (1.6 m ha), the United Arab Emirates (1.3 m ha), and Japan (0.3 m ha). The locations of this "world land grab" included Indonesia (1.6 m ha), Madagascar (1.3 m ha), the Philippines (1.24 m ha), Sudan (1.1 m ha), Pakistan (900,000 ha), Laos (700,000 ha), and Mongolia (270,000 ha); Laos's numbers, given its relatively small size, made it the most "grabbed" country shown.[18]

The feature also included a feature story from Laos, which was arguably the most important piece of the set since it helped ground the almost unbelievably large numbers shown on the map.[19] Echoing *The Economist*'s concern with national elites benefiting from foreign land deals at the expense of local citizens, the *Guardian* feature implied that Lao officials had abdicated their public duties and were instead giving away land to line their own pockets. "The situation is completely out of control," it quoted one foreign adviser in Vientiane as saying; "It's a fire sale. People in power are just desperate to get their hands on the money so they don't miss out. For the companies coming in it's a massive land grab." The feature also quoted a prominent historian of modern Laos, who described the situation as "simply a matter of greed. Officials are grabbing what they can. Companies need land and are prepared to pay well. It all goes under the table."[20]

These passages exemplify a common way of talking about transnational land deals. Using what I call an "authority gap" narrative, they examine the interests and motivations of companies and governments that seek land abroad, but focus exclusively on corruption and elite self-interest when trying to explain the actions of host states. The phrase itself comes from a 2010 story in the *Asia Times Online*, a widely read English-language media outlet in Southeast Asia, that decried what it termed "Chinese expansionism" across northern Laos, in special economic zones, corporate rubber plantations, and the growing (and allegedly underestimated) Chinese population in northern Lao cities. The article bemoaned what it called "the authority gap in a growing number of areas in the country where Vientiane has effectively ceded sovereignty to Beijing."[21] In this narrative, as in the other pieces quoted above, local elites and corrupt officials are the ones in charge: foreign land deals and actually *governing* are framed as mutually incompatible. The authority-gap narrative has a number of variants, including references to "weak governance"—a staple of the development industry—or, in some cases, "anarchic" or "frontier" development.[22] Whatever the language, the message is the same: "The situation is completely out of control."

Despite their popularity, these explanations miss a lot. First of all, they ignore the significant role of host states in creating both the legal and the economic feasibility for large-scale land deals. By conjuring a weak or absent state, authority-gap narratives ignore the histories of progressively stronger state ownership of rural hinterlands, first during the colonial era and, more recently, by newly independent countries of the global South, whose nationalization of untitled lands during the 1950s, '60s, and '70s reflected both elite self-interest and the prevailing socialist winds of Third World nationalism.[23] Authority-gap narratives likewise miss the more recent policy changes, often from the 1990s, that drastically lowered taxation rates (on land, profits, and commodity exports) and altered national land laws in a bid to attract greater foreign investment to poor countries.[24] While often implemented by Southern governments under pressure from Northern lenders—whether as part of structural adjustment packages or more "voluntary" alternatives—these adjustments imply strategic state action under conditions of structural duress, not the absence of governing per se.[25]

Most importantly, authority-gap narratives ignore the socio-spatial unevenness that transnational land deals invariably manifest. Because they are negative descriptions—accounts of what is missing rather than what *is* actually going on—authority-gap narratives have little to say about why foreign land deals have been targeted into certain regions with good farmland but not others, or why they achieve large-scale enclosures in some places yet run up against prohibitively strong resistance elsewhere.[26] As researchers have studied the global land rush over the last decade-plus, they have become increasingly convinced that, as one senior scholar put it, "an accelerated process of dispossession is clearly in motion."[27] Yet as agriculture, energy, and finance merge, and as sovereign wealth becomes an increasingly global force,[28] questions of *how* and *where* this "accelerated dispossession" is taking place are increasingly intertwined. If accelerated dispossession is "clearly in motion," what enables that motion to gain traction on the ground? What makes a land *rush* into a land *grab* in some cases, but not others?

GOVERNING ENCLOSURE

Echoing earlier studies of globalization, scholars have been quick to point out that transnational land deals complicate traditional notions of territorial sovereignty, especially when the areas involved—some exceeding tens of thousands of hectares—are large enough that they spill from economic space (property) into political space (territory).[29] The legal scholar Liz Alden Wily, for instance, offers an excellent account of the new land rush's enabling conditions, from colonial land law to postindependence hinterland nationalization to neoliberal-era structural adjustments of national tax and land policy.[30] Similar ingredients drive anthropologist Pál Nyíri's theorization of Chinese land deals abroad in the wake of the country's "Going Out" policy, announced in 2000. Positing a "return of the concession"—a colonial-era model of outsourced political space aimed at stimulating global trade—Nyíri builds on anthropologist Aihwa Ong's studies of "graduated sovereignty" in the special economic zones created during the 1990s across the global South.[31] Nyíri emphasizes the sharing or blurring of national sovereignty by large-scale Chinese land deals in sub-Saharan Africa and the Southeast Asian borderlands; the difference now, as compared to the 1990s, is that zonal exceptions, formerly limited in size and number, have become so extensive that they seem to be changing the fabric of "normal" political space itself.

Noting the prevalence of state-linked firms in these "new enclosures," many scholars have used the Marxian language of primitive accumulation to link land's removal from the protective arena of national law and regulation to a new round of imperial plunder.[32] The sociologist Saskia Sassen, for instance, sees the new land deals as "contemporary versions of primitive accumulation" and argues that the abandonment of Keynesian commitments to social protection that flourished across the global South during the mid-twentieth century has begun "a systematic repositioning of territory" away from national space and instead as "'needed' resources" for the rest of the world.[33] "One brutal way of putting it," she writes, "is to say that the natural resources of much of [the global South now] count more than the people on those lands count as consumers and as workers."[34]

Scholars also highlight the rising material stakes of land loss as communities throughout the global South have been excluded from the economic benefits of globalization. As anthropologist James Ferguson points out, during the last few decades "whole regions and populations [have found] that they have no '[comparative] advantage' of any kind and are (in some significant measure) simply left out of the global production regime."[35] This has had important implications for the so-called agrarian transition, which under traditional modernization theory would have viewed state-managed enclosure and resulting forms of social differentiation as a *good* thing because they helped move labor off the farm and into better jobs and greater productivity in the city.[36] A half century later, these expectations have given way to the more pessimistic reality of today's highly uneven global economy. As anthropologist Tania Li notes, land deals threaten to displace rural producers "from their 'inefficient' farms" amid this "truncated" agrarian transition, where "the anticipated transition from farm to factory is nowhere on the horizon."[37] In such a context, Jacques Diouf's warning in the report quoted above—"you can easily imagine the risk of a social outcry when [farmland] falls into foreign hands"[38]—is not just about the "old" nationalisms of blood and soil. It is also, just as importantly, about the heightened stakes of land dispossession today.

I had initially been drawn to northwestern Laos because local authorities there seemed to be trying to take this threat seriously. In late 2005 three northwestern provinces—including Luang Namtha, the gateway to China's

Yunnan province and the location of the Vieng Phoukha district—had made a public commitment to embrace Chinese rubber investment using a contract-farming model. Centering on a smallholder-based business model, this contrasted strongly with the large-scale, long-term concessions of putatively state-owned land that predominate in central and southern Laos as well as throughout the global land rush more generally.[39] While hardly a cure for the structural marginality that Laos's upland farmers faced at the precarious end of global commodity chains, market integration based on local land-ownership rather than state-assisted enclosure seemed like an alternative worth studying. In the months after our initial visit to the Bolisat Ltd. nursery, however, as my colleagues and I developed a better understanding of the new geography of rubber in the area, what we found was initially hard to classify. Our efforts allowed us to make sense of the map described above, as well as the operations of other rubber plantation schemes across the northwest. What we found was a hybrid that combined the state-managed enclosure of a concession scheme with the regulatory invisibility of the "contract farming" label. Buried under the rhetoric of contract farming and cooperative investment with farmers on their own land was a concession-like model of rubber-planting "promotion" that was all the more insidious because of the mostly invisible—and highly socially uneven—land grabbing it facilitated.

Smallholder rubber had indeed taken root in some areas, but its success was modest at best. Independently owned rubber plantations are expensive to establish and thus remained out of reach for most farmers, while contract farming was not taken up widely because of the poor terms that companies typically offered (see ch. 1). A third type of land deal thus emerged to fill the perceived investment gap. This was a type of rubber plantation "promotion" based on state-managed enclosure and wage labor—a model that, despite being officially labeled as a type of contract farming, was in fact much closer to a concession. This regime relied on coercive land zoning to pry land away from local users and allocate it to Chinese companies, and its invention and proliferation across the northwest gave the lie to the promise of "cooperative" investment based on a smallholder model. This concession-like variant was operating in the area that my colleagues and I had visited, and its existence as a sort of dark twin to the much-heralded smallholder model was the wider context of the map we had encountered. In retrospect, it is hardly surprising that project developers and local authorities had kept their maps vague.

It is this mix of enclosure and invisibility that I find especially compelling. If the scholarship summarized above highlights the potential rescaling of political and economic space, as well as the heightened material stakes involved, it also raises the question of how transnational enclosures actually work. While Marx's work on primitive accumulation remains an important touchstone, Li's point that alternatives to agriculture are increasingly hard to come by in many corners of the global South suggests that the classic model of forced displacement from (rural) farm to (urban) factory is increasingly out of date. Add to this the often nationalist-tinged resistance that, as Diouf warned, has in fact materialized when transnational land deals are seen to benefit primarily foreign actors.[40] Designers of transnational land deals have thus had to think not just about the material logistics of enclosure—how to gain access to good land, water, labor, and infrastructure, and how to process and market the commodities they produce—but also the wider political optics of signing away land to "foreigners." The bad old days of colonialism and empire are supposed to be over, after all, and development cooperation is ostensibly based on a promise of mutual benefit.[41] As my colleagues and I discovered, managing these optics—via the social targeting of land deals, the controlled and (at least initially) only partial application of enclosure, and the framing of all of this as pro-poor development—was a key part of the enclosure process itself. This was a far cry from the authority gap of a missing state; it was, by contrast, the governing of enclosure by a variety of state officials and institutions, using a whole set of tactics that spanned the realm of the discursive to the intimately material. It is this set of practices—the *governing* of enclosure—that demands critical attention and that this book examines in detail.

UPLAND GEOPOLITICS

In the chapters that follow, I describe this governmental dimension of transnational land deals in terms of upland geopolitics. The "uplands" of mainland Southeast Asia, including but not limited to the uplands of Laos, are often characterized as the semiforested hills and mountains that separate the region's major river basins (the Irrawaddy, Salween, Mekong, Red, and so on) where, historically, intensive wet-rice cultivation supported high population densities and state formation. By contrast, the uplands were the spaces in between, traditionally home to ethnic minority groups who practiced dryland shifting (often called "upland" or "hill") rice cultivation.[42] The mix of physiographic, ecological, and sociopolitical factors here is deliberate and unavoidable: the uplands are a biophysical and socio-ecological landscape, and like the concept of "landscape" itself, they are at once spaces themselves and a way of looking at space—typically, in this case, from the state-centric vantage point of the lowlands.[43] Depending on *when* one is referring to them, Southeast Asia's uplands have thus been characterized as a collection of nonstate spaces located outside the reach of premodern states, a geopolitical fracture zone produced by Cold War conflict, or a resource space inhabited by socially marginal peoples where modern technologies (from roads to gasoline-powered earthmovers to state-defined property rights) are today enabling what James Scott evocatively terms a "last great enclosure."[44]

In such a context, upland geopolitics refers to the complex relations, both within and among states, that target the uplands, their resources, and their inhabitants as objects of development, extraction, improvement, and control.[45] That the uplands form what geographers call a governable space is reflected in local terminology as well.[46] "Upland geopolitics" is thus a contemporary riff on the Lao word for "politics" (*kan-muang*), which literally means "the affairs of the *muang*"—historically, the fundamental unit of political space in lowland Southeast Asia. Today, *muang* carries both wider and more bounded connotations than it did in precolonial times, but still means something very much like "territory" or "realm." The difference is that it now also encompasses the upland spaces that were formerly defined in physical, political, and cultural opposition to the lowlands.[47] In contemporary Lao usage, for instance, *muang* refers both to local administrative districts (e.g., *Muang* Vieng Phoukha) and to the country as a whole (*Muang* Lao).

In my usage, this local dimension is especially important because of the ways that politics and economics intersect in hinterland spaces like the uplands. It is not simply that the governing of land, population, and socioeconomic affairs in a given area is inherently political owing to questions of resource allocation—although it certainly is. Today, even as scholars have largely moved beyond the authority-gap narrative and its variants, the explanatory focus, whether one is looking at the global land rush or more recent variants such as "global China," often remains at the national scale.[48] Without discounting the role of national laws or international relations, or the dilemmas that central-level authorities face when pursuing economic development and national sovereignty simultaneously, my focus is on the ways that local authorities influence and manage transnational land access because of their administrative proximity to putatively "available" upland areas. These on-the-ground workings of transnational land deals are, as we will see, crucial to determining the social distribution of enclosure, as well as to mediating the relationships between land deals and a range of other state-territorial processes.

Micro-Geopolitics

A central aim of this book is to help explain the uneven geography of transnational land access by showing how legacies of geopolitical conflict can help facilitate enclosure. Transnational land deals often pull in opposite directions at the same time: they are seen as desirable for host states charged with creating economic development; yet they can easily turn politically volatile if the optics work out wrong. The case study at the heart of this book shows how the history of US intervention in the Lao uplands during the Cold War continues to haunt contemporary Lao-Chinese development cooperation, weighing most heavily on those who are not only among the most vulnerable to land loss today but who were also on the losing end of earlier "win-win" strategic cooperation schemes. Given the extensive reach of American intervention abroad, these sorts of multi-decadal legacies are worth taking seriously.

Development projects traffic in the complex and inevitably negotiated politics of force and consent, and transnational land deals in particular incite struggles over enclosure, dispossession, and compensation that wrestle as much with questions of sociopolitical legitimacy as with those of formal law and policy. The terms of engagement for all of these turn on citizenship in practice: the ability to choose a livelihood, to select between competing risks, to have a voice in defining what improvement itself looks like.[49] Property is always a social relation, and especially in legal-pluralist contexts like Laos where multiple factors shape the control over land, land conflicts are never solely about land; the ability to resist or negotiate the terms of development often depends on the capacity—whether individual or collective—to articulate one's role as a worthy citizen.[50] Conversely, when nationalist-tinged aspersions articulate with long-standing prejudices against certain forms of land use, the enclosure process can operate that much more easily.[51]

Attention to this sort of historically sedimented, place-based "micro-geopolitics" has begun to emerge in recent scholarship, but it remains in short supply.[52] By adding an extended case to the literature, my hope is to help push both popular and scholarly understandings of transnational land politics beyond negative explanations like weak governance or the "authority gap," and beyond national-level explanations like authoritarian governments or (post)socialist property systems. As a growing literature on resistance in authoritarian contexts shows,[53] the politics of dispossession are invariably more local and contingent. This book examines the long historical dimension of these contingencies, drawing on scholars of empire, property, and postcoloniality to examine the ways that place-based politics can span multiple eras of transnationality.[54] As the following chapters show, the remnants of American empire's reach into the Southeast Asian uplands—and indeed into the very concept of "the uplands" themselves—have helped create powerful tools for managing dispossession. If the repositioning of territory is key to making space for land deals today, it is important to see how this process accumulates over decades. Especially at a moment when American empire's more recent forays seem to be on the wane (in Iraq and, most recently, Afghanistan, for example), the longer-term perspective offered by the case of Laos has potentially wide-reaching application.

Methodologically, I have been inspired by the work of economist Michael Perelman, who highlights what can be gained by examining the logic and practices of those he calls "primitive accumulationists": the planners and administrators who sit at the nexus of state and corporate power.[55] One of many scholars who, in tracing capitalism beyond Europe and into the global South, have emphasized the overtly coercive dimension of accumulation as not just fundamental to *initial* inequality but as an *ongoing* process that keeps people poor, Perelman is especially interested in land.[56] These interests go hand in hand. Especially in the global South, land is a key means through which economically marginal people access and mobilize wealth.[57] Yet Adam Smith's retrograde explanation for why some are rich and others poor—Marx summarized it as the narrative of the "diligent, frugal elite" versus the "lazy rascals who spend their substance, and more, in riotous living"[58]—still appears with startling regularity among both policymakers and development professionals.[59] Seeing how the coercive redistribution of wealth continues to operate at a structural level provides an important corrective.

Perelman is an especially useful theorist of what we might call partial enclosure. Through his studies of colonial plantation systems, Perelman noted that the model of primitive accumulation described by Marx for England—the full enclosure of land and resulting displacement of the rural population to the city (factory, poorhouse, slum, etc.)—did not occur in situations where, for various reasons, colonial officials and plantation managers preferred to keep rural populations in place. For Perelman, the calculus was one of profit: leaving rural workers enough land for self-provisioning would allow them to survive on lower pay.[60] In the context of transnational land deals, I have found that a similar method—studying the state and corporate planners who calibrate land deals to specific contexts in order to make them work—helps explain the uneven geography of enclosure. By targeting the greatest enclosures at those communities and landscapes least able to resist them, *and* by keeping the resulting enclosures partial and out of the way, contemporary "primitive accumulationists" in the Lao-China borderlands seem to have found a winning formula for making transnational land access work.

This "working," however, looks very different from the vision of permanent livelihoods—spatially fixed, market-integrated production that is accountable to the state both economically and politically—that initially inspired the development schemes examined below. My account of the micro-geopolitics that ultimately made transnational land deals work is thus not just about space, but also about change over time. This operates on two temporal scales, first in the transition from the pre-1975 upland territoriality of American Cold War intervention to the Lao (postrevolution) government's management of upland territorial affairs during the 1980s' geopolitical turmoil; and second, during the 2000s, in the slippage from the rhetoric of "win-win" development cooperation with Chinese rubber companies to the realities of managed enclosure. Rather than being a "triple win" for upland farmers, Chinese companies, and Lao authorities, the working of transnational land deals has turned out to be one of cheap land access created and sustained through sociopolitical marginality—a version of the racialized accumulation that underpinned colonial capitalism and, as elsewhere, has been carried forward by postcolonial regimes to do political-economic work in the present.[61] In this case, that work is not only the cheapening of land access but doing so in a way that minimizes potential nationalist-tinged objections about "giving land away" to "the Chinese."

Illegibility

The politics of spatial information within the state figure centrally here. Exploiting historical legacy to manage land grabbing is a double exploitation, not just of the communities involved but also of a whole country's tragic past. While there are important nuances and ambiguities, I would like to believe that the managed land grabs I describe below would not have survived close scrutiny by higher-level authorities, especially given the official smallholder-favoring policy rhetoric at the time. So a second issue this book takes up is how and why transnational land deals remain largely out of the view of even the regulators tasked with monitoring them on behalf of national governments. This gets back to the opening sketch above, where my colleagues and I found ourselves lost in the field, so to speak, because we had yet to break through the various barriers that had been quietly erected to avoid revealing too many details—even to the central government. These barriers turned on a wider political economy of how land is allocated for "development," and in particular on the control of forests and potential timber rents. This struggle within the state over land-based value remains alive and well across much of the world and plays a key role in maintaining the opacity that continues to surround many transnational land deals.

As with the place-based politics of enclosure, these internal politics of transnational land access have not been as fully examined as they need to be. Much attention has deservedly gone to critiquing the land-deal inventory efforts that have emerged at a global scale during the first few years of the global land rush.[62] But the subnational, domestic politics of land-deal information are a key reason why global inventory efforts were so fraught in the first place: many states did not know where their own land deals were. Part of the way states achieve what geographer Matthew Hannah calls "the mastery of territory" is through the creation and maintenance of institutions that collect, amalgamate, compare, and analyze statistics about land and its inhabitants. These "statistics"—literally the knowledge of the state—are tools for governing from afar, and their quality and reliability determine in large part the extent to which the everyday work of governing can be centrally managed versus ceded to local authorities.[63] The situation in Laos is thus not an abdication of sovereignty to some foreign power like "Beijing," but rather a field of struggle within the state over issues like timber rents, land taxes, and the right to regulate business. Central-level authorities sometimes prevail in these struggles.[64] But in other cases, including the Chinese rubber deals in northwestern Laos, the state authority that is present is far more localized and the power of the center much more attenuated.

Bringing these politics of legibility into the story helps resolve one of the long-standing questions about the global land rush: Why has it been so hard to quantify? As soon as GRAIN began publishing maps and statistics about the "global land grab" back in 2008, a debate began—quietly at first, and then more loudly in the sessions and hallways of conferences and the pages of academic journals, white papers, and online databases.[65] These exchanges highlighted the poor quality of the numerical data about transnational land deals, while also converging on a general consensus that the global land rush was a clear and present danger.[66] But what has always been just out of reach is a compelling explanation of *why* quantitative and cartographic data about the new enclosures is so consistently hard to get. Examining the role of spatial-data politics in ongoing state formation, I show how the paucity of good spatial data is an *effect* of internal territorial politics within host states like Laos, and is thus *part* of the global land-rush story rather than simply a barrier to understanding it.[67] The global land grab began as a numbers story: a million hectares here, tens or hundreds of thousands of hectares there. One key advance made by scholars such as those involved in the Land Deal Politics Initiative was to help move the debate past the numbers alone, so that critical, engaged research would remain primary when statistics inevitably became destabilized by closer scrutiny.[68] This book takes up this challenge, not as a way to "get past" the numbers, but to locate them within the wider field of social and political struggle within which land deals occur.

The stakes of this struggle matter because even as the "land rush" has itself subsided, transnational land-deal details remain important, whether in the aftermath of earlier land deals or as highlighted in recent scholarship on agrarian change (on contract farming and the "broader forms of dispossession") or on "global China," among others.[69] Across the global South, middle-income countries have begun to experiment with redistributive ("neo-welfare") policies like direct cash transfers as a way to correct the mismatch between the social need for high employment and the much lower demands for labor in today's global economy.[70] Poor countries like Laos have, thus far, resisted these policies and, in essence, tried to make transnational land deals do the same work of generating rural employment while also maintaining economic growth. If this sounds like wishful thinking—especially in light of the outcomes so far—it is worth noting that the active presence of sovereign wealth in many of the new land deals makes them somewhat different from the resource concessions that have featured in development schemes since the colonial era.[71] While this explicit state role has generated perhaps overly optimistic accounts of "inclusive development" (e.g., in China's Belt and Road Initiative), it is also a key finding of more critical scholarship, such as the sociologist Ching Kwan Lee's study of Chinese state capital in Zambia.[72] In the rubber deals of northwestern Laos, what Lee calls the "socially encompassing" flexibility of Chinese state capital ("in contrast to the profit-maximizing logic of private capital"[73]) is represented by a generous Chinese government-subsidy program aimed at replacing opium with licit crops like rubber in the uplands of Myanmar and Laos. While the plantation "promotion" schemes examined below have thus far failed to generate the sorts of social inclusiveness hoped for by both Lao and Chinese policymakers, this stemmed in part from the relatively opaque forms of internal legibility on both sides of the border. In the current era of development cooperation, the more active turn toward the state seems to be here to stay. This means that the sort of legibility politics examined in the latter half of this book will remain key to future debates, even as the specifics of transnational land access continue to change.[74]

This book draws on research conducted in Laos and the United States between 2004 and 2018. It began, as many projects do, with questions that have remained even as the locations where I went looking for answers changed. As a doctoral researcher interested in the political ecology of Western development, I initially became interested in Laos thanks to the World Bank placing the country in its global crosshairs with the Nam Theun 2 hydropower project, the first large dam to receive World Bank financing after the late-1990s reform efforts of the World Commission on Dams.[75] My interest then shifted to northwestern Laos during 2005 and 2006, as land politics became a topic of extensive domestic debate and as it became increasingly clear that Chinese development financing was giving Western donors and lenders a run for their money. As the idea of a Beijing rival to the Washington Consensus began to coalesce, northern Laos offered as good a place as any to see if there was indeed a "there" there.

Northwestern Laos drew my attention because of the confluence of two processes there. The first was the rubber boom sketched out above, which resonated with many of my informants not just because it involved China, but also because rubber had become something of a metonym for foreign investment and development cooperation more broadly across rural Laos. With Vietnamese companies in the south, Thai companies in the central provinces, and Chinese companies up north, conversations about rubber had a way of turning into reflections on development more generally, including all of the complexity that the term implies.[76] Rubber was a way to talk about, among other things, the risks and opportunities of modernization, Laos's place in an increasingly global Mekong region, and the livelihood implications of maps whose legal status was highly ambiguous.

The second process that drew me to the northwest was the building of the Northern Economic Corridor, a road project connecting China's Yunnan province to Thailand's Chiang Rai province through the uplands of northern Laos. Built in the early to mid-2000s, this piece of infrastructure helped channel new investment in rubber plantations to places like Vieng Phoukha and exemplified the vision of economic connectivity and regional cooperation embodied in spatial imaginaries like the Greater Mekong Subregion and the Golden Quadrangle. I made a preliminary visit to the northwest in 2005 and eight additional trips there during 2006, 2007, and 2008, during which I observed the corridor's development and the rubber boom, and assisted Laos's National Land Management Authority (NLMA) in its effort to get a better inventory of investment projects (both foreign and domestic) in the area. This period comprised the bulk of my fieldwork in the north. Additionally, I made brief follow-up visits in 2013 and 2018, although only the latter generated sufficient ethnographic data to be included here.

During all of these visits, I focused my research efforts on processes linked to what scholars call the agrarian question: What happens to traditional land use when capitalism arrives?[77] In this case, "capitalism" meant the Northern Economic Corridor, the Chinese rubber boom, and various state efforts to manage their interaction. These efforts produced maps like the one that initially eluded my NLMA colleagues and me, as well as various planning and property-formalization programs for land use that had preceded both the road and the rubber boom, but were also aimed at making land more accessible to economic development. This broader work of studying the multiple *formal* geographies of land management led me to three additional "research sites" that gave this book its ultimate form. The first two of these were sites for me in the archives only, while the third was both my home base and, as it turned out, a crucial field site, too.

The first is an area called Nam Nyu, located in a remote corner of Laos's northwestern Bokeo province. The site of a clandestine base built and used by the US Central Intelligence Agency between 1961 and 1972, Nam Nyu sat outside my fieldwork area but its influence drove the historical-legacy angle of my northwestern case study. Various trajectories of human movement connected the uplands of Vieng Phoukha to Nam Nyu and its surroundings during the base's heyday in the 1960s, as well as during the post-1975 period when the security-oriented resettlement of upland communities occupied the military and civilian agencies of the newly created Lao People's Democratic Republic. During my fieldwork, I was able to reconstruct some of these resettlement trajectories using interviews and document sources; I later complemented these with historical sources, many of which were available in the secondary literature thanks to a wealth of scholarship on Laos's "secret war."[78] Tracing these various upland trajectories provided key linkages between the remnants of Nam Nyu and the uneven enclosures of the contemporary era.

This project also detours through a second historical landscape, located in the uplands of Bolikhamxai province, in Laos's central panhandle. Between the eras of US and Chinese cooperation that bracket my study, a third development partner made a key imprint on the upland geopolitics of rural Laos: Sweden. The Lao-Swedish Forestry Project, active in the forested areas east of the national capital between the late 1970s and the mid-1980s, provides a crucial missing link between the upland geopolitics of the "hot" Cold War—America's secret war in Laos, which ended in the early

1970s—and the techniques of differential and managed enclosure that animate the contemporary rubber boom in the northwest. Focusing on an area called Muang Houng, I use archival sources collected in Laos and the United States to chart the emergence of a suite of techniques that, following the discourse of Lao officials in the late 1980s, I refer to collectively as "population management work." Spanning the gray areas between coercion and consent, these methods ranged from village relocation and consolidation for purposes of securitization and service delivery, to land-use zoning, property formalization, and agricultural extension. My focus on Muang Houng and its surroundings stems from convenience and access—I am aware of no other area with a comparable public archival record. Despite the challenges inherent in archival sources, the Muang Houng landscape illustrates a crucial dimension of what I call "postwar Laos" by showing how population management work arose in a period of national insecurity and was then repurposed, beginning in the late 1980s, for economic development. Tellingly, Lao leaders at the time referred to this era of transition as "a new battlefield where no gunfire can be heard."[79] They meant it literally.

Third and finally, Laos's capital Vientiane provided me with an important gateway to both archival sources and the urban milieu of development professionals, bureaucratic politics, and land and natural resource policy. My archival work there provided access to most of the policy documents examined in the chapters that follow, as well as to various development project documents that drew me toward more detailed historical research after I returned to the United States. My time in Vientiane also yielded contacts in the development community without whom this research would have been impossible. These included staff at international organizations, donor and lender offices; government staff in various ministries and other offices; private-sector consultants; and members of Lao civil society. In addition to providing institutional support for my fieldwork, my time in Vientiane alerted me to, and then steeped me in, the regulatory struggle *within* the Lao state. These struggles, almost as much as those on the ground, are central to the analysis that follows.

This book constitutes what I think is best called an ethnography of upland government. I use this phrase to distinguish my efforts from an impressive body of ethnographic work that uses long-term fieldwork with single or multiple communities to bring local, often indigenous, perspectives into more public view.[80] My project is somewhat different. For both practical and ethical reasons, I chose not to get too close to the communities that populate my field site, many of which were on the losing end of the land deals I studied. While some of their experiences and perspectives come through—as they must, in order to convey the processes of land grabbing that occurred—my ethnographic attention is directed more upward than downward: to the practices of governing that form the nexus of interaction between land, local populations, and the state. My work thus fits more directly into a long line of research on "studying up" to examine the workings of power in practice, although in my case that means looking at multiple actors whose power interlocks and often competes: initially, provincial Lao authorities in the northwest, development bank planners, and Chinese policymakers; and then later, by turns, American Cold War strategists, foreign and domestic advisers to state forestry operations, Lao district authorities, Chinese companies, and central-level Lao authorities.[81] Together, these examinations add up to a study of contemporary "primitive accumulationists," actors whose efforts—whether in concert or in competition with one another—produce the uneven enclosures and complex geopolitics that comprise the recent land rush. I begin this examination on the ground: where the rubber meets the road.

CHAPTER ONE

Where the Rubber Meets the Road

Uneven Enclosure in Northwestern Laos

The location, weather, and land are suitable for rubber planting, and the target is shifting-cultivation fallow land and people who are interested in planting rubber. . . . The population will receive permanent livelihoods, will be able to alleviate their hardship via this stability, and will have an elevated standard of living compared to the past.

—CHINESE RUBBER COMPANY PROPOSAL, 2005

S ITTING on the table in front of us, the piece of tuber is roughly the size of an adult's fist. It is early July of 2018, and I am back in Vieng Phoukha, following up on the rubber planted here during the boom years of the mid-2000s. My informant is a Lao man of about fifty, a village official who is telling me about his days as a labor broker for Bolisat Ltd., the Chinese company whose plantations are at the center of the rubber boom here. We are sitting outside at a small wooden table, under a sunshade next to the village's single dirt road. I have been here before, a few times, mostly in the months after my colleagues' and my run-in with the company map recounted above. For all the changes that the last decade has brought to northern Laos, the village looks remarkably similar. The houses are still mostly old and wooden; the road is still unpaved, although the rain from earlier this morning is thankfully keeping the dust down; and upland rice fields, green with this year's new growth, still line the surrounding hills. My informant is telling me about the past, and about the transition to the present.

A few minutes earlier, he had called over a child from the village and had him go get something from a nearby house. This something, it turns out, is a piece of "wild cassava" (*man pa*) that he uses to punctuate his story. During the mid-2000s my informant had been in charge of recruiting, training, and managing residents of this and the surrounding villages to work for Bolisat Ltd., first clearing and terracing the land, then planting and weeding the company's young rubber plantations. But as the seedlings matured and planting and weeding gave way to rubber tapping—and here his account takes the turn that it must in order to accommodate the current situation— the jobs had gone largely to imported workers from a neighboring district. Their dormitory (he gestures to a nearby ridge) is just over there, down a feeder road that bisects one of the company's large plantations.

"Our village is Muser," he says, referencing one of the ethnic groups who live in the mountainous borderlands of northwestern Laos (the term is from the Burmese word for "hunter"), "formerly based in the mountains, in the forest, moving from place to place." He refers to the community inclusively ("Our village"), but from his description and his own roles as a labor broker and village official, it is clear that he is himself an outsider, appointed by the district government to help bring development to a village that is seen as among the poorest of the poor. "The people here are very poor; they do shifting cultivation," he explains, rehearsing the link between poverty and upland rice farming that one often hears across Southeast Asia and beyond. As he returns to the community's relationship with Bolisat Ltd., his account becomes pointed again. "But this year the rats came a lot to the upland fields. There are limited lands in the village because the company has a lot of the land, which limits agricultural production. For households without lowland rice paddies"—in this hilly landscape, this means the majority—"they have to eat wild cassava because of the rats."

We are sitting in the middle of an area local authorities call Khet Nam Fa, a small upland valley in Vieng Phouka district, located in northwestern Laos's Luang Namtha province. In Lao language, *khet* means "area" or "zone," and the Nam Fa is the local river, a tributary of the Mekong that joins the larger river about halfway between where it flows out of China and its passage through the tri-border "Golden Triangle" where Laos meets Thailand and Myanmar. Here, and across northern Laos more broadly, the rubber boom of the 2000s was supposed to embody the win-win development cooperation conjured in the epigraph above and evoked by Laos's so-called "3 + 2" policy, a loose reference to contract farming coined around 2005. Under this policy, Chinese companies would provide the financing, markets, and technical training (the "3") to Lao farmers, who would use their own land and labor

FIGURE 1.1   Chinese rubber plantations, c. 2008, Khet Nam Fa.

(the "2") to grow rubber. A decade ago, as I finished the bulk of the research for this book, this promise of cooperative development was already fraying, as Chinese companies' large rubber plantations (fig. 1.1) had already far outpaced smallholder contract farming. In the intervening years, the land grab whose early stages I witnessed in 2006–8 had been cemented into place. Bolisat Ltd.'s plantations had matured and expanded, rubber tapping and processing had begun, and the already limited wage work had gone increasingly to outsiders. The tuber on the table summed up this transition poignantly.

Today, plantations like the ones in Khet Nam Fa—variously referred to as "demonstration gardens," "concessions," or "4 + 1," a variant on "3 + 2" discussed below[1]—have become widespread in northern Laos. While the statistics about their size and location remain uncertain, they are extensive, covering multiple thousands of hectares across dozens of plantation sites, and frequently occupying the good land near the roads.[2] Although they are often believed to exemplify Laos's lack of regulatory muscle—the "authority gap" discussed in the introduction—the story of their creation is in fact much more interesting and complex.

These quasi-concessions should absolutely be seen as land grabs, but not because of the abdication of regulatory responsibility by a state missing in action. Paradoxically, they are the result of a regulatory *push* by Lao authorities that dates from the earliest days of Lao-Chinese bilateral rubber cooperation: the same moment that launched the rhetoric of "3 + 2 cooperation" mentioned above. Today this may seem like authoritarian doublespeak, a way to gloss over what was always a plan to create large swaths of land for foreign capital. Not so. Uncovering the process of divergence between the official discourse of Lao-China bilateral rubber cooperation and the actual landscape of specific rubber deals that emerged alongside it—in part *from* it, in part *despite* it—is essential to understanding northwestern Laos's uneven geography of land grabbing. Getting the story right corrects the narrative of pliant host states that often underlies discussions of transnational land deals.[3] More importantly, it shows how regulatory pushback over a key policy question—in this case, whether bilateral rubber cooperation should follow a contract-farming or concession-based business model—can actually open up space for hidden and uneven dispossession, despite intervening in the name of protecting the local population.

This question of "business models" may sound arcane and specialized, but it exemplifies a key issue in the larger world of international development cooperation. Amid the structural labor-shedding that has characterized the global economy since the 1970s, many development cooperation schemes have tried to implement "alternative business models" that add social objectives like job creation and enhanced land-tenure security to traditional goals like commodity production and, more generally, economic growth. These schemes often take cajoling, negotiation, and—crucially—the addition of government subsidies, especially when the actors deputized to represent the wealthier countries in "development partnerships" are themselves companies. The case of Laos-China rubber development cooperation exemplifies this quest for the appropriate mix of private interest and public benefit. Playing out through the regulatory struggle over "3 + 2" cooperation in Laos's Northern Economic Corridor, a landscape that has subsequently become discursively enrolled into China's Belt and Road Initiative (BRI), the emergence of land grabs like those in Khet Nam Fa is symptomatic of these politics of social inclusion that remain at the fore with the intertwining of international business and development aid.

PERMANENT LIVELIHOODS

Rubber is a relative newcomer to montane Southeast Asia, and especially to northern Laos. In the early twentieth century, French-colonial planters introduced the crop to southern Laos as part of their development of large plantation complexes in Cambodia and southern Vietnam. But their rubber varieties, imported from the Brazilian Amazon via British Malaya and London's Kew Gardens,[4] were adapted to the humid tropics and thus limited to the southern part of the Indochinese peninsula. The cold-adapted varieties found today in the mountainous uplands of southern Yunnan, northern Laos, and northern Myanmar were developed much later by Chinese agronomists during the Korean War, as China faced a Western blockade that shut the country off from the rubber supplies of Malaya, Thailand, and Indonesia. The Chinese varieties' lower rates of production made them uncompetitive for export, but they served important domestic purposes. Helping create self-sufficiency during the embargo and aiding Chinese officials in their efforts to "modernize" the uplands of southern Yunnan, rubber played a key role in China's Cold War–era agrarian transformation of its upland borderlands.[5]

The Cold War also helped bring Chinese rubber varieties to northern Laos. During the upheavals of the 1960s, '70s, and early '80s, a number of Lao refugees had fled across the border to Yunnan, where they learned rubber tapping in the state plantation system created in the 1950s around the new cold-tolerant varieties. In the late 1980s and early 1990s, some of them returned, bringing both the technical skills and the social connections that allowed northwestern Laos a degree of informal incorporation into China's rubber sector.[6] In 1991 Luang Namtha's provincial Party Congress got on board, officially declaring rubber "a key poverty alleviation strategy and an instrument to stabilize shifting cultivation."[7] This signaled state enthusiasm for the crop as a "modern," market-based livelihood distinct from the "natural economy" of subsistence production, and provided both political cover and a limited amount of economic support for some farmers to experiment with its development.

For Lao officials, rubber fit the governmental ideal of "permanent livelihoods" (asiip thavon or asiip kong thi). This concept drew on both indigenous and imported notions of proper settlement and economy. Generalizing the ideal of flooded-paddy rice production long practiced in the lowland parts of mainland Southeast Asia, it exemplified the legible farmer: fixed in space, market-integrated, and taxable by the state.[8] The concept of permanent livelihoods also echoed colonial-era anxieties about shifting cultivation, which at the time was by far the dominant form of upland farming. French-colonial foresters echoed their British and Dutch colleagues across the region in calling indigenous shifting cultivators mangeurs du bois (wood eaters), and subsequent generations of officials and bureaucrats from India to Indonesia inherited the tradition of trying to "stabilize" shifting cultivation in favor of more commercially oriented and spatially fixed forms of agrarian production.[9]

While Lao authorities embraced rubber nationwide in the late 1990s and early 2000s, the crop had a particular significance in the north, where opium production had long been part of at least some upland farming systems. As a licit and legible crop, rubber symbolized stability and market integration where opium and upland rice evoked mobility and independent subsistence.[10] And while the material similarities of opium and rubber were not lost on state officials—a provincial official once explained to me that both were latexes extracted through skilled-labor tapping—this was seen as a good thing because it meant that farmers familiar with opium production would readily take to rubber. But in the boostering that surrounded rubber development in the early 2000s, the differences were what mattered. Rather than being harmful and subversive, rubber was seen as secure: economically, socially, politically. It was a permanent livelihood par excellence.

This was easier said than done, however. Throughout the 1990s, as Laos had transitioned out of the socialist-bloc isolation of the late Cold War and into regional and global markets, officials across the country had exhorted upland farmers to intensify and sedentarize their agricultural practices. Often this "encouragement" came in the form of a village-scale zoning program called Land and Forest Allocation (hereafter LFA), which was rolled out in thousands of upland villages in the late 1990s and early 2000s. But despite leaving behind colorful land-use maps and pages of rule-laden documents, LFA failed to provide the resources—in particular the financing—that would allow the intensification conjured by its maps. The program thus had the effect of criminalizing shifting cultivation further by drawing village-scale land-use maps that could only be followed if long-fallow farming was abandoned.[11]

Rubber first emerged in contrast to this top-down approach to sedentarization, as a smallholder-led initiative in a handful of borderland villages in Luang Namtha, where residents had access to two ingredients missing from LFA: social networks that extended into the Chinese rubber sector, and credit.[12] This happened most famously in a Hmong village just outside the provincial capital, where a former vice-governor helped members of his home community (some of whom had recently returned from China) get a sizable loan from a state development bank to finance the establishment of their plantation.[13] Planted in the mid-1990s, their rubber matured to tapping age in the early 2000s, just as Lao-China development cooperation took off in the wake of China's recently announced "Going Out" policy. This village, Ban Hat Nyao, was not the only place where state banks provided financing to establish rubber plantations, or where smallholders successfully mobilized capital to establish their own plantations. But it became by far the most famous, exemplifying for some the possibilities of smallholder entrepreneurialism and for others the need for organized management of the five key ingredients for rubber production: financing, market access, extension, land, and labor.[14] The latter lesson would later form the grammar of the "3 + 2" policy.

For many Lao officials, this first generation of Lao rubber provided a proof of concept, while also emphasizing the imperative for outside assistance. China's rubber sector, widely seen as the only commercial outlet for rubber produced in northern Laos, remained protected; despite joining the World Trade Organization in 2001, Chinese leaders had successfully exempted the sector from liberalization by referencing the Western blockade of the 1950s as evidence of its "strategic" importance.[15] Lao rubber producers thus faced significant hurdles in selling their crop to processors in Yunnan, and often relied in the early years on informal methods to get their crop across the border.[16] If rubber production in northern Laos was going to scale up, this would have to change.

Moreover, the key role of the state bank loan in enabling Laos's most widely celebrated smallholder rubber success story highlighted the significant financing that would be needed if rubber was going to power the agrarian transition to "permanent livelihoods" that Lao authorities hoped for. While the cost of establishing a new rubber plantation would become a matter of some debate, the capital inputs were significant. In Luang Namtha alone, provincial Agriculture and Forestry officials had, by 2002, classified almost 200,000 hectares as land that was "suitable for rubber or eucalyptus plantations."[17] With authorities across the region thinking big about rubber, the roughly $400 per hectare needed for seedlings and other capital inputs was widely seen as prohibitive for both farmers and the Lao state.[18]

These issues were taken up when Chinese president Jiang Zemin made a state visit to Laos in November 2000 and signed a joint declaration on development cooperation, along with economic and trade agreements that included agricultural production.[19] This diplomatic push helped usher in the northern Lao rubber boom of the mid-2000s by addressing financing and export in ways elaborated below. Widely framed as a win-win-win for Lao farmers, Lao officials, and Chinese companies, bilateral rubber-cooperation rhetoric combined social, economic, and environmental objectives. As one proposal put it at the time: "The population will receive permanent livelihoods, will be able to alleviate their hardship via this stability, and will have an elevated standard of living compared to the past; the state will benefit from reforestation, protection of the environment, and increased taxes and fees; and the investor will benefit from rubber processing and trade."[20]

"UNBLOCKING" LAOS

Bilateral rubber cooperation between Laos and China blossomed at a time when governments from North America to Europe to East Asia were widely embracing regional connectivity in the name of economic prosperity.[21] In the 1990s and early 2000s, the once "isolated" and "remote" borderlands of northwestern Laos thus became progressively enrolled into regional imaginaries like the "Golden Quadrangle," the "Greater Mekong Subregion," the "Northern Economic Corridor," and (later) China's "Belt and Road Initiative." As a 1997 Asian Development Bank proposal for the Northern Economic Corridor put it, the goal of these efforts was to reanimate "natural economic areas" like the one spanning northern Thailand, northern Laos, northern

Myanmar, and China's Yunnan province, which had once "thrived" as part of the ancient silk route between Sichuan and Assam but had been "disrupted by colonialism and the Cold War."[22] Such regional boostering channeled state and private resources into new geographies of connection and played on a mix of similarity and difference. If northern Laos's "location, weather, and land" were "suitable for rubber planting" just like in Yunnan, bilateral cooperation was also premised on an economic division of labor. Laos would be the producer, and China the financier, processor, and consumer.

Efforts to enhance regional connectivity were, of course, nothing new.[23] In the 1860s French-colonial explorers had taken a great interest in the connectivity of northern Laos, which they reluctantly termed a "region of rapids."[24] France's Mekong Exploration Commission had been hoping to discover a river route to southern China that would have allowed Phnom Penh and Saigon—farther down the Mekong and, at the time, newly under French possession—to compete with British Hong Kong for access to trade within the Chinese interior. When the Mekong turned out to be hopelessly unnavigable, the commission turned its attention to the territory itself. Issues of connectivity interested them highly, as evidenced in their report, written by the geographer and military officer Francis Garnier. Highly impressed with the northern Lao city of Luang Prabang—"the first time since our departure [from Phnom Penh] that we had found a market in the sense this term has in Europe"—Garnier linked the economic prosperity of what the French called "upper Laos" to its isolation: "The distance of Luang Prabang from the theater of the wars which tore Indo-China apart in the eighteenth century contributed greatly to assuring its prosperity, no doubt after having been one of the determining causes of its foundation. . . . Today, the kingdom of Luang Prabang is the most important Laotian center in all Indo-China, the place of refuge and the natural focus of support for all the peoples from the interior who want to escape from the despotism of the Siamese."[25]

French interest in Laos's connectivity with its neighbors was, of course, highly geopolitical. Historically, "upper Laos" had been linked by overland and river-based trade routes that ran from southwest to northeast, connecting regional centers like Luang Prabang and Muang Sing (in present-day northern Laos) to places like Nan and Chiang Rai (today in northern Thailand) and Jinghong and Kunming (in present-day Yunnan) and beyond.[26] In the late 1800s these connections posed a real challenge to the French, whose recently formalized protectorate over Cambodia was just the latest step in assembling what would become French Indochina. During the commission's stay in Luang Prabang in 1867, Garnier waxed poetic about offering a similar "protection" arrangement to the Lao king there, hoping the French might replace the historical role of the Chinese empire in "exercising a domination benevolent and wise, which stimulated production . . . and increased the welfare and vital energies of the subject populations."[27] In return for protection, he hoped for infrastructural changes (both political and material) that would undo the inconvenient truth that upper Laos was far more closely linked to Siam than it was to Cambodia or Vietnam.[28] The French, Garnier wrote, "would only ask him [the Lao king] to favor the development of commerce toward the southern part of the [Indochinese] peninsula, to help us do away with fiscal hindrances, and to improve the roads in this direction."[29] This idea, it turned out, was premature—but not by much. Luang Prabang sought and received French "protection" in 1887 amid a deadly mix of refugee flight, social banditry, and local uprisings linked to China's suppression of the Taiping and various Muslim rebellions in the 1870s, and by Siam's efforts to consolidate its periphery against rising European interest in the chaos that followed.[30] By the early twentieth century, when French concerns were focused not on acquiring Lao territory but on governing it, this same concern with connectivity took the form of what colonial administrators called "unblocking."[31]

"Unblocking" was a strategic description par excellence: it was not that Laos was "blocked" per se but that it was connected in the wrong directions. French administrators treated Laos until the 1930s not as a distinct national space but as a resource-rich hinterland for Vietnamese industry and excess population.[32] In the early twentieth century, colonial administrators thus sought to minimize Laos's connections to Siam and China while building roads to Vietnam over the Annamite Mountains and, to a lesser extent, constructing railways around the unnavigable sections of the lower Mekong. These infrastructure plans were consistently undercut, however, by a reluctance to spend scarce state resources. Colonial officials thus left the task largely to a mix of *corvée* labor ("tax" paid by the local population in the form of work, often on roads) and private-sector investment, often from Europe. Both spectacularly failed to deliver at scale; the former was beset by local resistance while the latter crashed hard in the Great Depression.[33] Laos thus entered the period after the Second World War as a regionally "remote" and "isolated" country, a leading example of what would come to be called Asia's vast infrastructure deficit.[34]

While the Cold War period is largely remembered as one of regional fracturing—as in the Asian Development Bank (ADB) proposal quoted above, and as elaborated in the next chapter—the 1950s and 1960s also saw the birth of a new imaginary of connectivity based on the Mekong River. Like French efforts to "unblock" Laos, this imaginary was more often aspirational than actual, but it nonetheless inspired the idea of a Greater Mekong Subregion (GMS), a vision of regional connectivity that embraced both old forms of French-era connectivity (between Laos, Cambodia, and Vietnam) and earlier historical forms (between Laos, China, and Thailand) that the French had sought to minimize or interrupt. Articulated in the early 1990s as Southeast Asia's regional leaders sought to "turn battlefields into marketplaces" at the end of the Cold War, the GMS, like other regional imaginaries of the neoliberal era (and like the BRI, into which the Northern Economic Corridor has subsequently become enrolled), posited shared prosperity through enhanced connectivity and comparative advantage.[35] While exemplifying the shades of economic imperialism that critics called Thailand's "resource diplomacy"—strengthened political ties with Laos, Cambodia, and Myanmar seemingly aimed at helping Thai businesses access those countries' timber, mineral, and hydropower resources—the GMS was a distinctly multilateral initiative.[36] Yunnan was also part of the GMS from its initial formalization in 1992, and made up the northern end of multiple regional "economic corridors" that gave the GMS its internal structure (map 1.1). Lao leaders, having long viewed the country's landlocked status as a hindrance to development, widely embraced the "corridor" approach in hopes of becoming instead a "land-linked crossroads" of the region.[37]

Laos's Northern Economic Corridor (hereafter NEC), a major road upgrade built between 2002 and 2007, thus played a key role in connecting wider regionalization efforts to the geography of Lao-China rubber cooperation. Linking southern Yunnan with northern Thailand through northwestern Laos, the NEC had been originally envisioned back in the late 1980s as the Lao portion of the so-called Golden Quadrangle, a ring road that boosters hoped would one day connect the region's two biggest economies via both northwestern Laos and the eastern part of Shan state—essentially a bid to have Laos and Myanmar compete with each other for lower transport costs.[38] In 1994, with the Shan portion hampered by ongoing political instability, ASEAN representatives declared Laos's NEC a "high priority" project, and after a delay due to the 1997 Asian economic crisis and an unsuccessful effort to get the road built by a private concessionaire, the project went ahead in the early 2000s. Under a joint agreement facilitated in 2001 by the ADB, Laos agreed to finance the road using loans—each covering roughly a third of the project—from Thailand, the ADB, and China.[39]

ADB planners enthusiastically described the NEC as an "initializing project" that would "serve as a 'locomotive' for subregional economic

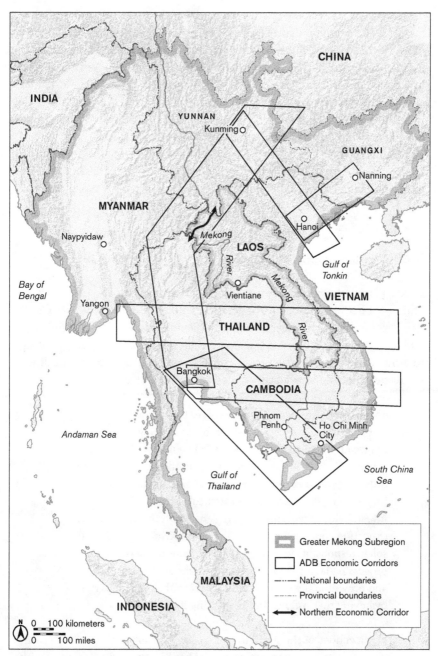

MAP 1.1   The Greater Mekong Subregion, regional economic corridors, and the Northern Economic Corridor. Map by Ben Pease. Based on ADB, "Greater Mekong Subregion Atlas," 120.

development . . . along the north-south axis" of the GMS.[40] This description proved to be apt, although the development that emerged would be highly uneven. In 2004, as construction was beginning, the bank's consultants worried that while the project would "automatically benefit" entrepreneurs in China and Thailand, it would not do the same for "subsistence-oriented ethnic minority shifting cultivators inhabiting the road impact zones"— in other words, uplanders like the residents of Khet Nam Fa. "Hence, there is a strong risk that the economic opportunities and benefits of road upgrading will bypass these rural communities, which will still be exposed to the associated potential negative consequences."[41] These fears proved more than justified.

"CERTAIN CONTENTIOUS ISSUES"

In early 2001, as the NEC agreement was being finalized, and in the wake of Jiang Zemin's state visit to Laos, provincial officials in Luang Namtha outlined a plan to their subordinates. It focused on developing 10,000 hectares of new rubber plantations in cooperation with the Sino-Lao Rubber Company, a joint venture between Chinese rubber and import-export companies with whom they had been in discussions since the previous year.[42] Writing to provincial- and district-level agricultural extension agents, they outlined the respective roles of what they called the initiative's two "sides":

> The province of Luang Namtha agrees to facilitate rubber planting and factory construction by convincing upland farmers to give up shifting cultivation-based livelihoods and plant rubber; to assign government staff from the relevant offices in order to coordinate with the Chinese investor side; and to implement rules, laws, etc. in order to assist the Chinese investor side in working in accordance with the policies of the exporting country [i.e., Laos]. The Chinese investor side will be solely responsible for investing in the building of the rubber-processing factory, contributing the relevant technical inputs, and providing the market for Luang Namtha's upland farmers by buying their rubber and processing it for export.[43]

Carrying echoes of the 1991 Party decision on rubber, this passage summarizes a development cooperation model based on contract farming, with the Chinese investor "side" in the role of the contractor (providing inputs, technical specifications, and a guaranteed market) and the province in the role of recruiting Lao farmers to join the scheme. Rubber is framed in the language of permanent livelihoods, and the organizational division of labor evokes at once the sort of comparative advantage envisioned by regional economic boosters and the mutual assistance typical of South-South cooperation since the 1950s.[44]

Contract farming, however, was not the vision of cooperation that Sino-Lao Rubber Company representatives had in mind, as evidenced by the conflict that followed. For the next five years, Luang Namtha provincial officials and Sino-Lao representatives remained at odds over the question of whether to grant the company a large land concession, an arrangement that would have let Sino-Lao develop its own plantations using hired labor. The half decade from 2000 to 2005 followed the launch of China's "Going Out" policy, and came both in the immediate wake of Jiang Zemin's state visit to Laos and at the beginning of what has since become arguably Laos's most important bilateral relationship.[45] Yet it saw a flagship project of bilateral rubber development—Sino-Lao's investment in Luang Namtha, a province often called Laos's "gateway" to China—stall because of what well-placed observers, in early 2005, called the persistence of "certain contentious issues."[46] This conflict concerned the details of transnational land access, and it played out broadly across northwestern Laos in the early and mid-2000s between Chinese rubber companies and various levels of the Lao government. Sino-Lao figured especially prominently in it because the company was negotiating with provincial authorities in not just Luang Namtha but also neighboring Oudomxai and Bokeo provinces (located to the southeast and southwest, respectively). This seems to have helped drive the three-province decision in late 2005 that originally drew me to the northwest. But the struggle over the concession issue was hardly limited to a single company.[47]

A pair of competing proposals from this period are worth looking at for a few reasons. On the one hand, they illustrate the extent to which regulatory politics at the time focused on the question of Lao state assistance for Chinese companies. At the time, this was being negotiated separately by a handful of different companies across various locations and jurisdictions, so the proposals provide a view into the mechanics of an already emerging geography of uneven enclosure. In the proposal language, the question of state-managed enclosure manifested as a debate about which business model—company-controlled plantations or smallholder contract farming—would form the core of the 10,000-hectare Sino-Lao partnership being planned in Luang Namtha. (The 30,000 hectares in the passage quoted below refers to the three provinces of Luang Namtha, Oudomxai, and Bokeo collectively.) On the other hand, the two proposals also show the significant room to maneuver that existed in policy language, and that was exploited by companies like Sino-Lao, Bolisat Ltd., and a few dozen others in their efforts to secure land access during the boom years of 2003–8. In practice, these ventures reflected aspects of both proposals, which helped maintain the discourse of smallholder-centric development while also creating quasi-concessions like the ones in Khet Nam Fa.

Titled "Draft Plan for Cooperation in Rubber Planting between Lao PDR and the PR China, 2005–2007," the first proposal was circulated by the Lao Ministry of Agriculture and Forestry shortly after a visit by Sino-Lao representatives in early 2005 aimed at resolving the "issues" mentioned above.[48] The document was addressed to the ministry's provincial-level offices in Luang Namtha, Oudomxai, and Bokeo, and outlined a concrete plan for rapid, yet still smallholder-centric, rubber cooperation. Covering topics from physical geography to economics, it converged on a proposal that echoed the contract-farming language of provincial officials, quoted above, from a half decade earlier. This began by dangling the carrot of 30,000 hectares of land and corresponding labor availability:

> Laos has an area of 236,000 square kilometers . . . [and] three target regions for rubber [in the north, center, and south]. . . . These three regions comprise sixty percent of the country, or 140,000 square kilometers, within which twenty percent is capable of production, or roughly . . . 2,800,000 hectares. Therefore, planting 30,000 hectares of rubber [in the northwest] will not be a problem. . . . Based on national statistics, Luang Namtha contains roughly 150,000 people; 23,000 families and 50,000 labor units [i.e., adult laborers]; Oudomxai roughly . . . 80,000 labor units; and Bokeo . . . 45,000 labor units, providing sufficient labor capacity to plant an additional 30,000 hectares of rubber.[49]

After conjuring a landscape ripe for rubber development, the proposal then explained that *four-fifths* of this area was intended for contract-based smallholder production, with the remaining 20 percent under direct company control. This plan was offered under the heading "Company + People" (*Bolisat + Pasason*), specifying 10,000 hectares per province, each to be divided into 2,000 hectares of company plantations and 8,000 hectares for local farmers. It also laid out a timeline for getting these planted rapidly, by the end of 2007.[50] Crucial to the ministry's strategy was the balance of give-and-take: it was offering to actively "supply and provide land" for the project, "organize the population to participate in a united and disciplined manner, and coordinate the relevant state organizations." On the other hand, the land promised directly to the company was comparatively small: the 2,000 hectares offered in each province was four times less than the land planned for contracted smallholders.

Three months later, Sino-Lao came back with a very different counteroffer. It began on the same terrain as the ministry's plan, noting Luang Namtha's proximity to Yunnan, its favorable mix of land and labor availability, and the mutual benefit that each side would gain by working together.[51] But on the details that mattered most, Sino-Lao's plan was far less inclined toward working with smallholders. Against the ministry's proposal of 80 percent smallholder land, the company proposed that "regarding the gardens produced by cooperative investment with the population, these will be divided 50–50 by total area via a division [between the company and local farmers] that will occur one year after planting, and then each side will take care of its own."[52]

On one level, this can be read as a modest, if nonetheless significant, counterproposal. While a 50–50 rather than 80–20 split would hardly have been a trivial alteration, it could still have been interpreted as a compromise, proposing an equal division between the company and smallholders rather than a model dominated by either side. But a second crucial issue concerned the timing: Sino-Lao proposed that the plantation be divided "one year after planting." This implied a planting process that was intensively planned and managed, and would have needed to include an active reconfiguration of land-tenure arrangements. Rather than distributing seedlings to farmers who would then plant them on their own land and with their own labor, Sino-Lao's proposal relied on the up-front development of company plantations with wage labor; the 50–50 division would come subsequently. Such a plan was closer to the model of state farms or resettlement areas (*nikhom* in Lao and Thai), where rubber tapping might be farmed out to individual households or labor groups, but the initial planting was company-managed and based on alienated land and labor.

A second indicator of the distance between the two "sides" was how they valued their own relative contributions (table 1.1). Input values are crucial for negotiating cooperative business arrangements because the distribution of the final product should, in theory, reflect each side's contribution. Using a per-hectare basis, the ministry's "Company + People" proposal estimated the total cost of establishing a plantation and maintaining it for one year at almost $1,500; of this, it estimated that almost 70 percent came from smallholder labor inputs like land clearing, terracing, fertilizing, planting,

TABLE 1.1   Rival cost estimates for rubber plantation establishment, per hectare (in 2005 USD)

STEP	LAO MINISTRY OF AGRICULTURE AND FORESTRY	SINO-LAO RUBBER COMPANY
1. Land preparation	720	149
Clearing	216	50
Plowing and hole digging	324	95
Fertilizing	90	4
Terracing	90	*
2. Plantation establishment	270	45
Planting seedlings	90	*
Spraying	90	5
Weeding 1 year	90	40
3. Seedlings (495/ha)	297	325
4. Pesticides	90	5
5. Technical instruction/extension	90	10
Total	1,467	534
Value from smallholder labor (steps 1 and 2)	990	194
% from smallholder labor (steps 1 and 2)	67%	36%

* Activity not listed in Sino-Lao estimate. Derived from figures in MAF "Draft Plan" and Sino-Lao "Project proposal document" discussed in text. Original figures in renminbi have been converted at the 2005 rate of RMB 1 = $0.12.

weeding, and spraying. (The balance went mostly to seedlings, but also included things like pesticides and agricultural extension.) Sino-Lao's proposal was accompanied by a set of figures that roughly mirrored the ministry's categories. But the company's counteroffer came in much lower, largely owing to how it valued smallholder labor. Against the ministry's figure of almost $1,500, Sino-Lao estimated overall plantation establishment costs at just $534, and within this much lower estimate, it valued the share of smallholder labor at just over a third of the total, against the ministry's estimate of over two-thirds. Each side's valuation supported its own proposal, and each differed most in its valuation of the scheme's central ingredient: the upland smallholder. Thus, as late as mid-2005, despite their agreement in principle—on cooperating to stabilize shifting cultivation, alleviate upland poverty, and create mutual economic benefits—the two "sides" remained miles apart when it came to how to actually work together.

AREAS OF INFLUENCE

My own research in the northwest began during this period of nascent but uncertain bilateral rubber cooperation on the one hand, and rapid construction of the Northern Economic Corridor on the other. While often discussed as separate sectors or projects, rubber and roadbuilding were in fact closely linked, both being parts of the wider effort to connect the hinterland of northwestern Laos with surrounding areas.[53] More specifically, roadbuilding drove rubber planting. Suitability for rubber, after all, is not just a function of biophysical characteristics like soil quality, temperature, topography, and water availability. It is also intimately social, depending in particular on accessibility, availability of land and labor, and complementarity with other local sources of livelihood.[54] The building of the NEC rearranged all of these social "variables" significantly.

The risk of various forms of land grabbing was identified during the NEC planning process; road corridors are a relatively mature technology, and their effects on newly opened hinterlands have been recognized for centuries.[55] While critics of the GMS and similar geographical imaginaries often interpret enhanced regional connectivity in terms of states' and businesses' ongoing search for cheap resources—what economic geographers call capitalism's "spatial fix"[56]—infrastructure practitioners tend to deal with the downsides of economic expansion in the language of risks, acceptable trade-offs, and mitigation plans. At the scale of specific projects like the NEC, a key question developers faced was thus how far outward in space the corridor's "area of influence" stretched. This had been flagged as an empirical question back in the late 1990s when the ADB took over the project, and it was still being addressed in 2006 when I began my fieldwork.

"Project area of influence" is a term of art that entered the development lexicon as a result of the struggles over accountability in the 1980s and 1990s.[57] On the one hand, it allows lenders of public money like the World

Bank and ADB to evaluate, measure, acknowledge, and discuss the range of impacts that their projects create, often at significant physical distances from projects themselves. "Areas of influence" are thus part of a wider discourse of spatially nuanced impact analysis that includes terms like *direct* impacts, *indirect* impacts, *induced* impacts, *cumulative* impacts, *regional* impacts, and *in-combination* impacts.[58] These terms operate inevitably within what Michel Foucault called power-knowledge, wherein the meanings of words and the statements they produce are linked to high-stakes questions like, in the case of the NEC, how far from the road the protective mitigation activities required by the ADB would extend. Operating within the norms shared by multiple development banks, the mitigation of "indirect" impacts gave the NEC's developers significantly more latitude than "direct" ones.[59] Specifically, the notion of a "project area of influence" allowed planners to acknowledge that the NEC would likely have significant negative impacts away from the immediate roadside, while nonetheless limiting their mitigation activities to the roadside itself. This had important consequences for the rubber development efforts that were getting started in the early 2000s, just as the NEC's mitigation studies were getting off the ground.

The ADB hired the American firm Nathan Associates to do the project's social and environmental impact assessment; this began in 2002 and was completed early the following year, right in the middle of the Sino-Lao rubber impasse described above. The Nathan study made it clear that the NEC's anticipated "area of impact" would extend well beyond the ninety-seven villages through which the road would pass directly. In addition to the roadside villages, "other villages, which are *not seen from the road but are affected by its commerce*, further expand the ethnic and cultural diversity found in the Northern Economic Corridor. Most of the inhabitants of these villages are engaged in subsistence agriculture . . . [and have] some of the highest rates of poverty in Laos. . . . Appropriate development measures taken in conjunction with the improvement of the Project Road will be needed to help to bring these inhabitants to above poverty level standards."[60]

This call for "appropriate development measures" was elaborated in the study's section on social impacts, which, along with the ADB's final recommendation for financing to the bank's board of directors, highlighted a pair of issues that have proven prescient. The first was the mismatch between Lao property law, which recognized "intensive" land uses like lowland rice paddies and tree plantations—permanent livelihoods, in other words—and the "extensive" and often illegible land uses like shifting cultivation, livestock grazing, and forest harvesting that predominated in the NEC's area of influence.[61] Tightly echoing the ADB's own recently published *Participatory Poverty Analysis for Lao PDR*,[62] the Nathan study noted the "severe hardships" caused by LFA (the government's village-scale mapping program mentioned above) throughout Laos's northern uplands via its largely unsuccessful effort to create "'permanent' livelihood substitutes." These included exacerbated land-tenure insecurity ("issuing . . . land certificates to upland farms only if they meet the 'permanent' criteria") and increasing soil exhaustion as a result of the shorter upland fallow rotations induced by the zoning process.[63]

Second, and somewhat ominously, the chapter on social impacts noted that a huge amount of land—some 196,615 hectares in Luang Namtha alone, comprising 82 percent of the province's officially designated agricultural production land—had been classified by provincial authorities as "suitable for rubber or eucalyptus plantations."[64] This pairing of policy-induced tenure and livelihood insecurity with the conjuring of large-scale conversion to industrial plantations gave substance to the report's call for appropriate measures to protect upland villages. It also echoed requests from local officials documented in the NEC's Social Action Plan for "assistance to protect the needs and rights of the existing communities" from the already-apparent commercial pressure on the corridor's land base.[65]

The NEC's planners ultimately settled on a pair of compromises that, proponents argued, would help prevent land grabbing within the corridor.[66] The first was to issue land-tax certificates to residents whose land parcels fell within fifty meters of the NEC's centerline. This distance was judged to be that of "direct" impact and led to the documenting of over seven thousand parcels along the length of the road.[67] While these documents were widely referred to as "titles" by foreign consultants I met in the field as well as by subsequent official reports, they were in fact land-tax documents that provided a limited form of recognition—that of *existing* use and thus the "right" to pay tax—rather than a future right to permanent use. This point was emphasized by the Nathan-study authors who, writing just a few months after ADB planners had speculated that "all households in the project villages [might] be issued with land titles on a priority basis,"[68] noted that "the government places higher priority . . . on extending the land tax document to all homeowners as a means of increasing tax revenue and broadening administrative documentation."[69] The NEC's so-called titling component was thus widely perceived as a twofold compromise, given its spatial narrowness and the limited form of security it conveyed.[70] Various people I spoke with in 2006 acknowledged these shortcomings but expressed hope that any form of land documentation was better than none, given the rising pressure on land that was already becoming apparent from, among other things, rubber projects.[71]

The second piece of the compromise addressed the land *outside* the fifty-meter buffer but still within the NEC's official area of influence, which was defined as the ninety-seven villages through which the road passed directly as well as twenty-five "other villages" mentioned above that sat away from the road but were nonetheless "affected by its commerce."[72] (This was a conservative accounting; as noted elsewhere in the Nathan study, the NEC was "more realistically" defined in terms of the full three districts through which the road passed.[73]) Reflecting the room to maneuver on so-called indirect impacts, NEC planners removed responsibility for areas outside the fifty-meter buffer to a different project entirely: a grant-based initiative from the Japanese government. This project sought to pilot what the Nathan study called "scientifically designed, participatory, and well-implemented land-use planning and allocation in conjunction with integrated rural development and capacity building."[74]

This spin-off project targeted entire village territories rather than just the immediate roadside strip. But it came at a cost: the nine-village pilot was budgeted at $1.5 million, which would have translated to roughly $20 million if applied to all 122 villages in the NEC's official area of influence. As a development professional affiliated with the NEC told me in 2006, even $10 million would have been "way too much" for the project's mitigation budget; the loan needed to stay simple and lean, he explained, rather than trying to "do everything."[75] Moving the burden of dealing with the land-grab threat to a different project thus allowed the ADB and the three national governments to have their proverbial cake and eat it too. As they proceeded with construction in 2004, they had a loan with an impressive 20.9 percent estimated internal rate of return.[76] They also had at least a claim—for themselves as well as for any potential critics—that the land-grab threat was being taken seriously.

AVAILABLE LAND

Events on the ground rapidly proved otherwise. Throughout the mid-2000s, numerous land deals involving "investors" of various kinds took place within the NEC, especially in the areas beyond the project's fifty-meter mitigation buffer. Some of these were just a few minutes' walk from the main road, like the large rubber plantation (thirty hectares or so) established in one of Vieng Phoukha's roadside villages by a businessman from the district capital. Established in 2005, this deal was especially embarrassing for the organizers of the spin-off project discussed above because it sat in the middle of their main pilot village's agricultural land.[77] While it exemplified the "delay in implementation" that the ADB would later use to rate the project less than satisfactory,[78] in fairness it simply illustrated the difficulty of stopping a land rush that was already underway. It was, moreover, entirely typical: entrepreneurial, ad hoc land-finding was taking place across the northwest, and indeed more generally across rural Laos.[79] Typically, it followed the roads.

During my research I heard multiple descriptions of how various entrepreneurs—foreign and domestic, private and state-affiliated—gained access to land; these ranged from accounts of "informal" or personal access to highly bureaucratic processes of approaching this office, then that, then another, and producing documents X, Y, and Z at each stage along the way.[80] While the differences often testified to internal jurisdictional struggles within the state (see ch. 5), their agreement on the need for actual, on-the-ground surveying and negotiation highlighted a common disregard for existing land-use maps. And while this sometimes frustrated technocratically inclined participants and observers both in and out of government, there were good reasons for going to the field to survey. One was the dynamism of the moment—the confluence of the rubber-planting boom and the new hinterland access created by the NEC. A second related to a longer-standing issue with how village-scale maps were produced. As noted above, LFA maps often depicted land use in aspirational terms, and the impossibility of farmers following them meant that across the country, both poor farmers and wealthy entrepreneurs had been violating them for years. Occasionally, LFA's restrictions on land use came up in my and my colleagues' discussions with farmers, but often things tended in the other direction.[81]

Let me give an example. In late 2007, my research assistant and I had a chance to speak with a man who was in the process of developing a modest (roughly two-hectare) rubber plantation. We had been traveling on one of the NEC's feeder roads, about ten minutes from the main highway, when we spotted the telltale contours of a new rubber garden. The man was working with two laborers, and he chatted with us while the three took a break from hacking the new terraces out of the hillside. He was from the district center, and explained that he had recently purchased the land from a relative who lived in the village where the plot was located. Recently cut rice stalks were still standing, showing that the field had been used for shifting cultivation the previous growing season. When we pushed for the details of the sale, he told us readily that it had been approved by the local village head, and that he planned to take the sale documents to the district tax office to register it as soon as he finished planting. Over the weeks that followed, the plantation took full form. The terraces were completed within a week of our conversation, and within two weeks they were completely planted with young rubber seedlings.[82]

The man's account echoed what we had been hearing from local officials. According to local tax officials, land sales were typically approved at the village level and came under their (the tax department's) purview relatively late in the process—often not until the new owner brought the previous owner's land-tax receipt (transferred during the sale) to pay the next year's land tax. The sale was also divorced from the zoning map, which was kept in the local Agriculture and Forestry office and should, in theory, have been consulted before the sale was approved. This did not necessarily happen, however, and this particular sale had almost certainly been illegal because it sat inside the village's "local use forest" (*pa somxai*)—the area where residents were permitted to gather building materials and nontimber forest products.[83] As evidenced from the previous year's upland rice stalks, the parcel had actually already been out of conformance with official zoning, even before the sale. This too was unsurprising. Local Agriculture and Forestry officials had told us a few times that LFA was unpopular with farmers in the area because of its efforts to limit them to three agricultural plots. Many had thus expanded their fields into new areas—often including those zoned as "forest"—for various reasons. In one of our meetings, a government staffer who knew the local situation especially well confided that these expansions were not just due to demographic causes; they also reflected the increasing encroachment of rubber on land used for food production.[84]

Rubber companies like Sino-Lao and Bolisat Ltd. fit into this dynamic landscape in multiple and often complex ways. On the one hand, despite being part of the wider land rush, they were also subject to a regulatory check in ways that smaller land deals by local elites were not. In Vieng Phoukha, for instance, it was clear that Bolisat Ltd. was in competition with people like the land buyer described above; both were pursuing land along the NEC's feeder roads in the same general vicinity. One of my informants told me that local elites were in fact strongly opposed to Bolisat Ltd.'s operations because the company was beating them to land that they were hoping to develop for themselves. The district governor, my informant explained, had embraced working with Bolisat Ltd. for precisely this reason. Even if it meant giving up land to the company's plantations, the logic was apparently that doing so would be more manageable than having poor villages' land base eroded piecemeal by numerous and essentially unregulated land sales.[85]

This protective dimension was also apparent in the creation of the "3 + 2 policy" in late 2005, which was put forward as a putative solution to the impasse described above in the Sino-Lao case. The agreement was described by a team from Laos's National Agriculture and Forestry Research Institute in language that emphasizes its departure from the concession model:

> A meeting was held on 10 October 2005, in Luang Namtha,
> where representatives from . . . Bokeo, Luang Namtha and
> Oudomxay gathered to discuss foreign investment in rubber.
> Representatives from the three provinces agreed that providing
> land concessions to investors to manage rubber plantations will
> not resolve rural poverty, as farmers lose access to agricultural
> land and are merely hired by investors as laborers. On the other
> hand, representatives of the three provinces agreed that foreign
> investors should promote smallholder rubber plantations with a
> general profit-sharing arrangement of 70% for farmers and 30%
> for companies. They also agreed to support foreign investors
> that are willing to provide inputs on credit, and purchase latex
> from farmers.[86]

The "3 + 2" agreement was also sometimes called the *songserm* policy, using the Lao term for "promotion" (as in the paragraph above: "investors should promote . . ."). It was also formally spelled out in the meeting minutes authorized by Luang Namtha's provincial governor: "The cooperative investment mode is hereby agreed to be the 3 + 2 model, namely: Investors are responsible for three aspects: (1) capital, (2) technique, and (3) marketing. Villagers are responsible for two aspects: (1) labor and (2) land, in accordance with state land management."[87] While both the final caveat on "state land management" and the concept of "promotion/extension" (*songserm*) left important room to maneuver, the expectation that bilateral rubber cooperation in the north would operate under a smallholder- rather than a concession-centric business model was widely shared.[88] Indeed, when problems with Vietnamese rubber concessions in southern Laos blew up as a national issue in 2007, Laos's prime minister held up the "3 + 2" model as the "strongly promoted" alternative when he announced a national moratorium on concessions.[89]

On the other hand, the land-finding efforts of at least some Chinese rubber companies proved quite successful. In part, this was no doubt due to their employing the same sort of opportunistic resourcefulness as local Lao entrepreneurs. In one of my interviews at a Chinese rubber company office in Luang Namtha, for instance, the bulk of the talking was done by an older Lao man who was a former provincial Industry and Commerce official and had gone to work for the company after retiring from his government job.[90] As I elaborate in chapter 4, this sort of reliance on local officials to navigate the terrain of land access was highly successful in areas like Khet Nam Fa.

But another part of rubber companies' success involved the logic of wage work, which fit the economic realities of upland livelihoods much better than the "long pay" of contract farming with a slow-growing tree crop. Rubber may have fit the ideal of the permanent livelihood, but successful smallholder rubber typically involves at least some degree of state support during the six to ten years between initial investment and harvest.[91] This support is missing from all accounts of "3 + 2" that I am aware of,[92] and is reflected in a common answer to the question of how farmers were supposed to survive during the transition period: that it is possible to intercrop upland rice "for a few years." A flimsy excuse, this nonetheless acknowledged the difficulty of the transition for farmers who depend on annual production for their food and livelihood security.

It was thus unsurprising that even the allegedly smallholder-friendly "3 + 2" schemes proved widely unattractive to most upland farmers. This was already apparent when I was doing fieldwork in 2007 and 2008. The lack of farmer interest was often explained to me in terms of the splits being offered: as I heard from numerous village heads, even the 70–30 split outlined in the official version of "3 + 2" was widely seen as unattractive since farmers wanted to own their plantations outright; many actual "3 + 2" deals were even worse, offering 60–40 or even 50–50.[93] But while this gave a reason, it also avoided a larger and more uncomfortable issue, given the widespread official boostering for rubber as a livelihood-improvement mechanism for the upland poor. Time and again, the "smallholder" rubber producer fit the profile of the man I met along the road, or the businessman from Luang Namtha: urban people with means who might own farms but were not typically identified as "farmers." And even the so-called poorer farmers who participated in "3 + 2"—people who could not afford to finance inputs on their own—were still relatively well-off compared to their even poorer neighbors. Both groups tended to have multiple existing livelihood options. For the northern uplands' majority, on the other hand, smallholder rubber, even with contract farming, was a leap too far.

Wage work, on the other hand, was not. This was where the Sino-Lao counteroffer examined above carried a logic that traveled widely: that of combining wage work with a division of plantation *land* rather than a share-cropping arrangement based on the division of the rubber (latex) *crop*. Between 2005 and 2007, a variant on "3 + 2"—sometimes called "4 + 1"—was developed in various pockets around the northwest. In some places its genealogy was obvious. Even though Sino-Lao's proposal was ultimately rejected in Luang Namtha,[94] the company took the same plan to Oudomxai province, where it applied the wage-work-with-land-division model to a 5,000-hectare "3 + 2" agreement it negotiated with local authorities. As in Luang Namtha, provincial Agriculture and Forestry officials had objected to the scheme, but the company made an arrangement with the provincial governor's office and used district-level technical staff to circumvent the objection.[95] Back in Luang Namtha, the same basic template of wage labor plus land partition was applied by other companies, including Bolisat Ltd., whose "4 + 1" arrangement in Khet Nam Fa bettered Sino-Lao's Oudomxai deal by a full 20 percent: Bolisat Ltd. was promised a 70–30 land split in their favor, and in the end no partition took place at all (see ch. 4). Other variations on "4 + 1" occurred across the northwest (map 1.2).[96] Targeting the "lower uplands" under 800 meters where the risk of frost was low, these deals homed in on the region's abundant supply of former shifting-cultivation lands (*pa lao*), frequently accessing high-quality land close to roadsides.

In 2008, as I was finishing my main research period, it was already clear that this concession-like variant had become "the predominant contracting mode," as political scientist Weiyi Shi noted in the first major study of northern Laos's rubber boom.[97] At the time there was already much debate about this "other" sort of contract farming, both in and out of government, since it used the heavy hand of "state land management" to secure company plantation lands. This meant using the basic tools of concession-making to create available land, either by invoking state claims of direct ownership over forests or invoking the state's exclusive right to "manage" (*khoumkhong*) or plan agricultural land use through the zoning (*chatsan*) process. Moreover, the very thing that made these deals more compatible with upland livelihoods—their use of wage labor—also made them more concession-like. Echoing Shi's worry that "it is not enough to ban the concession only to have its problems disguised under a new face called 'contract farming,'" a provincial official complained to me in mid-2007: "There is a problem with contract farming. [It's] not really like contract farming—it's like a concession to a company: a big area. The company says it's contract farming but it's not actually contract farming."[98]

These quasi-concessions were not properly inventoried at the time, in part because national-level land management authorities deemed them

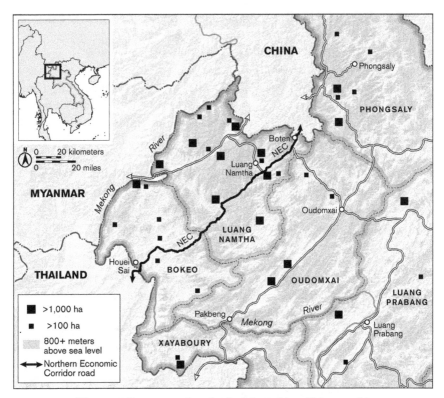

MAP 1.2 "Not actually contract farming" projects: large Chinese rubber plantations in northwestern Laos. Map by Ben Pease. Based on Hett et al., *Land Leases and Concessions in the Lao PDR*, 23, 29, 39, 46; and Thongmanivong et al., "Concession or Cooperation?," 13.

outside the purview of their already limited concession-inventorying efforts.[99] Even a decade later, provincial-level technical staff in Luang Namtha and Oudomxai admitted that they were still unsure how much land had ended up in each "contract farming" category.[100] In 2013, Luang Namtha's Agriculture and Forestry office published a "concept note" on rubber production in the province that is nonetheless illuminating in its nonchalant reference to rubber as needing huge amounts of alienated wage labor rather than relying on the household labor of smallholders. While acknowledging the crop's origins in state efforts "to generate income and alleviate poverty, stop slash-and-burn and poppy cultivation, and create more permanent jobs for people of the province," the document makes clear the shift since those hopeful early days.[101] Calculating a labor shortfall of *forty-nine thousand people* between the plantation owners and the working bodies necessary for tapping their rapidly maturing holdings, the "concept note" reflects the slippage from the type of smallholder conjured by "permanent livelihoods" rhetoric—the stabilized shifting cultivator turned household-scale rubber grower—to the larger plantation owners described above: Chinese companies and various levels of Lao elites.[102] And as we have already seen in Khet Nam Fa, even this "opportunity" for local people to "get some income by selling their labor power" did not always pan out.

While scholars have rightly pointed out the extensive conjuring of empty land that often underlay Laos's representation as "a business-friendly resource frontier,"[103] this chapter tells a subtly different story. Some Chinese rubber companies did indeed buy into the myth of empty land, reflecting Laos's frequent portrayal in China as underpopulated and resource-rich.[104] But a better reflection of investment politics appears in the materials examined above, drawn not from the public transcript of boostering and the media but from the more guarded arena of regulatory debates and specific investment projects.[105] Contra land being empty or unused, this material shows that land was instead what we might call "socially" available: accessible to certain preferred uses like rubber even if it was already being used in other ways, and even if the channels for availability—Chinese rubber "promotion" projects, Lao elites' plantation schemes—remained themselves subject to ongoing deliberation, debate, and state intervention. Land's social availability also appears in the statistical conjuring exercise quoted above, where Lao officials asserted that developing 30,000 hectares of new rubber plantations would "not be a problem." Ministerial officials may not have known precisely where those 30,000 hectares would go, but that was beside the point. Their proposal was about recombining land and labor—the "hectares" in the three northwestern provinces and the local population's "labor units"—in new ways, precisely because their existing configuration was seen as undesirable.

This recombination could have gone a number of ways, in part because of the possibilities created by the Chinese central government's "opium poppy replacement" program. Established in late 2004, the program used a mix of tax credits, import allowances, and direct cash subsidies to support Chinese companies in developing rubber and other agricultural-commodity "promotion" schemes across northern Laos and northern Myanmar.[106] On the one hand, given Beijing's apparent seriousness about using alternative-livelihoods development to help stem the flow of Southeast Asian opium into

China's heroin market, the program might have used its significant resources to help finance the smallholder rubber transition, much like state enterprises did decades earlier in Malaysia and Thailand.[107] This would have been consistent with the program's purpose of facilitating Chinese investment by lowering the costs of working with upland farmers in new and economically risky contexts.[108] Moreover, it would have followed Lao officials' request for smallholder-centric rubber cooperation, mirroring both China's long-standing commitment to "noninterventionist" international cooperation and more recent rhetoric, such as that accompanying the BRI, about using state resources to do international development better than under the prevailing neoliberal model.[109]

On the other hand, the devolution of the program's oversight to the provincial level—and in particular, the decision to give Yunnan's provincial commerce department administrative power over the program's operations—articulated with a narrower pursuit of business interests.[110] The poppy-replacement program thus exemplified Yunnan authorities' wider strategy of tapping into China's national policy aims and associated revenue streams by becoming "a grand passageway to Southeast Asia" via official channels like the "Going Out" policy and the GMS economic corridors.[111] To the extent that it more narrowly supported the interests of the companies involved, the program risked being simply financial fuel for an upland land rush, wrapped in the legitimating guise of alternative development.

The evidence points toward the latter, but also highlights the persistence of significant opacity when it comes to what happened where, why, and how. This illegibility obscures crucial details. Of all of the places where rubber cooperation was "promoted" by Chinese companies and local Lao authorities, only some communities lost land. The socially uneven distribution of enclosure and dispossession has been noted throughout Laos's concession boom, as well as more widely throughout the global land rush.[112] In Laos, it jibes with a long-standing recognition that land policy is subject to differing interpretations by local authorities, often due to how it connects with various "local interests and power struggles."[113] While this can have positive implications in some cases, it also has clearly negative ones in circumstances like those discussed here. In contexts like the NEC's upland villages, where property formalization was still in flux, and where the "promotion" of rubber was often paired with a strong dose of coercion to accept any development assistance on offer, negotiating with "investors" and government officials demands both political acumen and active citizenship. The lack of spatial detail about where and how Chinese rubber schemes operated leaves unanswered the questions of how land's social availability was negotiated on the ground and how this differed from place to place.

We need to look carefully at the historical terrain on which citizenship is created and negotiated if we are to make sense of the uneven enclosures exemplified by Khet Nam Fa and the slippage to "4 + 1" more broadly. While mainland Southeast Asia's economic integration has been famously called "turning battlefields into marketplaces," this phrase is usually interpreted both regionally and metaphorically by critics and proponents alike.[114] Instead, we need to take this phrase more literally by examining Southeast Asia not just as a Cold War landscape in a general sense but also as an interlinked network of actual, local landscapes where Cold War conflict took place on the ground, and where place-specific struggles over land access continue today. It is in these groundings that we see how the slippages from protective efforts like "3 + 2," a regulatory pushback against large-scale land concessions to Chinese rubber companies, came about, and how the quasi-concessions of "4 + 1" became targeted into particular communities and landscapes. Examining the "global" land rush in the landscapes and communities of northwestern Laos thus illustrates not just the mechanics of land grabbing but also shows the ways in which legacies of geopolitical conflict can linger on the ground, animating the micropolitics of land access far longer than they have any right to.

CHAPTER TWO

A Real Country?

Denationalizing the Lao Uplands, 1955–1975

We live in a revolutionary world in which internal war is a basic fact
of life. . . . Studies of the techniques by which internal wars can be
molded and channeled are therefore of the utmost importance. The
Machiavellian overtones, the apparent cynicism, may make such
studies repellent, but that cannot be helped.

—FROM *SOCIAL SCIENCE RESEARCH AND NATIONAL*
SECURITY, a 1963 report by the Research Group in
Psychology and the Social Sciences, Smithsonian
Institution, Washington, DC, for the US Office
of Naval Research

I N 1971, as part of its ongoing efforts to advise the US military on Cold
War strategy, the RAND Corporation hired a man named Douglas
Blaufarb to chronicle the lessons of the "unconventional" war the United
States had been fighting in Laos since 1962.[1] Blaufarb had been the Vientiane
station chief for the Central Intelligence Agency (CIA) from 1964 to 1966,
and would later write an authoritative insider account of US Cold War counterinsurgency efforts across the global South.[2] His report combined big-
picture strategy with cool technical precision, and argued that the "quiet
war" the United States had been fighting in Laos had "largely achieved its
aim."[3] Declassified in 1997, it makes for chilling reading.

Central to Blaufarb's analysis is his account of a shift that took place in
1960–61 among key American policymakers and advisers, as the out-
going Eisenhower and incoming Kennedy administrations confronted

what came to be called "the Laotian crisis." The shift concerned the onto-logical status of the political-geographic entity, Laos, that the Americans were dealing with. In the years leading up to the so-called crisis, US engage-ment there had aimed to make Laos what Blaufarb called "a firm anti-Communist 'bastion' on the borders of China and Vietnam,"[4] and had focused largely on the urban milieu of Vientiane. But as US frustration with electoral and coalition politics grew, the Americans began to rethink what Laos actually *was*. The premise of creating a strong "bastion" had presumed that Laos was an actual country, ontologically the same as the others that surrounded it: Vietnam, China, Thailand, and so on. But as Blaufarb's account reveals, the Laotian crisis was not just an outward political crisis, a series of events centered on a 1960 coup by a Neutralist army captain who leaned distinctly away from US interests.[5] It was also an internal, analytical crisis among US strategists and their advisers, who began to suspect that Laos was not what they had previously thought. Increasingly, they began to doubt whether it was a real country at all.

Blaufarb's opening pages describe Laos as "hardly a country except in the legal sense,"[6] and his subsequent elaboration reflects the opinion of the vari-ous policymakers, advisers, and clandestine operatives he worked with:

> History and terrain have divided the land into separate regions,
> with little to bind these together. The population is a mixture of
> races and religions, of primitive hill tribes and lowland paddy-
> growing Lao peasants, who regard each other with fear and
> hostility. Although in control of the government and its military
> forces, the ethnic Lao comprise less than half the population.
> The elite of this Lao minority is a collection of rival clans, who
> share little in the sense of national purpose but regard the
> government and the public service as an arena where they
> compete for influence and power to enrich themselves. The
> country as a whole is underdeveloped in every way. A limited
> road network connects the main towns along the Mekong
> [River] but, with few exceptions, avoids the hinterland, a rugged,
> roadless expanse of jungled hills and limestone ridges.[7]

Today, similar discourses of national unreality permeate global geopoli-tics in "fracture zones" across the Middle East, sub-Saharan Africa, and South Asia, where discourses of "tribalism" and "rival clans" are regularly invoked to explain ongoing political crises from Iraq to Sudan to Afghani-stan, among others.[8] These explanations are, of course, highly selective, leaving out the trajectories of foreign intervention that, like the 1963 report quoted in the epigraph above, reflect the premise held by some state officials and their so-called expert advisers, both then and now, that molding and channeling the "internal wars" of other countries is something to be embraced and undertaken, however reluctantly.

While no longer riven by the "unconventional" conflict that Blaufarb summarized fairly accurately as "a civil-war-cum-foreign-invasion,"[9] Laos still bears the scars of the days when it *was* the Afghanistan of its time. These scars are partly physical; Laos's status as the most-bombed nation on earth is rarely far from popular accounts of the country.[10] But the legacies are also socio-geographic in the sense described in this chapter, which focuses on the upland landscape. Laos's uplands—today a target of many development projects, including but hardly limited to the transnational land deals discussed in the last chapter—cannot be understood merely in the biophysical and human-ecological terms usually used: a mountainous region where population and road densities are thin, where forests are historically abundant, and where shifting cultivation has long been a dominant form of agricultural production.[11] The uplands are also a political landscape where questions of governance, resistance, and security are rarely far from the surface, even if their depths are, as elaborated in later chapters, highly variable and often hard to see.[12] If, as James Scott argues, upland Southeast Asia is today a key site of the ongoing "last great enclosure" through which modern states "climb hills,"[13] the unevenness of this process should not be underestimated. The Cold War history of Laos's uplands—both in general and in the northwest in particular—has shaped this unevenness significantly. In the northwest, this history revolves around a place called Nam Nyu.

Nam Nyu was the site of a clandestine military and spy base run by the CIA from 1962 to 1973 in what is today the remote hinterland of the Northern Economic Corridor. While now relatively a nondescript, rural corner of Laos's Bokeo province, until the mid-2000s Nam Nyu was one of a handful of military "special zones" that dotted the uplands of northern Laos and reflected the legacy of events discussed in this chapter and the next. At 600 square kilometers, the Nam Nyu special zone was comparatively small, at least relative to the larger and better-known Saysomboun special zone, a 7,000-square-kilometer area formerly located in north-central Laos that makes an appearance in chapter 3. (Saysomboun is now a province of its own, while the Nam Nyu special zone has been absorbed into the surrounding districts.) But even at 600 square kilometers—60,000 hectares in the units used in chapter 1—the special zone that was created in the wake of Nam

Nyu's destruction in 1973 testifies to the ease with which postwar events overspill earlier boundaries. This overspilling was substantial.

In Laos, Cold War–era logic and practices sought to create a form of upland political space that was explicitly, deliberately, and strategically *denationalized*. Today, we often associate territorialization efforts with processes of integration, whether for nation-building, regionalization, or both—the NEC, for example.[14] Here, in contrast, territorialization focused on exacerbating the *dis*connectedness and internal fracturing that, as in Blaufarb's description quoted above, US strategists increasingly associated with Laos after around 1960. The geography of infrastructure specific to this form of territoriality was not roads, but roadlessness supported by small aircraft, and the sociopolitical space it thus strove to create was one of remoteness, isolation, and autonomy for the upland "hill tribes" that the CIA and their collaborators worked with. This embrace of the uplands, and of upland peoples as political allies and "assets" (in the blunt language of Cold War espionage), was a direct response to the Laotian crisis of 1960–61, and it drew for inspiration on French military efforts of the 1950s to pit upland communities against the nationalist Viet Minh. But it was also a response rooted in multiple decades of French colonialism, in both its logics and its shortcomings. For most of their rule the French never imagined Laos as a distinct nation, seeing it instead as an underpopulated and racially inferior borderland whose "ordained role" would be, as historian Martin Stuart-Fox explains, eventually being absorbed into "a greater Vietnam."[15] But systematic underinvestment by the French made this incorporation a slow process, and the fragmentation that formed the basis of the US turn to the uplands was as much an effect of colonial neglect as it was of explicit policy.

The US reorientation away from the Lao urban milieu was enormous, both at the time and in terms of its enduring legacies. The most well-known of these was, as mentioned above, the unacknowledged air war that, between 1964 and 1973, gave Laos the unhappy distinction of being one of the most bombed countries of the twentieth century.[16] But the shift to treating Laos not as a nation per se but as a postcolonial terrain, to be understood and exploited militarily in the context of the wider Cold War in East and Southeast Asia, also dug deeply into what twenty-first-century military strategists have come to call the human terrain.[17] In the process, cold warriors like Blaufarb and others who appear below rearranged sociopolitical relationships within and across upland Laos in ways that would have long-lasting impact.[18] Given the emphasis on the "denationalization" of territory that has come to characterize scholarly understandings of transnational land access today,[19] earlier histories of territorial denationalization—especially where they underlie and influence later processes of land grabbing—are essential to bring into the picture.

EMBRACING THE UPLANDS

Most Americans had never heard of Laos before the so-called "Laotian crisis," which confronted the newly inaugurated President John F. Kennedy in the winter and spring of 1961. Over those months, Kennedy learned to pronounce the name of an unfamiliar country ("Lay-oss" in February, "Laos" by April) and adopted his predecessors' domino theory of Southeast Asian geopolitics. "If Laos fell into communist hands," Kennedy fretted, "it would increase the dangers on the northern frontiers of Thailand, would put additional pressure on Cambodia, and would put additional pressure on South Vietnam, which themselves would put additional pressure on Malaya."[20] These sorts of worries, at once hemispheric in their perceived importance and yet also intensely local, tasked American policymakers in new ways during the Cold War and led them to rethink assumptions and come up with new methods that were at once inventive, difficult to categorize, and tragic for many of those they entangled. The desire to create replacements for traditional military engagement—to wage wars that were not quite wars, yet were at the same time "politics by other means"[21]—had pushed the US military to develop its social-scientific capacities in new ways after the Second World War. Engaging some of the brightest minds of the day, the challenge of manipulating "internal wars" in other countries found fruition in early-1960s Laos.

At the end of the Second World War, President Franklin Roosevelt had outlined a doctrine of American support for Third World decolonization, but also simultaneously began a process by which the United States—first passively, then actively—came to support France's reoccupation of its Indochinese colonies after the war. This reversal stemmed largely from the changing calculus of global hegemony that we have come to know as the Cold War. While Roosevelt believed that Japanese aggression had been abetted by weak colonial governments around the Pacific Rim, the shift toward countering Soviet "aggression" demanded, he believed, a strong and thus colonially reequipped France to help shift the balance of power in Europe.[22] As recolonization stumbled with the outbreak of the First Indochina War in 1945 and, a decade later, the French defeat at Dien Bien Phu, the United States increasingly took up what its leaders saw as the anticommunist mandate in Indochina.

During the mid-1950s, the US government launched and scaled up both civilian and military aid programs to Laos and "South" Vietnam, aiming to create what the rhetoric of the day called "anticommunist bastions" to contain China and "North" Vietnam.[23] The "domino theory" that Kennedy would later take up had been first articulated in 1954, as President Eisenhower tried to mobilize public support for the French in the weeks before Dien Bien Phu fell;[24] later in the decade it would become a key talking point for US policy in the Mekong region. By the late 1950s, however, the American aid programs in both Laos and South Vietnam had become mired in corruption, fueling conspicuous consumption among urban elites but making minimal inroads into rural areas and the improvement of the respective local militaries.[25] Despite making Laos the greatest per capita recipient of American aid at the time—$150 per year, more than twice the average annual income[26]—the effectiveness of US support for Lao nation-building was limited. By one estimate, almost a third of all annual American aid revenues were linked to scandals or fraud involving "virtually every member of the country's ruling elite."[27] The same observer wrote that the situation was "made to order for the communists."

By January 1961, just as Eisenhower prepared to pass the American presidency to John F. Kennedy, events in Laos confirmed the American program to be failing badly, and the situation escalating—as it also was in the newly independent Congo—toward proxy war with the Soviet Union. As they did across the global South, US efforts ran increasingly into the politics of "nonalignment," an effort among Third World leaders that, following the Bandung Conference of 1955, attempted to delink international development assistance from Cold War geopolitics.[28] In Laos this came in the form of a military coup in mid-1960, led by an army officer and self-proclaimed Neutralist who, with substantial popular backing, reinstalled a prime minister who had been deposed only months earlier by an American-backed candidate in an election that was widely seen as rigged. Almost immediately a countercoup returned the anticommunist faction to power, but in doing so drove the Neutralists—including a large slice of the army—into alliance with the Marxist Pathet Lao (Lao Nation) party. In late 1960, as the Neutralists began receiving airlifts from the Soviet Union and with the Pathet Lao advised and assisted by the North Vietnamese, the US strategic position was seen to be deteriorating badly. This was the "Laotian crisis" that precipitated Eisenhower's famous warning to the incoming President Kennedy: "If Laos is lost to the Free World, in the long run we will lose all of Southeast Asia."[29]

The response to what Blaufarb later called the unsuccessful US "effort to make political bricks without straw"[30] centered on a reorientation to the uplands. First and foremost was a scaling up of the US "tribal program," which allowed Washington to distance itself from the Royal Lao Army, which was linked to the embarrassing visibility of the countercoup, while simultaneously maintaining and even enhancing its military capabilities despite the international commitment to "neutralize" Laos formalized in the Geneva Accords of 1962. Although US work with Laos's "hill tribes" had begun in the late 1950s, it was not until early 1961—the peak of the crisis— that the program began to occupy center stage with the launch of Operation Momentum, authorized during Eisenhower's final weeks in office.[31] This initiative brought together two earlier trajectories of irregular warfare in the region: on the one hand, French efforts begun in the early 1950s to channel "minority grievances" into anti–Viet Minh resistance, mostly in Vietnam but also in parts of Laos; and on the other hand, American efforts in Thailand begun during the Korean War to defend against a possible Chinese invasion by mobilizing ethnic-minority groups along the Thai-Burma border as paramilitary allies of the Thai state.[32] These experiences formed the raw material for much of what followed.

Before 1961, US military advisers had done a limited amount of work with what remained of the ethnically organized, geographically localized militias (*maquis*) set up by the French counterinsurgency specialist (and later theorist) Roger Trinquier.[33] Having started his career in French Indochina, organizing upland militias for customs enforcement in northern Tonkin, Trinquier later became notorious for his advocacy of torture during the Algerian War of Independence.[34] As the United States took over French anti-communist efforts in the late 1950s, they retained his model but had to recruit and train their own fighters, since most of the French-trained militias had been killed in the months after Dien Bien Phu.[35] Operation Momentum focused on reassembling one of these units, a Hmong *maquis* based in the mountains northeast of Vientiane, which boasted the leadership of Vang Pao, then a mid-level army officer and later a famous Hmong leader in the United States. Already up and coming—he had been sent to a seminar on counterinsurgency in the Philippines in 1958—Vang Pao was a key reason why the Hmong of northeastern Laos became, for the United States, what one historian of the secret war called "the right tribe in the right area at the right time."[36]

Seeking to minimize the visible US presence in Laos while also scaling up its military capabilities, Operation Momentum also brought in a program from Thailand developed there by the CIA: the Police Aerial Reinforcement

Unit, or "Paru." Created in the 1950s, the Thai Paru forces worked to develop *maquis*-style relationships with the upland "hill tribes" of northern Thailand, whom they saw as a potential first line of defense if US support for the Chinese Nationalist Kuomintang (KMT) were to erupt into a wider war.[37] As Operation Momentum grew into a full-blown military apparatus, first in northeastern Laos and then in the northwest, the Paru played key roles as officers and trainers. In both locations, and especially in the latter, the Paru would be supplemented by additional "third-country nationals," elaborated below, to help displace the visibility of Americans when it came to actual military activity.

Operation Momentum's third leg was civilian logistical and infrastructural support, which had played a role in American operations in Laos before 1960 but was scaled up and militarized as the "tribal program" expanded and took increasing precedence. In keeping with the need to roll back visible US military involvement, the US Agency for International Development (USAID) became a hub for both military advising and logistics through the use of retired military "specialists," as well as for coordinating the refugee relief effort; Blaufarb described this as "an AID-sponsored program fully integrated with the tribal effort, which sustained the families of the guerillas and thereby provided a reassurance essential to morale."[38] Momentum also drew extensively on the services of Air America and a few other nominally private airlines owned by the CIA.[39] Negotiating the upland landscape reliably meant flying in and out of short, often steeply sloped and roughly cleared landing strips. This in turn required the services of specially developed "short-takeoff-and-landing" (STOL) airplanes, along with specially trained pilots. These three pieces—well-placed "hill tribes," "third-country" adviser-coordinators like the Paru, and a nominally civilian logistics support network—were the key components of an upland territorial apparatus that came together in 1961 and expanded over the decade that followed.

NAM NYU

The decision to expand the CIA's tribal program from the Hmong *maquis* in the northeast into the Burma-China borderlands of the northwest came in mid-1962. After a turbulent and politically ambiguous 1961, the armed forces of the Royal Lao government, advised and assisted by American Green Berets, had lost the northwestern provincial capital of Houakhong in the spring of 1962 at the Battle of Namtha. (After 1975 Houakhong would be divided in half, forming today's Luang Namtha and Bokeo provinces.) The loss had far-ranging repercussions. Locally, it posed the threat of an unchallenged communist advance to Thailand, via a route that would later become the NEC. Nationally, the battle shifted the political terrain, giving the Pathet Lao additional leverage that produced a tentative agreement with the Royalists and Neutralists in the weeks that followed. In June 1962 all three factions went to Geneva for further negotiations, and in July they signed the Geneva Accords, formally "neutralizing" Laos and mandating the withdrawal of all foreign forces by October. As Blaufarb later acknowledged, the agreement did not actually mean that the US military presence in Laos came to an end. Instead, it "imposed certain constraints upon US military and paramilitary activity which greatly increased the delicacy of this involvement and complicated the operational problems it entailed."[40]

Operation Momentum, begun the previous year, had already developed the basic spatial model that the United States would use to quietly violate the Geneva Accords via the operations that Blaufarb would later classify under the umbrella of "unconventional war." The program exemplified the US shift to the uplands, as well as the reconceptualizion of Laos's abundant rugged and forested terrain—including its corresponding lack of roads— from national liability into tactical advantage. Officially ending the earlier "White Star" military assistance program, the USAID program converted an old White Star base in the mountains north of Vientiane into a publicly acknowledged "refugee relief" center (run by USAID and serviced by Air America), and opened a secret military installation in the secluded mountain valley of Long Cheng just ten kilometers away—a long walk or a short STOL flight.[41] This model, predicated on remoteness, small airplanes, and "civilian" aid, was replicated in the northwestern uplands, after the Battle of Namtha, in a place called Nam Nyu.[42]

Although Laos's "secret war" is usually discussed within the wider context of the Vietnam (or Second Indochina) War, Nam Nyu's development was both motivated and influenced by US involvement in the Cold War's "China theater." Since the early 1950s, the CIA had been supporting the Chinese Nationalist KMT in the borderlands of Yunnan and then, after the KMT's failed invasions in 1950, 1951, and 1952, in northern Burma and Thailand. As KMT soldiers remained in this landscape throughout the decade that followed, their recruitment of local allies—for purposes that combined ongoing insurgency with drug trafficking—brought them into the regional trade in arms and opium, as well as into alliance with future members of the Shan independence movement in Burma.[43] The government of Burma objected to the KMT's presence and took the issue to the United Nations in the mid-1950s, and when this produced limited results, appealed to Beijing for help "demarcating" the common border between the two countries in 1960. In late 1960 and early 1961—just as the "Laotian crisis" emerged farther to the south—thousands of Chinese People's Liberation Army troops came across the Yunnan border into northeastern Burma. They destroyed some KMT units but scattered others into the area that became increasingly known as the Golden Triangle.[44] As US officials in Laos looked to take Operation Momentum into northwestern Laos in late 1962, they faced not only the Geneva Accords but also the immediate aftermath of this process. This turned out to be a mixed bag. On the one hand, the increased presence of the Chinese People's Liberation Army in the region created the risk of escalation; on the other hand, the CIA had the old "assets" of the KMT at its disposal. In the effort that followed, it put them to extensive use.

The CIA's base at Nam Nyu was set up in late 1962 and 1963 by a man named William Young, the CIA's so-called tribal expert in the region.[45] Young had grown up in northern Thailand, part of an American missionary family who had come—first to Burma, then to Thailand—in the early 1900s, and had ended up working for the CIA during its support for the KMT in the 1950s.[46] Young had grown up speaking a number of local languages that would serve him well in Laos, including Hmong and Lahu, discussed below. After helping to get Operation Momentum off the ground in the Hmong area northeast of Vientiane, Young was sent to build an American *maquis* in Houakhong province, an ethnically diverse and especially roadless area that made up much of what the United States called Military Region I (map 2.1).[47] The province's southern extent covered the northern reaches of the old kingdom of Luang Prabang and went as far north as the Mekong River, spanning the Lao portion of the old caravan-trade routes between Yunnan and Thailand that would later be reimagined as the NEC (see ch. 1). In addition to the diversity brought by being a historical trading crossroads, northwestern Laos was also something of a melting pot owing to the in-migration of upland Hmong-Mien and Tibeto-Burman peoples who had fled various uprisings and pacification campaigns in nineteenth-century China. To tackle and exploit this diversity, Young drew on the legacy of French colonialism, although he did so differently than Operation Momentum had done with the Hmong in the northeast. He also drew heavily on his family's connections with the upland "tribes" that the CIA had helped mobilize in support of the KMT.

As Young developed a guerrilla force at Nam Nyu, he based the model on the same approach that the CIA used in Operation Momentum in northeastern Laos, but with a key difference. Lacking a local hill-tribe *maquis*—a local equivalent of Vang Pao's Hmong militia—Young borrowed the only

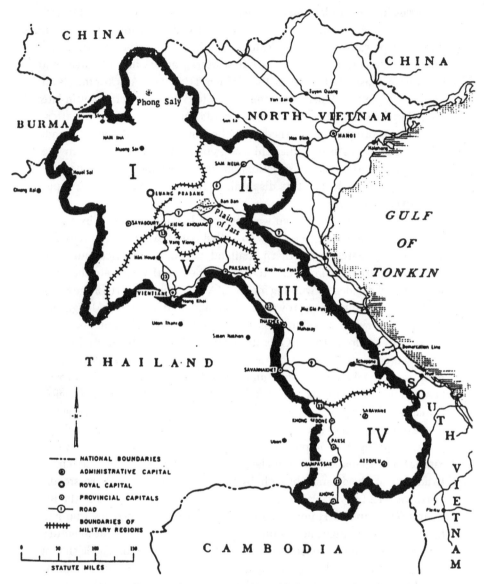

MAP 2.1 The roadless northwest. Originally published in Blaufarb, "Organizing and Managing Unconventional War in Laos," xv. Reprinted with permission.

recently defunct French-colonial structure of indirect rule, recruiting a pair of leaders from the Iu Mien ethnic group, Chao Mai and Chao La. (*Chao* means "lord" or "head.") As anthropologist Hjorleifur Jonsson, who studied this community after many of its members became refugees, explains, "The father of Chao Mai and Chao La [who were brothers] . . . was known as *Phya Long Hai*, 'cruel great chief,' which suggests something other than an unqualified admiration." Phya Long Hai's political rise, Jonsson notes, was "not because he was the only leader" but due to his overshadowing of rivals "through tax collection and military suppression campaigns for the benefit of French colonial rule."[48]

The Iu Mien were opium growers, and were thus one of the ethnic groups that French colonial authorities classified as "evolved" in contrast to the indigenous Mon-Khmer groups like the Khmu, whom they viewed as backward.[49] Opium was one of three state monopolies in French Indochina, along with salt and alcohol. It was thus central to the French policy of *mise en valeur*, an effort to make colonies economically self-sufficient by "developing" their resources; according to historian Geoffrey Gunn, opium "never contributed less than half the revenues of the general colonial budget" of French Indochina.[50] Opium was thus at the heart of indirect rule throughout the uplands of northern Indochina. While high taxes—paid in opium, cash, or corvée labor—led to material hardship and even revolt (especially before the 1930s),[51] by the late-colonial period a number of the "evolved" upland leaders— people like Phya Long Hai and Vang Pao's mentor and patron Touby Li Fung—had forged close and lucrative working relationships with colonial authorities.[52] In setting up the anticommunist *maquis* units, both before 1954 (in the northeast) and after (as in the northwest), cold warriors like Trinquier and Young drew on these leaders' coercive capabilities to provide soldiers, maintain social order, and otherwise staff the "unconventional" military activities of their respective countries.[53]

To organize these activities spatially, the United States drew heavily on what has been called France's *montagnard* (uplander) strategy. The essence of this approach had been to refashion the administrative architecture of colonial indirect rule into a human terrain of military resistance and upland autonomy. Where colonial rule had played ethnic tensions and hierarchies off each another to knit the social landscape *together* in a system of coercion-based extraction facilitated by upland middlemen like Phya Long Hai,[54] the building of *maquis* units reinvested these tensions and hierarchies with a politics of local autonomy amid a wider landscape of late-colonial military strategy. As historian Alfred McCoy explains, the French *montagnard* program was the upland component of "a vast chessboard" that the French developed during the First Indochina War, "where hill tribes, bandits, and religious minorities could be used as pawns to hold strategic territories and prevent Viet Minh infiltration. . . . The French hope was to atomize the Viet Minh's mobilized, unified mass into a mosaic of autonomous fiefs hostile to the revolutionary movement."[55] Young repeated this basic atomization approach at Nam Nyu, recruiting hundreds of troops for the base's defense force from the followers of Chao Mai and Chao La, who had fled west from northeastern Houakhong province in the aftermath of the Battle of Namtha.[56] Enrolling an authority structure that had been built up by French rule, Young put it to work defending and monitoring the territory around Nam Nyu.

Young recruited from the other local "hill tribes" as well, drawing to Nam Nyu members of indigenous Mon-Khmer groups such as the Khmu and the Lamet. Here he seems to have drawn on the remains of the precolonial *sakdina* system, through which indigenous upland groups had forged mutually beneficial, if highly unequal, political relations with lowland states.[57] Especially in the north, this had left the Royal Lao Army well staffed with skilled and dedicated soldiers from a number of upland groups; a prominent historian of Laos's secret war describes Mon-Khmer soldiers as "fierce fighters" who "signed up in droves" for guerrilla forces like those deployed at Nam Nyu.[58] Young's other major source of recruits came from the Lahu, the minority group that his family knew best, and whose presence in the borderlands of Burma, Laos, Thailand, and China made them ideal for CIA espionage work.[59] Given Washington's broader plans for military escalation (visibly in Vietnam, quietly in Laos), a key dimension of the CIA's expansion into northwestern Laos was to be on the lookout for signs that China might be responding in kind.[60] The Young family's special relationship with the Lahu was integral to this effort.

William Young's grandfather had been a Baptist missionary who arrived in Burma's Shan states around 1900 and focused his efforts on the Lahu. His son had expanded the family's mission northward into the Wa states, close along the Chinese border, in the 1930s. After being forced to move to Thailand after the Second World War, the Young family maintained their ties with Lahu communities in the Shan and Wa states, and as the KMT opened up a second front against China's People's Liberation Army in 1950,[61] Young's father and older brother—the future anthropologist and "hill tribe" expert Gordon Young—ran a CIA intelligence network using Lahu and Shan agents to report on troop movements in Yunnan. In 1962 and 1963, William Young integrated northwestern Laos into this already existing KMT-CIA network, bringing to Nam Nyu a group of Lahu and Shan intelligence veterans to coordinate Nam Nyu's cross-border program and to recruit members of the local upland communities for US intelligence work. Trainees would go first to Thailand, where they received radio and paramilitary training from the Paru, and then go on either three-to-four-month espionage missions into Yunnan or to one of two listening posts that the CIA maintained along the Burma-China border. As McCoy describes, this was quite an operation: "Using four-pound radios with a broadcast range of four hundred miles, the teams transmitted . . . directly to a powerful receiver at Nam Yu or to specially equipped Air America planes that flew back and forth along the Lao-Chinese border. . . . By . . . 1967, [Young] had opened three major radio posts within Burma's Shan states, built a special training camp [in Phitsanoulok, Thailand] that was graduating thirty-five agents every two months, and sent hundreds of teams deep into Yunnan."[62]

In the mid-1960s, as the "unconventional" operations overseen by Blaufarb and others expanded throughout Laos, Nam Nyu matured into a full-scale military base. By 1967 its military force numbered almost seven thousand, making it second only to Long Cheng, the Hmong *maquis* base in the northeast, discussed above.[63] Like Long Cheng, Nam Nyu had an openly acknowledged "refugee center" a few kilometers away where USAID delivered food, supplies, medical assistance, and even education to families who had fled Namtha after its "fall" to communist forces.[64] And as it did in Long Cheng, Air America connected Nam Nyu to urban hubs like Vientiane, Luang Prabang, and Houei Sai, as well as to an ever-growing network of CIA-managed remote upland airfields, or "STOL sites." This infrastructure was extensive. The 1970 edition of Air America's *Facilities Data* book lists 281 STOL sites in Laos, while maps printed in 1975 by the US government's Defense Mapping Agency Topographic Center in Washington, DC, show over 450.[65]

By the mid-1960s, Nam Nyu had blurred the boundaries between what Blaufarb described as the "tribal" program's key pieces: its most important "third-country advisers" (the so-called Sixteen Musketeers who managed cross-border operations) were "tribals" themselves, and the nominally "private" and "civilian" Air America was thoroughly imbricated not only with the logistics of aid provision but also with Nam Nyu's espionage program.[66] This blending was precisely the point in that it facilitated the outsourcing of the war effort, maintaining significant capacity with low US visibility. In the remote mountain base of Nam Nyu, the various pieces—hill tribes, the CIA, upland missionaries, the Paru, Air America, USAID, and the KMT—had jelled into one of the "various devices and expedients" that Blaufarb later described as allowing the United States to develop "a rather sizeable military response" in Laos while officially maintaining precisely the opposite.[67]

Writing in 1971, Blaufarb found it difficult to fit US operations in Laos into familiar categories: "Perhaps," he wrote, "we should simply style it an unconventional war, a term which calls attention to its outstanding characteristics."[68] One category of which Blaufarb was especially wary was one he later wrote a book about: counterinsurgency. In part, his reluctance had to do with the extent and devastation of the American bombing program. While the US Air Force did not play a role at Nam Nyu for reasons discussed below, its operations loomed extremely large in other parts of Laos; between 1964 and 1973, according to one historian, "the U.S. military dropped almost two million tons of bombs, which worked out to two thirds of a ton for every man, woman, and child."[69] Some of this was aimed at supporting the Hmong *maquis* northeast of Vientiane, while much of the rest of it targeted the Ho Chi Minh trail system in central and southern Laos.[70] Bombing was still ongoing when Blaufarb was writing, and his report gave sample data from 1969 and 1970 that showed an average of over ten thousand attack sorties (individual plane flights) per month—and this *excluded* B-52 runs.[71] He did not shy away from the bombing's destructiveness, noting the "obliteration" of various district towns in both the northeast and the south ("Xieng Khouangville, Phongsavan . . . , Mahaxay and Tchepone"), although Blaufarb—ever the analyst—noted that "of course, such destruction did not stem from a deliberate decision but was a consequence of relaxed ground rules [and] a huge increase in available sorties."[72] His point, however, was that the destruction of the bombing pulled so obviously away from "winning hearts and minds" that there was no way the US operation could be classified as a counterinsurgency effort.

But there is an even more important dimension, for my purposes, to Blaufarb's insistence on the term "unconventional." This matters because it speaks directly to the strategic shift behind the upland reorientation at the heart of this chapter. Blaufarb was emphatic that "the tribal program . . . cannot be equated with a standard counter-insurgency effort aimed at rebuilding security and effective government in the countryside."[73] The reason had to do with the political geography of the conflict: "The [Lao Communist Party], in its own name and that of the dissident Neutralists, claimed control of most of the territory in which the tribesmen lived. Some it had in fact controlled and governed since the early 1950s, particularly in [the northeast]. The [Hmong] and other tribal movements were in large part popular resistance *against* a government perceived as oppressive, rather than an effort to secure the countryside *for* a threatened government."[74]

Here, Blaufarb was describing the mosaic *maquis* geography exemplified by bases like Nam Nyu and Long Cheng, contrasting them with standard counterinsurgency operations to secure the countryside "*for* a threatened [national] government." The US military was certainly familiar with counter-insurgency, having practiced and studied it extensively in the Philippines and Central America during the 1920s and 1930s, and having attempted it with the strategic-hamlet program in both Vietnam and Laos beginning in the mid-1950s.[75] In 1957 the CIA had actually sent an agent, Rufus Phillips, to Laos to set up a USAID "civic action" program inspired by the strategic-hamlet program in Vietnam, which he had just helped the famed counter-insurgency specialist Edward Lansdale develop.[76] But as Blaufarb explained (and Phillips later lamented in his memoir),[77] Washington abandoned this earlier program of civic action, nation-building, and counterinsurgency-oriented development in the wake of the Laotian crisis of 1960–61; it opted instead for the operations described above.

Blaufarb explained this change carefully, beginning with the assertion that the earlier US policy on Laos contained "one crippling flaw": the assumption "that Laos was a nation with sufficient national unity, leadership, and political and social infrastructure to use U.S. aid effectively in a policy of firm resistance to its enemies."[78] This culminated in the passage quoted at length at the beginning of this chapter. In arguing that "history and terrain" had divided Laos "into separate regions, with little to bind these together," that the population was "a mixture of races and religions" who regarded each other "with fear and hostility," that the elite were little more than "rival clans" competing for riches rather than popular allegiance, and that the territory itself was "underdeveloped in every way" (lacking infrastructure and comprising instead "a rugged, roadless expanse of jungled hills and limestone ridges"), Blaufarb could have been offering a withering critique of France's colonial legacy in Laos.[79] He was not; his purpose was far more practical. In his estimation, building "a firm anti-Communist 'bastion' on the borders of China and Vietnam"[80] would have required raw materials that were far more *nation*-like than Laos had to offer: a better infrastructure network, greater regional integration, a public ideal among the elite and members of the government, and an ethnic landscape that was more unified than it was divided and tribalized. Blaufarb's account of Laos's national shortcomings was in this regard not so much a critique of French colonialism as an acceptance and even a tactical embrace of its legacy. Laos, he argued, did not merit being considered on its own terms, but was better thought of—and after 1960 had been treated—as a "buffer zone against North Vietnamese pressures" and "a secondary theater" relative to Vietnam.[81] Once American policymakers decided that Laos was not a nation to be defended but a fractured terrain whose physical and social characteristics could be exploited for larger geopolitical purposes, the uplands turned from a strategic problem into a strategic asset, and tactical failure into tactical success.

"THE CHINESE BORDER HAS ALREADY BEEN SHIFTED SOUTHWARD"

Even in Blaufarb's Machiavellian use of the term, however, this success was short-lived. Less than four years after its writing, the Pathet Lao declared victory and, in December 1975, announced the creation of the Lao People's Democratic Republic. With this, the Lao uplands would revert to being a national problem space much as they had been before 1960, albeit with postwar complications.

But even as Blaufarb was completing his report, the denationalized landscape that was both premise and product of the system he described was being undone by an activity that increasingly became a target of US analysis and concern in the years that followed: roadbuilding by the Chinese military. As US involvement in Laos began to wind down as part of the Nixon administration's wider disengagement from Southeast Asia in the late 1960s and early '70s, American attention to northern Laos focused increasingly on monitoring a new road network that was undoing the very isolation and remoteness upon which its operations of the last decade had been premised. The roadbuilding had begun in the wake of the Pathet Lao victory at Namtha; but its slow start meant that its effects on the upland territoriality described in this chapter were initially minimal. But once in place, the infrastructure it created was a key progenitor of the regionalization-inspired connectivity that would follow in the 1990s and 2000s, and it helped lay the groundwork, quite literally, for what later became the NEC. The "Chinese road" (as the Americans called it) directly contributed to the Pathet Lao's overrunning the base at Nam Nyu in 1973. But in challenging the fractured territoriality that was central to US strategy, it also introduced a form of integration that, while theoretically conducive to nation-building and territorial integration, anticipated contemporary anxieties about Chinese influence in the northwest. In doing so, it helped set the stage—both alongside and in tension with the US activities discussed above—for contemporary events.

Chinese roadbuilding in Laos during the 1960s and early 1970s ambiguously blended economic aid with military strategy. The Lao government's initial invitation had come in 1961 during a diplomatic visit to Beijing by Laos's Neutralist prime minister, and was apparently aimed at counterbalancing

Soviet influence in the northeast, which was growing at the time via its resupply of the Pathet Lao, mentioned above. The Chinese road began as a single route, connecting the far-north province of Phongsaly, where the prime minister had political allies, with southern Yunnan; then, as now, roadbuilding was difficult to argue against in a landscape where connectivity figured so centrally to communication, trade, and the provision of government services. But as the plan was announced by Beijing, it morphed in both geography and direction, expanding significantly and heading south and west rather than simply east (see map on p. xvi). This seems to have been due in part to an unwritten request made by the Lao representative, a Royalist general and onetime prime minister himself, who had been sent to China to finalize the arrangement on the prime minister's behalf.[82] Then, on top of that, the unofficial request to extend the road to Luang Namtha expanded even more, for reasons that remain unclear. Shortly after this second visit, Chinese radio announced the roadbuilding aid as planning to extend not just to Namtha but also to Houei Sai, on the Mekong River opposite the Thai border. As the US ambassador to Laos who inherited this situation put it long after the fact, "confusion persisted" on multiple levels.[83] Why had a Royalist general—and close ally of the United States—invited "the Chinese" to build an extra road into a communist stronghold area? How had the further expansion of the project's scope—all the way to the Thai border— come about? What was its intent? The plans for the extra roadbuilding struck at the heart of US anxieties about communist expansion in the region: as the US ambassador's account explained, "The arm that could push down a row of dominoes seemed then to be stretching out to do just that."[84]

After the radio announcement in 1962, Chinese official communication about the road's progress ceased.[85] Over the decade that followed, however, the multiple roads that emerged in its wake would be monitored heavily by US intelligence, including by the teams based at Nam Nyu and their various forms of air support discussed above. The details—from the roads' orientation southwest toward Thailand, to their heavy equipment and, starting around 1970, the antiaircraft installations that in some cases accompanied their construction—ensured that as "confusion persisted," it was the sort of confusion that carried significant geopolitical weight. Both the CIA and US congressional representatives would have much to say about Chinese roadbuilding as they tangled with each other in the late 1960s and early 1970s over the scope and secrecy of ongoing US involvement in Laos. As the US ambassador noted, Chinese roadbuilding was "particularly laden with strategic and tactical considerations" and was never just about transportation and communication.[86]

The roadbuilding began slowly. During the first half of the decade it made only minimal inroads into the upland northwest, leaving the military situation there uncertain, if hopeful, for the United States and its allies. A US Intelligence Bulletin reported in June 1965, "the military situation" in Laos "remains fluid in several areas. . . . [In the northwest,] a Communist clearing operation southwest of Nam Tha along Route 3"—at the time an unpaved road that the CIA would later call a "long-disused French logging trail" in reference to its poor condition—"has apparently stalled. Government guerrilla units are now regrouping in preparation for a counterattack against Vien[g] Phou Kha, which Communists seized on 25 May."[87] Vieng Phoukha was a strategic location because it sat astride this old French road in the middle of the northwestern uplands, a key node between the provincial capital in Namtha and the town of Huei Sai on the Thai border. Vieng Phoukha changed hands a few times in the 1960s, reflecting in part the lack of reliable road access for the Pathet Lao and the associated viability of the "irregular" operations profiled above. In the months after the bulletin quoted above, for instance, the counterattack was indeed successful.[88] This success, however, was undercut by the bigger picture of Chinese roadbuilding from the north. The month before the recapture operation succeeded, a Chinese-built road from the northern part of the province reached the capital Namtha, only about thirty-five miles away.[89]

The half decade from mid-1968 brought a further expansion toward the south and west. The route that today comprises the eastern third of the NEC, from the Luang Namtha provincial capital to the town of Boten on the Lao-China border, was built by Chinese military engineers during the rainy season of 1968. So was a second road, a spur heading southeast to Oudomxai from the Namtha-to-Boten road.[90] In the two years that followed, the road expanded farther southwest from Oudomxai, reaching almost to the Mekong River town of Pakbeng, located in what is today the southwestern part of Oudomxai province. If the route to Namtha was hard to dispute on the merits of economic aid, the latter road toward Pakbeng was downright alarming, not only to US and Thai government observers but also reportedly even to the Lao Neutralists.[91]

Ironically, a 1971 US congressional investigation into ongoing CIA involvement in Laos helped bring to light the extent of the Chinese roadbuilding. Since earlier public knowledge had focused largely on the northeast (the focus of Operation Momentum, discussed above), the northwest figured centrally in congressional alarm at the wider extent of US operations.[92] As the summary of the congressional investigation, a report titled *Laos: April 1971*, noted with concern:

The Chinese presence has increased in northern Laos, from between 6,000 and 8,000, as of 2 years ago, to between 14,000 and 20,000 at the present time. The road the Chinese are building in northern Laos has been improved in recent months; and its antiaircraft and associated radar have been heavily increased. In the opinion of knowledgeable U.S. officials, from an antiaircraft standpoint that area is now one of the most heavily defended areas in the world. . . . The practical effect of the Chinese road is that the Chinese border has already been shifted southward to encompass a substantial portion of northern Laos.[93]

The road network's further expansion over the next two years helped usher in the defeat of the CIA's model of upland territoriality detailed above. The Oudomxai road reached Pakbeng, on the Mekong River, in March 1972, one part of the "mixed messaging" that American officials perceived the Chinese government to be sending: as the ambassador's account cited above noted, only weeks after President Nixon and Chinese premier Zhou Enlai released their "historic joint communiqué" from Shanghai on renewed US-China relations, "the first Chinese infantry regiment moved into the Muong Sai [Oudomxai] area of northwest Laos; and road-workers were completing the segment to Pak Beng, a sophisticated operation, with bulldozers, graders, and cement mixers."[94]

Farther north in Luang Namtha, roadbuilding also continued apace. This spur, which had reached Namtha in mid-1968, covered half the distance from Namtha to Vieng Phouha by late 1972, and by early 1973 had reached the village of Ta Fa, well past Vieng Phoukha and near the present-day Luang Namtha–Bokeo provincial border. As part of this continued push westward, the base at Nam Nyu fell to Pathet Lao forces in February 1973; CIA analysts writing at the time called this the loss of "the [Royal Lao] government's principal military base in the northwest." They also read the ramping up of Chinese roadbuilding in the geopolitical terms of a coming end to the war, which was now only a matter of time: "Peking apparently wished to have both [the Oudomxai and Namtha] roads, which might cause concern in neighboring states [i.e., Thailand], well under way before a Lao settlement in order to spare Prime Minister Souvanna difficulties in attempting to justify them as 'aid projects.'"[95] In the decades that followed, similar questions about aid, connectivity, and geopolitical intent—albeit in a post-Cold War world—would remain persistent features of the northwestern landscape.

The "various devices and expedients" of US upland war-making continued to influence events in Laos long after the formation of the Lao PDR in 1975. As anthropologist Grant Evans noted in his introduction to the 1999 collected volume *Laos: Culture and Society*, "One of the paradoxes of studying Laos is that even those people most engaged in its affairs have questioned whether Laos exists as a 'real' national entity."[96] As representatives of "those people most engaged in its affairs," Evans quoted such Cold War luminaries as Arthur Dommen, Bernard Fall, Arthur Schlesinger Jr., and the French novelist Jean Lartéguy—men who referred to Laos, respectively, as "more a conglomeration of 'tribes' than a people," "neither a geographical nor an ethnic or social entity, but merely a political convenience," "a state by diplomatic courtesy," and "a figment of the imagination of a few French administrators." Evans explained these descriptions as stemming from an ideology "of 'natural' nations rather than historical ones." While perhaps true, they were also driven by direct and often partisan involvement: Schlesinger was best known for being an insider historian of the Kennedy presidency, while Fall and Dommen were both journalist-historians who emerged as authoritative voices on "the Indochina question" during the 1960s; though at times critical of American policy, their analyses were firmly on the side of Western anticommunism.[97] Jean Lartéguy was a French novelist who lionized the "centurions" like Roger Trinquier, the architect of the French "*montagnard* strategy" described above, who guarded the gates of empire even as they were abandoned by the politicians back home.[98] Given these histories, Evans's "paradox" begins to unravel when the discourse of Laos's national unreality is placed alongside the upland reorientation of American policy detailed above. The men who suggested that Laos was not a "real" country were not merely ideological with respect to nations in general; theirs was a prejudice deeply embedded in the Asian "theater" of the Cold War.

There were, not surprisingly, dissenters within the camp of US advisers and operatives who were committed to nation-building, rather than denationalization, in the uplands. One was Rufus Phillips, the CIA operative mentioned above who was sent to Laos in 1957 to conduct a "civic action" program modeled on the one in Vietnam, but whose efforts ended up hamstrung by various political-bureaucratic frictions in both the American aid bureaucracy and the Royal Lao government.[99] Another especially telling critique came from Joel Halpern, a UCLA anthropologist who was based in Luang Prabang in 1957 as the USAID mission's northern field representative. His analysis sits uneasily on both sides of the reorientation described in this chapter. Halpern was clearly one of those who believed in anticommunist nation-building as both a program and a political possibility.[100] His critique of what he called "Little America" is chilling, however, in that it advocated precisely the sort of "up-country" move that the CIA would subsequently make, although with a very different analysis and a very different plan. Little America, wrote Halpern, "may be defined as the intellectual culture of official American government personnel residing in Vientiane, Laos, in 1957. It also includes the various American material imports which have made possible to a significant extent a way of life fundamentally similar to that of middle-class government workers in Washington, D.C."[101]

In Halpern's estimation, the "Little America" model of development assistance was fundamentally disconnected from the lives of 90 percent or more of the Lao population; it attended little to transferring actual skills via the cultivation of sustained personal relationships; and it was largely seen by "the Lao villager"—a figure with whom Halpern was especially concerned—as enriching the urban elite while doing little for anyone else.[102] Halpern's critique was a constructive one, however: he recommended transforming Little America into a different sort of aid apparatus by reining in the material excess of expatriate life in Vientiane and shifting US aid efforts toward the rural sphere where most Lao people actually lived. He suggested that American aid focus on knowledge transfer by fostering relationship development and explicitly putting "ideas before materials"; that it emphasize the need for its staff to learn local languages and appreciate "local cultural values"; and that it place more emphasis on developing a presence in the countryside, especially among ethnic minorities.[103] Halpern's critique was circulated as a report "prepared for limited distribution within the United States" and indicated that the danger was already clear and present in 1958. It ended with this: "The United States Operations Mission to Laos is by no means a lost cause, but present methods and procedures will not ensure success; new ways and ideas must be found and tried."[104]

New ways and ideas were indeed found, although in places that Halpern likely did not have in mind: the French rearguard strategy for fighting the First Indochina War, and the CIA's support for the KMT in the borderlands of Yunnan, Burma, and Thailand. Halpern's critique of Little America thus illuminates a key thread running between the "Vietnam" era, the late Cold War period of the 1980s (ch. 3), and the present day. As Washington abandoned its nation-building strategy in Laos as "unrealistic," it nonetheless continued to keep its eyes not only on the prize of geopolitical containment but on the tool with which to achieve it: local populations. As US leaders discarded the idea that Laos was a country that could be defended through political means, they stopped listening to men like Rufus Phillips and Joel Halpern in favor of those like William Young and Douglas Blaufarb—men who could see local populations in terms divorced from those imposed by the idea of the nation. Colonial anthropology and missionary work provided this framework readily: that of the tribe, and in particular the "hill tribe." In such a context, Blaufarb's comment that the unconventional war in Laos was not quite a counterinsurgency operation is an understatement. It was a military operation aimed at taking tactical advantage of the gap between people and geography on the one hand, and nation-ness on the other. In so doing, it further expanded that gap and helped spawn a whole discourse of Lao national unreality that, as Evans points out, remains a cliché "even among those people most engaged in its affairs."[105]

Laos was hardly the only place where this was happening. In 1976 Seymour Deitchman, a defense analyst, published an insider's account of Project Camelot, a Defense Department effort to recruit social scientists to counterinsurgency research in 1964 that was scrapped when news of it leaked out.[106] Deitchman's account quotes extensively from a number of official sources to describe what he calls the Cold War "mentality" of many Washington insiders in the early 1960s—a mentality illustrated by Blaufarb above and in the 1963 report quoted in the chapter's epigraph. One of Deitchman's sources, taken from anonymous congressional testimony from the 1965 "Hearings on Winning the Cold War," traces an arc from the US military's earlier experience during the Second World War with social science (aptitude testing, teamwork psychology, isolation and combat stress experiments, etc.) to its newfound needs with respect to the civilian populations of the developing world. In describing the US military's need to better deal with "the developing nations of Asia, Africa, and Latin America" in the context of the Cold War, the testimony highlights the dark utility of people like Young and Blaufarb: "The [Cold] war itself revolves around the allegiance and support of the local population. The Defense Department has therefore recognized that part of its research and development efforts to support counterinsurgency operations must be oriented toward the people, United States and foreign, involved in this type of war; and the DOD has called on the types of scientists—anthropologists, psychologists, sociologists, political scientists, economists—whose professional orientation to human behavior would enable them to make useful contributions in this area."[107]

The Pentagon's history of enrolling social scientists in counterinsurgency work has, by now, been well documented, and widely and critically discussed.[108] What is often downplayed, however, is the fact that social science—and in particular what came to be known in the 1960s as "hill tribe anthropology"—was also put to work doing precisely the opposite of counterinsurgency: exploiting ethnic and geographic tensions for wider political purposes because they worked *against* nation-building.[109] As Blaufarb emphasized and as this chapter shows, US efforts to meet the "communist threat" in Laos sought to recruit portions of "the local population" to *destabilize* a national landscape by exacerbating its political fault lines. "Tribal experts" like Roger Trinquier and William Young saw the upland landscape as the Achilles' heel of lowland nation-building. These men were not the trained academics whose intellectualism often frustrated military efforts to use their expertise.[110] They were more like right-wing versions of what political theorist Antonio Gramsci called "organic intellectuals," people whose life experience made them skilled practitioners, organizers, and strategists. In this case, those skills were aimed at assembling and managing the *maquis* landscapes of upland proxy war via the "devices and expedients" described above. Their efforts cast a long historical shadow in precisely the direction pointed to by Blaufarb's distinction between counterinsurgency and unconventional war. This distinction was anything but academic. In enrolling members of the population into a project of denationalizing the Lao uplands, the unconventional operations described above marked certain communities, through a mix of ethnicity and location, as being against the socialist nation-building project. In the years after Blaufarb, Young, and others left, these marks would not be forgotten.

CHAPTER THREE

The Geography of Security

Population Management Work, 1975–2000

The security situation may demand measures, e.g., in terms of movement and relocation of population, which are not conducive to development. . . . [But] as an improvement of the living conditions of the population is probably the most effective way of overcoming the security problems, there is a paradox that development efforts are most needed where the security situation makes them most difficult to carry out.

—"MUONG PAKSANE REGIONAL DEVELOPMENT STUDY:
PROPOSED LONG-TERM DEVELOPMENT STRATEGY,
PROPOSALS FOR ACTION" (1982)

IN FEBRUARY 1988 Laos's Council of Ministers issued an instruction to the nation's ministry staff, state committees, mass organizations, provinces, and municipalities on "stepping up population management work." Population management work, the instruction explained, covered a variety of tasks: "grasping population statistics, recording birth and death statistics, issuing identification cards, organizing population relocation, arranging domicile patterns, and finding and creating new occupations for multi-ethnic citizens who own no land on which to earn their living."[1] The sheer breadth of these responsibilities made population management work "an enormous and all-encompassing task," while its "fundamental principle"—"to allow Laos's multi-ethnic citizens to enjoy legitimate equal rights in all spheres of life and to further enhance their right to collective mastership and a sense of creativeness in fulfilling their two strategic tasks:

defending the country and building socialism"—meant that the officials who practiced it inevitably walked a fine line between coercion and consent. Population management work, in short, was about getting upland people to "do as they ought," as the English reformer Jeremy Bentham once put it, while simultaneously making them think their actions were undertaken voluntarily.[2] Reflecting this challenge, the council reminded its audience that to be effective, population management work required the utmost care, including "a high sense of responsibility," "capabilities in executing political, social, economic, national defense and public security work," and "skillful, subtle and careful methods of avoiding deception by the enemies."

The instruction was issued at a time of great transition and uncertainty. Having gained power in the revolutionary wave that swept the former Indochina in 1975, the government of the Lao PDR had survived its first decade, albeit with significant outside help. By early 1988 the regionwide geopolitical tensions that caused the young government much hardship earlier in the decade (see below) had begun to ease, in part thanks to the rapprochement between China and the Soviet Union heralded by Mikhail Gorbachev's famous Vladivostok address just over a year earlier. Later in the year, Thailand's prime minister would issue his famous call to "turn Southeast Asia's battlefields into marketplaces"; in the years that followed, similar calls for regional connectivity would be reflected in initiatives like the GMS and the NEC (ch. 1). At the time, however, these openings masked major difficulties at home. Like Vietnam, Laos was acutely feeling the effects of the Soviet Union's economic decline, and its embrace of regional economic integration in 1986 was largely due to the desperation born of losing the Soviet and other Eastern Bloc aid that had helped keep the Lao economy afloat over the preceding decade. Signaling their commitment to stay the socialist course despite a turn toward the market economy, Lao Party leaders even named their shift the "New Economic Mechanism" after Lenin's own equally desperate and reluctant turn to market-based policies in the 1920s.[3]

Military difficulties abounded as well, especially in the country's northern uplands. For the two months before the council's instruction was issued, Laos and Thailand had been engaged in a low-level war along part of their shared and historically contested land border in Xayaboury province, one of the few parts of Laos located west of the Mekong River. And internally, the Lao government was facing pockets of rural insurgency that had persisted in the footprints of upland *maquis* geographies described in the preceding chapter. Since the late 1970s, rebels had received external support, initially via northeast Thailand and often targeting areas in Laos's central panhandle.[4] After Laos was drawn into the Sino-Vietnamese conflict over Cambodia in

1979, foreign support for Lao insurgents came from China as well, often via the northwest.[5] The instruction's reference to unspecified "enemies" thus conjured threats that were both internal and foreign.

Together, these circumstances made Laos's forested uplands a site of complex struggles over "security" issues in the broadest sense of the term. Given this mix of old and new geopolitics, the location and activities of the upland population remained an ongoing military concern for the new Lao government throughout much of the north. The instruction on population management work lamented, for instance, that "a number of our Hmong tribal compatriots have moved back and forth in many localities, thus creating favorable grounds for the enemies to create rifts between them and the administrative power, and to instill a sense of animosity in our multi-ethnic people." Such comments referenced the specific security issues associated with the former northeastern *maquis*, where ongoing Hmong resistance—and external support from Thailand—were well-known. But they also served to obfuscate, blaming external and political threats on matters that were internal and economic. As elaborated below, the government's own nascent forestry operations also created serious potential for "rifts" between upland agriculturalists and "the administrative power." The council knew well that mitigating these potentialities demanded significant and ongoing attention to questions of livelihood and settlement.

Even in normal times, the enclosure of Laos's then-substantial forestry resource would have been no small undertaking given the extensive occurrence of shifting cultivation. But Laos in the decade after 1975 was also a postwar landscape, in multiple ways. One dimension concerned internal, war-related displacement. In addition to traditional practitioners of shifting cultivation, many lowland farmers had taken up the practice of upland farming after fleeing the northeast during the war, only to find that lowland areas were already occupied in the landscapes where they had settled. As the new government began searching for accessible forestry lands on which to base its nascent development activities, it found that it was often competing with its own citizens for these same lands. Moreover, the ongoing insurgency made the government heavily reliant on the Vietnamese military long after the war's official end in 1975. From the late 1970s, this made much of the forest area of central Laos feel, to its inhabitants, like occupied territory. Under such circumstances, asking local residents to give up land for "national" development—never an easy proposition, even in good times—became an even harder and more delicate demand.

During the decade of the 1980s, Lao authorities and their various advisers developed techniques aimed at addressing these multiple and intersecting problems of military and economic security. Later, during the post-2000 period, these same echoes of national security would creep into the management of land access in general and enclosure in particular, although they would do so much more quietly. The value of looking at this earlier moment is thus that the confluence of security's economic and political dimensions—of "defending the country and building socialism" via a single continuum of governmental practice—was much more out in the open. This openness was not merely discursive, although it was that, too: in texts of the day, such as the instruction quoted above and other project documents examined below, security issues often received explicit and central treatment. More importantly, it was a matter of spatial practice. During the 1980s, as Lao authorities sought to "bring tranquility" to the uplands by "limiting irrational migration" so that residents would "have ample time to concentrate . . . on . . . production and improving their living condition,"[6] they developed two spatial technologies that would outlast and outgrow the specific postwar landscapes in which they emerged. These tools—managed enclosures and concentrated resettlement in "focal development" sites (or focal sites, for short)—had complex genealogies, drawing on colonial forestry practices and actual counterinsurgency efforts (cf. ch. 2) from across the region. But as they arose in the specific landscapes and became applied to the specific subpopulations of postwar Laos, managed enclosures and focal sites took on their own governmental utility, especially—and perhaps paradoxically—after "security conditions" improved. As Lao authorities developed means for dismantling the upland territoriality of an earlier era, they actually smuggled aspects of US-style denationalization into their own territorial affairs.

To make sense of the evidence and events from this period, it is useful to have a broader notion of "security" than is common in accounts of contemporary Laos. The importance of security issues is widely recognized by other scholars, but typically in a way that opposes military and economic issues; "security," identified with the former, thus becomes the precursor to "development," their relationship being one of transition from the former to the latter. In such understandings, state-managed resettlement of villages is widely framed as being primarily security-oriented throughout the 1980s, and development-oriented during the 1990s and 2000s.[7] Transition narratives like this resonate with widespread understandings of the massive changes ushered in by market-based policy shifts during the 1990s and early 2000s, as the key pieces of the contemporary development landscape came into widespread use. But they also risk masking the ways in which security was *always* about economics *as well as* politics, even back in the early 1980s.

More importantly, they risk hiding the ways in which the politico-military variety of "national security" can be repurposed for political-economic ends.

The economic and military "moments" of national security are related contingently; sometimes they pull against one another, other times they resonate and reinforce. In the epigraph quoted above, the relationship is clearly antagonistic: insecurity undermines the potential to do development work, whereas that same development work, it is believed, would help alleviate insecurity—hence the "paradox." But those attempting to govern the uplands believed this antagonism was not inherent. Through various forms of socio-spatial practice, the techniques of population management examined in this chapter tried to mitigate the conflict between these two types of security and bring them instead into a relationship of coexistence. If these efforts led to indeterminate results, they also helped forge a series of methods that would become standardized in the spatial tool kit of rural upland development during the 1990s and 2000s. Later, this "hardening" of the experimental tools developed amid the difficulties of the 1980s would be put to very different uses.

NATIONAL VERSUS "REGIONAL" DEVELOPMENT

In the late 1970s and early 1980s, Laos's forestry professionals, along with their various international advisers and donors, faced numerous and diverse challenges. Working in the aftermath of two decades of war, and before that a half century of colonial rule that combined exploitation with underinvestment, would-be foresters found that they needed to address the basic question of locating the forest resource itself and derivative problems of how to bring it to market. They also faced the wider issue of a rural population that was broadly interspersed within, and often heavily dependent on, this same resource. Details varied by region, of course. But the overlap was especially acute in the landscape 100 to 200 kilometers northeast of Vientiane, in the so-called panhandle region where Laos's width is a mere ninety miles. Here, the nascent state forestry industry had access to a relatively rich and accessible resource, but this access was encumbered by a population that contained not only traditional upland communities but also recently displaced refugees and, at various times and places, an ongoing insurgency against the new government that lasted well into the late 1980s.

In such a context forest inventory presented a special problem, although one with historical echoes. In his account of the colonial period, historian Martin Stuart-Fox notes that "every French account of Laos listed the colony's natural resources, almost as a prospectus for potential investors."[8] But such lists were rarely sufficient for sustained economic activity. Although long famed for its abundant forest resources—a 1937 "economic map" of French Indochina, for instance, shows Laos widely covered by a mix of "dense" and "thin" forest and adorned regionally with teak, pine, and various nontimber forest products (benzoin, stick lac, resins, "forest oil")[9]—the colonial underinvestment in infrastructure noted in earlier chapters also extended to the resource-inventory process. Listing resources in "prospectus" form was thus essentially a kind of boostering, advertising investment potential in a general way without doing the expensive work of precise quantification, classification, and mapping. A US economic inventory of French Indochina conducted at the end of World War II made this point by noting that "most forest statistics in Indochina" omitted Laos entirely because it did not have even a basic forest bureaucracy. While noting that Laos "certainly has the largest forest area" of the five Indochinese states, its authors could only speculate hopefully: Laos "probably has much the largest quantity of exploitable timber" in Indochina, and "it seems likely that Laos will produce more timber when its industry is fully developed than of any of the other [Indochinese] states."[10]

Despite significant attention between World War II and 1975—with foreign assistance, the Royal Lao government established a forest service at the national and provincial levels, and timber exports increased significantly in the years leading up to 1970[11]—after 1975 forest inventory remained a source of ongoing frustration. Reflecting in 1983 on six years as the head of Sweden's forestry cooperation project with the Lao government, Reidar Persson lamented the failure to create a "reliable national picture" of Laos's forest resource. "This is a pity," he wrote in *Forestry in Laos*, a self-published report written toward the end of his tenure, "because the higher Laotian authorities have a tendency to over-estimate the forest resources. . . . As long as I have been working with Laos's forestry [efforts,] the lack of knowledge about forest resources has been one of the most serious obstacles."[12] Three years later internal evaluators of the Lao-Swedish Forestry Project (LSFP) were even harsher. Focusing on the lack of profitable forestry operations despite almost a decade of assistance, they complained about the Lao government's bureaucratic rigidity ("It is difficult to change a decision once it is taken"), and they seemed to include the LSFP's original Swedish designers (including Persson) in their criticism of the project's failure to adhere to what they called "the Swedish view, namely that all background facts should be known before a decision was taken."[13] Such an expectation, of course, was highly unrealistic, as Persson and other development professionals (both Lao and Swedish) knew well when they launched the LSFP in 1977. Indeed, it is precisely the circumstances that threw up the opacities and operational challenges that irked the LSFP's evaluators that make it interesting for my purposes. By offering a window into Laos's postwar industrial forestry landscape, the LSFP affords a chance to examine the specific geographies of field operations—both in forestry and otherwise—where population management work was explored and developed at a crucial moment of Laos's postwar transition.

Persson's 1983 report contained a map, reconstructed below as the upper-right portion of map 3.1, that provides a good jumping-off point. It showed the locations of the nine state forest enterprises (SFEs) created in the late 1970s and early 1980s, along with a table showing the area allocated and development partner associated with each.[14] In contrast with various spatially precise forest categories that would be gazetted later in the 1990s and 2000s (see ch. 5), the original SFEs had only the most approximate target locations. And of the nine, only four—the two supported by Sweden, plus two more supported, respectively, by the Soviet Union and the Asian Development Bank—had quantified allocations of area. Moreover, as Persson's map shows, even these were defined in only the roughest of terms.

State Forest Enterprise no. 1 (hereafter SFE 1), located in the northern portion of the Lao panhandle in what is now Bolikhamxai province, was in many ways the LSFP's flagship operation. The Swedish also worked with the Lao Department of Forestry and with SFE 3, but both of these were assistance to institutions that already existed; SFE 1, in contrast, was built largely from scratch.[15] Central to the LSFP's approach to cooperation was what is now often called learning-by-doing; at the time, this was described as a decision to prioritize collaboration over preproject planning and, once started, to undergo "continuous review and adjustment until [the project] found its final form."[16] As many aid projects still do, this quest for "final form" began with the question of location. From a few competing possibilities, Lao and Swedish officials settled, after "some months" and "certain irritations" resulting from differences of opinion,[17] on the area shown in Persson's map for SFE 1, a broad swath of forest upriver from the city of Paksan (map 3.1). Even with this location, Swedish officials were apparently reluctant to fund "such a grandiose beginning in a remote and unknown area," referring to the Lao government's initial request to build SFE 1's "heavy investments (sawmill, plywood, pulpmill, etc.)" in a place called Muang Houng, located some distance into the forest interior. As a compromise, Lao authorities agreed to locate SFE 1's main facilities in a place called Muang Mai (today the district capital Bolikhan), located still inland from Paksan but only about a third of the way to Muang Houng, and still in the lowlands of the Mekong Plain.[18]

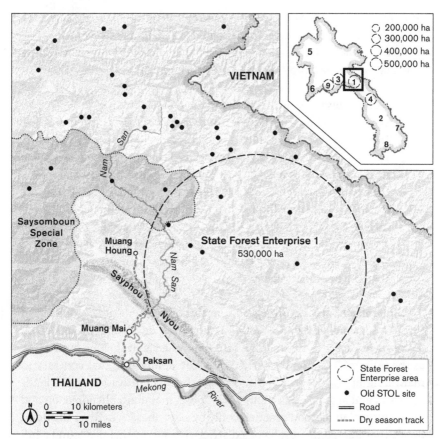

MAP 3.1   State Forest Enterprise 1 and environs. Map by Ben Pease. Based on Persson, "Forestry in Laos," 38; Thongphachanh and Birgegard, "Muong Paksane Regional Development Study"; US Defense Mapping Agency Topographic Center, Washington, DC, map series 1501, 3rd ed., 1:250,000 scale, sheets NE 48–01, NE 48–02, NE 48–05, and NE 48–06, compiled 1975.

In developing a new forest enterprise at Muang Mai, it became rapidly apparent that the LSFP could not be limited to forestry. In 1981 it thus began a subproject, financed under Swedish support for SFE 1 but targeting the greater landscape surrounding both SFEs 1 and 3, called the Paksan Regional Project.[19] As the study that helped launch this subproject explained, "Widespread shifting cultivation made isolated forestry development planning irrelevant" and required that the LSFP take "a broader view on the development potential and the development problems of the area."[20] This addition of a rural development objective to the LSFP's plans exemplified the abovementioned process of "continuous review and adjustment" and took the LSFP squarely into the realm of upland population management.

As the authors of a baseline study for the new subproject explained, the "regional" in the new project's title had a very specific meaning:

> [An] important aspect of the Muang Mai Project from a regional point of view is [to clarify and address] to what extent it is designed to benefit the region. For reasons which largely are acceptable, the Project has progressed to a considerable degree as an enclave in the regional economy with limited linkages and benefits to the region. . . . This is said *not* as a critique of SFE 1. It is merely a fact that a limited share of SFE 1's expenditure has gone to the region. Looking into the future it is important to recognize that the forest exploitation and processing activities will not benefit the *region* to any considerable extent even if they will benefit the country.[21]

Thongphachanh and Birgegard, the authors of this study, emphasized that this tension between "regional" and national development came down to competition for forestland due to the prevalence of shifting cultivation as the pillar of local food security. They noted, however, that contrary to many assumptions (both then and now), shifting cultivation in the landscapes in and around SFEs 1 and 3 was "not a mountain phenomenon and not a cultivation method practiced only by hill tribes."[22] To drive the point home, they quoted the results of a districtwide survey that had found a full third of the population fully dependent on shifting cultivation, and over two-thirds relying on a mix of shifting and fixed lowland production.[23] These numbers were conservative, moreover, since the sample had been forced to exclude, for reasons elaborated below, "the high mountain areas" where shifting cultivation was ubiquitous.

The dependence on shifting cultivation, even in the "nonmountain" areas close to Muang Mai, reflected the area's wartime and postwar history. During the early 1970s the Mekong lowlands, including the area around Paksan, had been a major destination for refugees fleeing the fighting in northern Laos, especially in the northeast. A 1976 report by USAID, for instance, which was intimately involved in support for internally displaced people before its departure in 1975, noted that in the Paksan area alone "twenty-one separate villages were constructed" by and for displaced people "in two long areas, one running 50 kilometers west from Paksan and the other area extending 27 kilometers north. Over 1,800 hectares of land were put under rice cultivation."[24] Almost a decade later, Thongphachanh and Birgegard made it clear that this significant investment in new land development had nonetheless been insufficient to support the area's new (and still growing) population. Northward expansion from Paksan had initially followed the potential for rice-paddy development along the Nam San River, but it was expanding into the uplands.[25]

This put the "regional" population on a collision course with SFE 1, whose foresters had identified "considerable areas with reasonably dense forest" to the east of the Nam San and to the northeast of the Sayphou Nyou, a narrow band of limestone mountains running northwest to southeast that separates the lowlands of Paksan and Muang Mai from the interior forests around Muang Houng (see map 3.1). "The exact extent of these resources remains to be determined," Thongphachanh and Birgegard noted (echoing Persson's point about forest inventory), "but they are large enough to permit a substantial logging operation for many years to come."[26] At the same time, however, shifting cultivation was expanding in precisely the same direction, "not so much because of a preference for *hai* [upland rice] cultivation" by the local population, Thongphachanh and Birgegard emphasized, which was mostly ethnic ("lowland") Lao, "but as a result of the scarcity of wet field paddy (*na*) land and the relative abundance of land that could be used" for upland (*hai*) production.

Noting with alarm that a majority of the farmers surveyed for the Paksan Regional Project reported upland fallow periods of less than five years, they predicted that shifting cultivation would continue to expand northward as "farmers will have no alternative but to look for new *hai* land," first in the areas along the Nam San and then in the watersheds above.[27] Arguing that what was "a moderate conflict at present" was "likely to develop into a more serious one over time,"[28] Thongphachanh and Birgegard emphasized the key question confronting the project: how to reconcile "the forest interests represented by SFE 1 and the legitimate interests of the local population to satisfy their basic needs for food."[29]

AN "UNCOMMITTED" POPULATION

Efforts to reconcile or at least mitigate this conflict focused on a suite of practices that Laos's Council of Ministers would later codify as "population management work." Why were these developed? If enclosing and developing a strategically important resource was an urgent national priority—and by most accounts of the time, forestry was atop a very short list of development options in the Lao PDR's first decade[30]—why not resort to coercion and violence, the "blood and fire" that Marx famously associated with primitive accumulation?[31] Why was it so important for foresters and associated development specialists to address the looming conflict between forestry and food security using "softer" methods rather than via what Thongphachanh and Birgegard called "law enforcement, fencing and guarding," which they recommended strongly against?[32] A partial answer no doubt comes from the ideological commitments of both of the governments involved. The Lao government, after all, represented a newly established "People's Democratic Republic" that, while ideologically willing to deploy coercion in the name of enforcing "the people's will," also faced practical threats to its legitimacy if it was seen as dispossessing the common people on a large scale. Similarly, the Swedish government, whose support for the new Lao government had as much to do with its earlier outspoken criticism of US imperialism during the "Vietnam" War as it did with forestry competence per se, was already well-known for its commitment to rights-based approaches to development cooperation.[33] Helping a Marxist-Leninist government dispossess its own people would not have been high on its agenda.

But there is much more to the story that comes through if we look closely at the landscape around SFE 1. My reference point here is security, both in the narrow politico-military sense in which the term is often used (and in which LSFP staff like Thongphachanh and Birgegard used it) and in the wider sense, also including economic issues, that appears in the instruction on population management work. The latter meaning echoes as well Michel Foucault's 1977–78 lectures on governmentality, which he titled *Security, Territory, Population*.[34] His focus was European history, but as geographers and other scholars have noted, his work highlighted a tension between two key forms of state power that have wider and contemporary relevance.[35] Inspired in part by Jeremy Bentham's ideas about designing prisons, factories, and workhouses for the poor, Foucault called the first of these "disciplinary" power; this focused on spatial arrangements that optimized social control, and the principles that emerged from it have been applied to numerous cases, from buildings like the ones mentioned above, to town planning, to state regimes for keeping track of landownership.[36] As Foucault also noted, however, economic processes like town planning, trade, and farming also depended on maintaining flows or adequate circulation. These ideas derived not from Benthamite notions about restriction and control but from French "physiocrat" economists who sought to "govern with nature" (*physio-cracy*), and whose ideas about enhancing productivity led them to embrace natural models like blood circulation through the body in their quest for "healthy" and "efficient" economies.[37]

This tension between control-based and productivity-based governing is a useful way to think about the often-conflicted spatialities of politico-military versus economic security. Laos's postwar experiences of industrial forestry exemplify this tension. Population management work sought to achieve both control and productivity, sometimes of the same people, as in the case of managed upland settlement; and sometimes of very different things, as in the case of upland farmers being kept away from forestry operations. Its methods were inherently spatial and often came up against the tension between control and production in their specific deployments. They also made use of force when they needed to; as Foucault and various political theorists have long pointed out, carrots work better when there are also sticks at hand.[38] But a key reason that Lao authorities and development planners were so keen to minimize the use of force, and instead manage the social geographies of hinterland settlement and production carefully, had to do with what LSFP personnel like Thongphachanh and Birgegard referred to as "the security situation." In the landscape of SFEs 1 and 3, there was an inherent tension between forestry and upland farming via the competition for land. But in addition, an antigovernment insurgency had emerged in the wake of the Lao PDR's establishment in 1975, largely in the footprints of former upland *maquis* areas. (STOL sites, discussed in ch. 2, are one indicator of this geography, and are included on map 3.1 above.)[39] Much of the insurgency was located north of the SFEs in what came to be called the Saysomboun Special Zone, but enough of it spilled south into the areas of SFEs 1 and 3 that it affected their operations significantly. The security situation was already sufficiently serious to warrant Thongphachanh and Birgegard's attention in 1981–82, and according to LSFP and other accounts it seems to have gotten worse in the years that immediately followed.[40]

The insurgency tended to be strongest in remote and forested areas; this has often been the case with so-called peasant insurgencies around the world, and in this case it followed specifically from the geography of earlier US war-making. In a context where shifting cultivation was socially and geographically widespread, and where it was not limited to "upland" ethnic groups, the inherent *economic* conflict between forestry and upland farming risked spillover into *political* sympathy for the rebels. In such a context, a 1986 LSFP report's comment that "it is often said, today, that the local population generally look upon the state forestry enterprises as their enemies" carries multiple potential meanings.[41]

Thongphachanh and Birgegard had interesting things to say about security and development, and their analysis and recommendations heavily inform the end of this section and the first part of the next. First, though, it is worth detouring to examine a key silence in their and other LSFP accounts: the heavy Vietnamese military presence in and around state forestry operations. This may have been deliberate, an example of the depoliticization that often accompanies development discourse.[42] But it also may have been too obvious to need saying. The presence of the Vietnamese military during this period is widely noted by scholars, and would have been well-known to the consultants' intended audience of government officials, technical staff, and LSFP advisers.[43] In contrast, it leapt off the page in the few popular accounts that were produced for a wider audience at the time.

In May 1987, for instance, a reporter for the Swedish newspaper *Svenska Dagbladet* visited Muang Mai to write a feature on Swedish forestry aid to Laos. The Vietnamese military figured centrally in the account:

> Swedes and other foreigners who visit Muang Mai say they are escorted by Lao soldiers or militiamen. But during *Svenska Dagbladet*'s visit, the Lao escort was replaced by a Vietnamese escort in Muang Mai. About twenty well-armed Vietnamese soldiers kept watch over our trip to the forest and our stay there.
>
> "Security is better now, but ever since 1984 we have had many clashes with Lao groups that came across the Mekong River from Thailand. A shipment was attacked recently," said Vietnamese Lieutenant Pham Van Thu, who has spent nine years in Laos.
>
> There are between 40,000 and 50,000 Vietnamese soldiers in Laos. A sizeable force is also stationed at the main camp in Muang Mai. They move about the area freely and sit in groups talking to the Lao workers. In the evenings, they go down to the little private market.[44]

A 1978 account that appeared in the *Far Eastern Economic Review* is also relevant. Even though it focused on an area significantly to the south of SFE 1, in Savannakhet province, it offers a glimpse of the negative entanglements between local agrarian livelihoods, security measures in general, and the Vietnamese military in particular. Written by an anonymous "Western student" who snuck into Laos for eight days, the account—based on "conversations with villagers, guerillas, an army officer who recently defected with ten men and their weapons, and an escapee from 'Seminar' (a re-education labor camp)"—made explicit the neocolonial dimension of the Vietnamese presence from the perspective of Lao farmers:

> The Laotians are fighting not only a rigidly authoritarian regime but, as they see it, one that is kept in being by the armed forces of an occupying power, the Vietnamese. The Vietnamese are said to be invariably in control of their Laotian counterparts. . . . Village leaders said that their villages were visited and searched by Vietnamese units up to five times a month. . . . . The villagers had an unalloyed hatred of the Vietnamese and disgust with Laotian officials and soldiers who were seen to be working for the Vietnamese and against their own people.[45]

It is in this light that Thongphachanh and Birgegard's comments on security deserve to be read. Outlining "three aspects of this problem," they distinguished first between "reactionary groups and bandits" and the rest of the population.[46] While not unconcerned by the former, it was largely with the latter—the main portion of the rural population—that their focus lay. This "reserved and uncommitted" population's allegiance needed to be *won*, they argued, counterinsurgency-style: "The situation has placed the rural population in a difficult position. The reactionaries are trying hard to alienate the population from the Government by threats and harassment. As an understandable reaction, the attitude of the population is reserved and uncommitted. Under these conditions mobilization for development becomes more difficult."[47]

"Mobilization for development" is often used today to mean uncompensated sacrifice to the national community.[48] There is certainly a hint of this in Thongphachanh and Birgegard's use of the phrase here. But given their concern for what might happen if the government pushed its citizens too hard in the name of the "national" interest, it is better to think of "mobilization" in this context via the quest for "win-win" efforts described by the Council of Ministers above. Given the right socio-spatial relations, planner-experts like Thongphachanh and Birgegard sought to achieve the simultaneous benefit of *both* citizens *and* nation through the judicious application of population management techniques. But this required taking seriously the needs of the local population so that their "attitude" would shift from "reserved and uncommitted" to mobilizable for various forms of development, which inevitably called for sacrifice.

Thongphachanh and Birgegard's final point on security, quoted above in the chapter's epigraph, outlined a conflict between development and security-related resettlement. The paradox they described built on their second point and highlighted the need to address upland resettlement with the utmost care: "Thirdly, the security situation may demand measures, e.g., in terms of movement and relocation of population, which are not conducive to development. Resettlement of whole villages and even entire *tasseng* [subdistrict] populations for such reasons may upset both short-term and long-term development efforts. As an improvement of the living conditions of the population is probably the most effective way of overcoming the security problems, there is a paradox that development efforts are most needed where the security situation makes them most difficult to carry out."[49]

Reading these comments in light of the Vietnamese military presence, the conflict between local and "national" development is especially delicate. If it was difficult to ask villagers to sacrifice for Laos's national development, the close working relationship between the Vietnamese military, the Lao military, and the Muang Mai forestry operations made this proposition even tougher. In this context, Thongphachanh and Birgegard's sympathy for the local population's "reserved and uncommitted" attitude toward SFE 1 and government intervention more generally, highlights the daunting nature of population management work in the postwar industrial forest.

THE GEOGRAPHY OF POPULATION MANAGEMENT

This characterization of the local population as understandably reserved and uncommitted vis-à-vis the Lao government was reflected in Thongphachanh and Birgegard's proposals for population management. The approaches they proposed followed a three-way distinction between the lowlands, the inner uplands, and the outer uplands, and sought to balance the need for state forestry in the latter two landscapes with the need for livelihood development in all three. Their recommendations anticipated and exemplified the rhetoric of win-win development and security that the Council of Ministers would articulate later in the decade, and the techniques that they proposed would reappear in the 1990s and 2000s as staples of state development practice. Given the lingering debates about the line between voluntary and coerced participation that these schemes trod, both in the rubber sector and elsewhere, their genealogies are worth examining.

Although Thongphachanh and Birgegard were skeptical of the potential for lowland rice production to meet the needs of the whole population of Muang Mai, they made paddy improvement and expansion one component of their population management strategy. Focusing on the Mekong lowlands southwest of the Sayphou Nyou, they recommended distributing improved plows to increase yields, redistributing fields that had been abandoned, and building new paddy land in areas where forest quality was already poor. This would help keep the "source" population that threatened the SFEs anchored as much as possible, while also following official policy preferences for lowland rice as much as the landscape would allow. The first of these also had an overtly strategic reasoning, targeting lowland farmers who already had paddy land of their own. Plow distribution, they argued, exemplified the "clear political dimension" of development work since it would "reach a large segment of the population, can be implemented without delay and without too much difficulty, [and will] have a visible impact."[50] In this, Thongphachanh and Birgegard echoed the kinds of high-visibility development that counterinsurgency strategists in the region had long advocated.[51]

They then turned to the area beyond the Sayphou Nyou, where the real challenges lay. They differentiated between the river and stream valleys of the inner frontier zone and the "high mountains" populated by the "Lao Soung"—a term that translates literally as "Highland Lao" and, in this context, would have referred to the Hmong. For the inner zone, Thongphachanh and Birgegard pushed for a generalized effort to "improve and transform" shifting cultivation through a mix of yield improvements and conversion to "permanent up-land cultivation." Proposing a long-term approach that would draw heavily on "experiences in other countries," they hoped that Laos would employ a version of the *taungya* cultivation system developed by British colonial foresters in Burma to enclose forests for state-managed extraction without provoking too strong a backlash from locals: "Protection of forest resources should be achieved by integration of shifting cultivators into forestry activities rather than by law enforcement, fencing and guarding. The integration should primarily take the form of development of agro-forestry (*taungya*) systems for reforestation. Areas for reforestation should be selected at the fringes of forest reserves where the encroachment by shifting cultivators is a threat."[52]

As this passage makes clear, the "agro-forestry" they had in mind was not the sort practiced in, for example, smallholder rubber systems in Indonesia.[53] Rather, "agro-forestry" was more of a euphemism for state-managed cultivation in which the agriculture was temporary and the forestry was long-term and state-owned; it was, in short, a form of managed enclosure. But it was intended to be subtle rather than overt. For Thongphachanh and Birgegard, physical alienation of land bred political alienation of the population; the line was almost one-to-one. Their recommendation against the use of "law enforcement, fencing and guarding" was based on the rationale that such an approach risked pushing locals toward the "reactionaries" discussed above.[54] "Integration"-based approaches that would keep the population in place while developing and managing the forest resource in their midst were, from this perspective, far more preferable because of their softer touch.

This approach seems to have taken root, although unevenly. In 1991 the anthropologist Ing-Britt Trankell spent seven weeks in the same part of Laos on a self-described "hit-and-run" anthropology project studying the effects of a road upgrade.[55] In some of the villages her team visited, she described a reforestation effort that had the essential features of the *taungya* method that Thongphachanh and Birgegard had advocated a decade earlier: "Villagers now receive plots from the forest company on which they are allowed to work for 2–3 years, on the condition that they plant tree saplings for the reforestation of the area. The work is performed simultaneously with the planting of rice. After the harvest, the area is marked with a fence in order to prevent cattle from damaging new plants. Villagers approve of reforestation programs and plea[d] for more such work to be done, but at the same time they resent the idea of being excluded from an area which they have themselves cleared and worked."[56]This ambivalence is a hallmark of many land allocation schemes that aim to rationalize upland farming through the offering of work (in this case) or formal tenure security (in others) in exchange for using less land. In Trankell's case, however, equally telling were her experiences in other villages, where residents were unwilling to even speak to her research team after having had their fishponds destroyed and "nutritionally valuable secondary growth" (i.e., swidden fallow forest) cut down following an earlier socioeconomic survey. As Trankell reported, "The issues of land use and land rights with regard to forestry and agricultural land are presently the most difficult and crucial problems. . . . Clashes with forestry company staff and forestry programs due to mutually conflicting views regarding the right to and the use of forestry products are reported."[57] Such heavy-handed approaches testify that the *taungya*-style approach of managed enclosure was not the only form of population management work local authorities were conducting to control village-scale land use; tactics varied significantly by time and place.

A second key strand of population management, echoing Thongphachanh and Birgegard's final point on security, was the managed resettlement of upland communities into concentrated areas. Spanning the entire decade of the 1980s—Thongphachanh and Birgegard did their fieldwork in 1981, Trankell did hers in 1991—in the areas around SFE 1, this focused on Hmong communities who populated what Thongphachanh and Birgegard described as the remote areas comprising SFE 1's mandate, and who Trankell (a decade later) noted were still "regarded as responsible for the occurrences of insurgent activities that regularly haunt the area."[58] (Trankell had been prevented from visiting what she called "villages in the hinterland," and had lamented the "certain 'shortage' of villages suitable for our project" as a result.) Concentrated resettlement was far less subtle and ambivalent than the *taungya*-style managed enclosures described above; provincial authorities in Bolikhamxai, for instance, described the establishment of the focal site at Muang Houng, discussed below, as requiring "tremendous effort to open the road in the middle of the forest" in part because of the "security problems [that] were an issue a few years ago."[59] They wrote this in 2000, implying that the insurgency persisted well into the 1990s. Trankell's description from a decade earlier, when the insurgency was still in full swing, described the "resettlement programs" as having been seen by local authorities "as a way to pacify the Hmong by bringing them down from the hills." Provincial authorities, she noted, "reported that at the time they had three different programs for 'the settlement and education' of Hmong groups in lowland areas."[60]

Thongphachanh and Birgegard's remarks about concentrated resettlement are especially interesting and relevant because they capture a key strand of official thinking at a key formative moment in Lao state forestry. In their report, concentrated resettlement offered a way to resolve the "paradox" mentioned above by bringing the population out of both the areas haunted by insurgency and the forests targeted for development by the SFEs. By stabilizing and fixing land use, they argued, it had the benefit of remedying the problems of what they took to be the Hmong's especially destructive style of shifting cultivation, which they described as moving from place to place "with no intention to return to the abandoned land after a fallow period" and leaving land with "little value either as agricultural land or as forest land."[61] Thongphachanh and Birgegard termed their resettlement-based approach "intensive 'sub-area' development," and they initially described it via "some general principles" due to their inability to access many of the areas they were seeking to manage:[62]

> Firstly it is suggested that the development of the mountain
> areas in the country as a whole as well as in Muang Paksan can
> *not* imply a development of the entire mountain areas (in terms
> of road networks, electrification, social services, etc.). Rather,
> development has to be *concentrated* to certain sub-areas and
> pockets with a relatively good economic potential. . . . A strategy
> of selective (and intensive) development in the mountains most
> likely presupposes a gradual out-migration from these areas.
> The reason is that it may be difficult (and economically unacceptable) to develop a sufficient economic base in selected areas
> for the entire mountain population.[63]

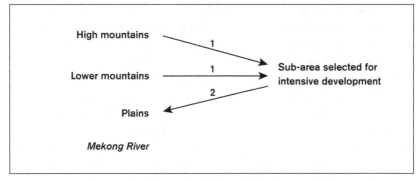

FIGURE 3.1   Schematic for "intensive 'sub-area' development." Diagram by Ben Pease. Based on Thongphachanh and Birgegard, "Muong Paksane Regional Development Study," 39.

This vision of upland relocation implied a squeezing of the upland population's economic base that would leave room for some, but not for all. The remainder of the population, they suggested, would be induced to relocate to the lowlands. Using a crude but clear graphic (reconstructed as fig. 3.1), Thongphachanh and Birgegard elaborated their "general principles" via a spatio-temporal proposal: "People from the mountains are to be encouraged to settle in the sub-areas selected for intensive development. This movement is illustrated by the arrows marked (1) in the [figure above]. The second movement involves an out-migration from the mountain sub-areas to the plains (arrow marked 2). After an initial period of settlement in the sub-areas (arrows marked 1), the two movements are expected to go on simultaneously. The time perspective involved is very long (25–50 years)."[64]

"INTENSIVE 'SUB-AREA' DEVELOPMENT": THE CASE OF MUANG HOUNG

The distinction between general principles and actual action plans dissolved in a place called Muang Houng. Located at the end of the road that offered access to the forest resource beyond the Sayphou Nyou, Muang Houng had been the Lao government's original proposal for where to build SFE 1, as noted above. After SFE 1 was moved to Muang Mai because of pushback from Swedish advisers, Muang Houng retained a focus within SFE 1's "regional" subproject, not for forestry but as a destination for upland resettlement. Muang Houng thus exemplified the Paksan Regional Project's cross-sectoral mandate of doing nonforestry development work that would nonetheless enable forestry to proceed.

Thongphachanh and Birgegard devoted almost four pages in their study to the "construction of a lower secondary school for the mountain *tassengs* [subdistricts]" that, they suggested, be built in Muang Houng. In contrast to the "general principles" above, their proposal for this school was quite detailed, covering "the proposed activity," "the buildings," "benefits and justifications," "implementation responsibility," "inputs required," a "cost estimate," and "agricultural activities to reduce boarding costs."[65] Education of upland communities was central to bringing state forestry and regional development into alignment, they argued, because it would facilitate the out-migration that was needed to alleviate the demographic pressure on forestry operations: "The provision of social infrastructure and services should purposively be used to influence future population settlement patterns. This means that priority should be given to (i) the plains along [the] Mekong; (ii) the pockets in the mountain areas identified for intensive development; and (iii) locations where agro-forestry systems are introduced (as an incentive to involve the farmers). To speed up out-migration of the high mountains it is proposed that even stronger efforts than hitherto are made to favor education of the children among the hill tribes."[66]

In the years that followed their proposal, Muang Houng became the home of Bolikhamxai's first "focal development" site. A *Socio-Economic Profile with Emphasis on District Development*, published in 2000 by provincial authorities and the United Nations Development Program (UNDP), describes in detail both focal-site development in general and Muang Houng in particular. Throughout the 1990s, focal-site development had been increasingly embraced as official rural development policy, and in 1998 Laos's central government had announced plans to scale up the "approach" nationwide.[67] Despite having arguably helped pioneer the approach via two decades of work in Muang Houng and its surrounding areas, Bolikhamxai authorities took care to frame their work in the language of official policy: "The essence of our Focal Site-based rural development is 'an area approach targeting rural poverty.' Our 'Focal Site' strategy is hence the 'bringing together of development efforts in an integrated and focused manner within a clearly defined geographical area, aiming at the eradication of poverty and at promoting sustainable development.'"[68]

Quoting official policy language like this downplayed the more heavy-handed dimensions of focal-site development, namely the massive relocation it often entailed and the fact that it was frequently a key part of active counterinsurgency operations. In their description of focal-site development in the district that now contains Muang Houng and Muang Mai, provincial authorities referenced Muang Houng as the first of the province's original two focal sites and emphasized its "accelerated development" compared to a second site "without any Lao Soung" where the administrative "structure was established but no development activities yet" undertaken. In contrast, the Muang Houng site was "half Lao Loum and half Lao Soung, with a minority of Lao Theung," and contained ten thousand people: ten times the population of the other focal site and a full *half* of the district's population.[69]

This concentration of population in Muang Houng and its immediate environs suggests a great deal of state intervention in the areas that Thong-phachanh and Birgegard had called the inner and outer forest frontiers. In contrast to the situation in the early 1980s, when the greater landscape of SFE 1 was extensively populated but only partly inventoried owing to the security situation, by the late 1990s "accelerated development" had rear-ranged both of these. As the provincial profile makes clear, these efforts spanned the spectrum between coercion and consent: "For us, focal site development must be ambitious and, at first, necessarily provincial govern-ment driven because of the basic need to first provide access, land clearing, etc. . . . We are aware that once the initial effort has been provided, a 'softer' approach has to take over."[70]

This "accelerated" process ("access, land clearing, etc.") was a sanitized way of referring to what the profile described elsewhere as a mix of logging and military operations that, in the case of Muang Houng, proved especially daunting. This began with "open[ing a] new road to the remote areas (with logging activities)," and as noted above, required "tremendous effort to open the road in the middle of the forest."[71] Part of this effort was certainly physical and logistical: Muang Houng was located well into the panhandle's forested interior, in the rolling uplands that ascend from the Mekong to the crest of the Annamite Mountains along the border with Vietnam. But the need to begin with "ambitious" rather than "softer" approaches also reflected the political difficulties that confronted the state push into the upland interior. The pro-file acknowledged as much, although it did so from the comfort of hindsight: "While security problems were an issue a few years ago, no troubles have occurred since accessibility has been improved, because improved accessibil-ity meant improved access to socio-economic development."[72]

Although the success of these "socio-economic development" activities is debatable,[73] it is clear that the development of the Muang Houng focal site figured centrally in the efforts—first of SFE 1, and then of provincial authorities, who took over the Paksan Regional Project in 1986 and SFE 1 in the years immediately after[74]—to separate the upland population from the forest resource. While the details of this process are beyond my present scope, the "two provincial saw mills" referenced in the Bolikhamxai provincial profile testify to its general direction, as does the almost complete surrounding of Muang Houng by provincial logging areas in the 1990s and 2000s.[75]

Finally, the Bolikhamxai provincial profile described the responsibilities of district-level Agriculture and Forestry officials. These were a far cry from the "integration of shifting cultivators into forestry activities" envisioned by Thongphachanh and Birgegard and observed fleetingly by Trankell in 1991. Instead, they focused on conducting land-use zoning—the LFA process, which was then in its heyday of nationwide implementation—and actively "prohibiting logging and wildlife hunting, as well as wildlife trade, by enforcing the law and punishing offenders according to regulations and rules."[76] This was precisely the "law enforcement, fencing and guarding" approach that Thongphachanh and Birgegard had written off in the early 1980s as both politically infeasible and unadvisable because of its security implications. By the late 1990s, in contrast, it was a different era entirely, and population management techniques had changed to fit the times.

In his lectures on governmentality, Foucault offered a conceptual distinction that is relevant to population management work. The population, he explained, was the collective who not only followed their own interests and desires but also acted in a way that was rational and could thus be governed, in pursuit of the greater good, using various policy instruments. This was the collective who would "do as they ought," as Bentham put it, with the right mix of incentives, rules, and, if necessary, force. As an essentially governable group, the population stood in stark contrast to what Foucault called "the people": the unruly mob who demanded that their needs be met even if doing so proved to be socially inconvenient. The people, unlike the population, placed themselves outside the collective, and thus by "refusing to be the population, disrupt the system" as a whole.[77] In the context of Laos's postwar uplands, this distinction between "population" and "people" was not inherent to the groups involved, at least from the perspective of the advisers, managers, and state authorities involved in and around industrial forestry operations and associated upland projects. Rather, the distinction was contingent on socio-spatial relations. Working in the name of development, state authorities and their advisers sought to manipulate these relations in ways that would render uplanders into the desirable category of population, "allowing" them, as the Council of Ministers put it, to direct their collective mastery to the "two strategic tasks" of development and defense.

The reality was considerably messier. But this messiness sheds important light on Laos's upland landscape at a key historical moment, showing how population management was not something that could be theorized from afar and then applied uniformly. Instead, it required a local praxis that experimentally combined analysis of the immediate terrain, prediction about future scenarios and competing needs, and deployment of available resources. The particular applications—*taungya*-style managed enclosures in some areas, focal sites in others; the deliberate avoidance of "fencing and guarding" in some circumstances and the embrace of laws, rules, and regulations in others—highlight the variation across space and time. But more importantly, they point to the family resemblance of different types of population management work that were being developed as a repertoire, a field of practical experience that could be drawn on in later situations. Scholars of development in Laos have tended to view the relationship between politico-military and economic issues through a lens of *transition*, emphasizing the shift from security-oriented interventions in rural development in the 1980s to development-oriented interventions in more recent decades.[78] This relationship, however, is better conceptualized as one of *interaction*. This theme of security as always both political *and* economic sits at the heart of population management work.

The Council of Ministers' 1988 instruction came in the early phase of Laos's official turn toward market-based development. This "Renovation Policy" or "New Economic Mechanism" was promulgated in 1986 and led, through the late 1980s and throughout the 1990s, to the devolution and in some cases privatization of various state enterprises, the writing and adoption of a constitution and beginnings of a legal code, and a range of state- and donor-led efforts to recruit foreign direct investment. This period gave birth to a number of widely known policies and interventions, including the formalization of focal-site development and the creation of the village-scale LFA zoning program.[79] It also launched a new discourse of postwar security talk that helped animate the application of these efforts by foregrounding the need for what state and party leaders called "heightened vigilance" as the country proceeded onto "the new battlefield where no gunfire can be heard."[80] An excerpt from a Lao radio broadcast from seven months after the council issued its instruction on population management work is exemplary, highlighting political leaders' anxiety about increased contact with the outside world and, tellingly, suggesting a link between social conflict and external interference that we will see again:

> The enemies have taken advantage of the conveniences of traveling in our country to send their spies in the guise of businessmen, traders, tourists, or workers to gather information about us and launch propaganda to create rifts between Laos and its friendly countries, between soldiers and police and civilians, between state officials and cadres and people, and among the people of different ethnic groups[. They] hope to cause mutual suspicion, antagonism and distrust between the lower and higher echelons, triggering internal conflicts so as to start riots and uprisings as they did in other countries. These are the most dangerous, subtle, and cruel of the enemies' tricks.[81]

As a way to combat these schemes, state authorities emphasized the need for diligence in population management work. Echoing the 1988 instruction, another radio broadcast from early 1989 exhorted cadres to "vigorously turn to the grassroots and build them into all-around strong localities," calling this "a foremost strategy in our party's and state's national defense and public security maintenance work."[82] As the examples above illustrate—from state forests to managed enclosure to focal sites—this idea of "all-around strong localities" captures the essence of multidimensional security intended by population management work.

Today, and even at the time it was issued, this security discourse carried the hollow ring of propaganda. Yet we should not confuse form with content. Events in the Lao uplands were existentially serious, both for the Lao state and for the many members of the population who found themselves living amid struggles both political and economic over which they had limited control. And population management work cannot be dismissed today as mere propaganda. As the 1980s turned into the 1990s and especially the 2000s, the government's quest for "all-around strong localities" drew increasingly on the outside world for economic resources and expertise. But to organize these in place, on the ground, Lao authorities drew crucially on the population management methods developed and honed during the earlier postwar period. It is with this history in mind that we can now return to the northwest.

CHAPTER FOUR

Micro-Geopolitics

Turning Battlefields into Marketplaces, 2000–2018

> Where it happens, war provokes a rearrangement of the ways
> territory and people are administered, . . . of the ways resources
> are tapped and distributed, of the framework in which disputes
> are settled.
>
> —ACHILLE MBEMBE

ESTLED among the government office compounds that sprawl
west from the town's main road, Luang Namtha's provincial
museum is easy to miss. A modest building, its single room contains displays that emphasize northwestern Laos's impressive ethnic diversity. Ornate bronze drums, richly patterned cotton weavings, and Chinese-style calligraphy line the walls, showcasing the "fine multi-ethnic traditions" lauded in the Lao PDR's constitution. Agricultural tools also feature prominently, highlighting the local diversity of farming traditions, from the wet-rice lowlands of the provincial capital and the Muang Sing Valley to the surrounding uplands that make up the majority of the province's land area.

Museums tell stories, and this one is no exception. As the exhibit winds its way around the building's interior, its artifacts narrate a shift from cultural heritage to political history, the mists of time and tradition giving way to the high drama of the mid-twentieth century. Highlighting the Battle of Namtha—the five-week campaign in early 1962 when the Pathet Lao drove the US-backed Royal Lao Army from the provincial capital and southwest toward the Thai border—the exhibit ends with an array of traditional weaponry and rusting yet fearsome machine guns. Conjuring a multi-ethnic population defined not just by its heterogeneous traditions but by its unified action, the exhibit is distinctly on message.[1]

Yet a closer look raises questions. One of the museum's most visible displays is a hand-painted wall map that dominates the building's entryway. On one level, it seems to tell a similar story of unity in diversity, showing the province's five districts dotted with "ethnic minority villages," each ethnicity marked by a corresponding color. The map's categorization and spatial precision exemplifies the legibility of the modern census, telling viewers that Luang Namtha's population is well inventoried, accounted for not just culturally and historically but politically and administratively as well.[2] But while many of the villages have a predictable geography—lowland groups like the Tai Lue and Tai Dam line the rivers, while Lao Theung and Akha villages are spread thinly across the uplands—other groups seem distinctly out of place. The "Yao" and "Kui," for instance, are widely celebrated as skilled hunters and upland farmers, both in the museum and elsewhere; the province's central massif is marked on old French maps as the Yao Mountains, for instance, while the Kui are famed forest hunters.[3] The museum map, in contrast, tells a different story. Yao villages are nowhere near the Yao Mountains, appearing instead as a string of villages on the Muang Sing Plain, outside the district center on the road to the Chinese border. Kui villages, similarly, comprise an enclave on the outskirts of Vieng Phoukha, a line of six gray dots along the road heading north from town (fig. 4.1). Meanwhile, the district's western region—the area where Kui and Yao villages appear on earlier maps—appears as empty space.

These mismatches are instructive. Even as the museum map simplifies (few villages in Laos are ethnically homogeneous), it hints at the extensive social reorganization that has taken place in the northwestern uplands over the last four decades. Some of this is well understood. Since the 1990s, upland reorganization in general, and involuntary village resettlement and consolidation in particular, have drawn increasing and often critical attention in Laos.[4] As numerous studies have shown, bringing remote villages closer to infrastructure and rural services, often apparently with a goal of freeing up hinterland forests for state use, has had major negative impacts, from the health consequences of moving highland villages down into warmer malarial zones to the consolidation-driven land loss and associated "new poverty" that geographer Jonathan Rigg has aptly called a "policy-induced Malthusian squeeze."[5] Yet as the museum map implies, there has been more to this than the corralling of upland populations and the primitive accumulation of forestland—space that is "uninhabited, covered by forest, and

FIGURE 4.1   Museum map detail.

administered by state agencies," as geographer Peter Vandergeest put it in
an early and thoughtful critique.[6] As in the central panhandle, the northwest was both a hot spot for antigovernment insurgency and a major center
for industrial forestry in the years after the Lao PDR's establishment. But
while territorial affairs there have followed a similar trajectory, combining
politico-military and economic rationales, their population management
dynamics have been more complex. As some upland groups were cleared
out, others were left in place or even brought in.[7]

Uneven upland reorganization has articulated with the enclosure processes of the rubber boom via what I conceptualize as micro-geopolitics, a
term that gestures to the ways that contemporary processes of enclosure
have become grounded in and shaped by earlier geopolitical conflicts. Enclosure is an enduring feature of capitalist development, and the differential
aspects of enclosure processes—some areas and some populations endure
far more than others—are inevitably a function of the interplay of historical and emergent geographies. Consideration of local, place-based histories,
rather than international relations per se, is important when analyzing the
geopolitical dimensions of transnational land deals, as are the ways that Cold
War violence continues to structure state-population relations in former

battlefield landscapes. Southeast Asia's transformation of "battlefields into marketplaces" began as an aspiration: a call to move beyond the political fractures of the Cold War toward a more prosperous and shared future. Yet as scholars like Cedric Robinson and Aihwa Ong have shown, preexisting social categories are all too often hitched to processes of differential value— of life, land, labor, rights, and so on—when such social and spatial differences help facilitate capitalist accumulation.[8] Cruelly, ironically, when examined on the ground, the transformation of battlefields into marketplaces appears more like a perpetuation of the Cold War's uneven human geography. Rather than replacing geopoliticized forms of social difference with modes of citizenship and equality appropriate to peacetime, development processes have capitalized on earlier fractures to facilitate ongoing enclosure and dispossession. This perpetuation, the smuggling of US-style denationalization into present-day Lao land politics, is a form of postwar legacy that demands our attention.

To show how this took place, I follow an approach that is broadly inspired by Michael Perelman's work on the history of enclosure, albeit with adjustments inspired by additional scholarship in the Marxian and Foucaultian traditions.[9] Perelman examined the logic and tactics of those he called the "primitive accumulationists"—plantation managers, colonial officials, and others who worked at the nexus of state and corporate power—to understand how enclosure practices became "calibrated" to particular historical situations. This is important since, as should be clear from my earlier discussions of population management work, fixity and integration via partial enclosure (rather than displacement via complete enclosure) have often been the aims of state action in the Lao uplands. But if Perelman's work focuses on the rationalities of those he studied, my interest is more in the emergent forms of territorial power that developed as multiple rationalities collided, competed, and combined. In northwestern Laos, this multiplicity is important: enclosure processes there involved multiple sets of actors—state authorities, rubber companies, development agencies, and upland residents themselves—each of whom had their own powers and liabilities, as well as their own internal differences. Within the state's horizontal bureaucracy, for example, provincial Agriculture and Forestry officials often tended to champion "3 + 2" rubber schemes, while their counterparts in Planning and Investment departments favored "4 + 1"; each reflected their own institutional interests. At the district level, meanwhile, territorial affairs reflected a range of intersecting concerns about local livelihoods, taxation, natural resource management, and security issues. Inevitably, these played out differently in various locales.

In such a context, some plans come to naught while others are twisted almost unrecognizably as they move from theory into practice. Enclosure is always a struggle—a *process*—and while it would be foolish to ignore plans and intentions completely, it is the outcomes that ultimately matter. Foucault's concept of micropolitics is useful here. Echoing Marx's critique of the "commodity fetish," Foucault advised against thinking of power like a simple object that can be passed from person to person.[10] Power is a social relation and needs to be studied in its native habitat, so to speak, from the ground up. This "ascending" approach to power, Foucault emphasized, differs markedly from a top-down approach focused on "who has power" ("What is going on in his head, this man who has power? What is he trying to do?"),[11] which often leads, in my experience, to variants on what I have called the "authority gap" narrative. If one begins only with plans, laws, and regulations, complexity on the ground all too often looks like implementation failure, illegality, even anarchy—terms that appear with some regularity in development discourse.[12] On the other hand, studying what Foucault called power's "infinitesimal mechanisms," each with "their own history, their own trajectory, their own techniques and tactics"—and examining how these get "invested, colonized, used, . . . extended, and so on by increasingly general mechanisms" of control[13]—offers an approach that, while hardly simple, is at least adequate to the complexity at hand.

THE SCRAMBLE FOR THE LOWER UPLANDS

The district of Vieng Phoukha illustrates the confluence of forces that brought Chinese rubber to northwestern Laos. For Lao leaders rubber exemplified both a vision for the desired upland agrarian transition to "permanent livelihoods" and, via the investment and state subsidies offered by China's "Going Out" policy, a means to finance it. Channeled through regional infrastructure initiatives like the NEC, and shaped by various regulatory disagreements, Chinese investment became grounded in Laos's upland interior. Vieng Phoukha, because of its location in the southwestern part of the province, was sufficiently removed from the immediate Lao-China border that local social networks had not already brought rubber to the district when investors' land-finding efforts began there in the early 2000s. These efforts targeted the lower uplands under 800 meters where rubber was most likely to survive and produce economically, and focused especially on interior regions where rubber was not already established: Vieng Phoukha, Long, and Na Le districts in Luang Namtha, and provinces like

Bokeo, Oudomxai, and Luang Prabang, located respectively to the west and south of Luang Namtha.

While some of these efforts were successful, a number of Chinese companies nonetheless ran afoul of the regulatory struggle described in chapter 1. Vieng Phoukha exemplified this as well. The Sino-Lao Rubber Company, for instance, whose disagreement with provincial authorities led to their ultimately giving up in Luang Namtha and focusing instead on Oudomxai and Luang Prabang, undertook significant surveying and negotiation in Vieng Phoukha in the months leading up to mid-2006. In May of that year, the company reached what it thought was an agreement with district authorities to "cooperate for poverty alleviation" through the development of "about 1,000 hectares" of rubber in six villages in the southwestern part of the district (map 4.1). But reflecting the significant room to maneuver that remained almost a year after the three-province "agreement" on "3 + 2," the Sino-Lao plan was amended—fatally, it turns out—by district authorities barely a month after it was signed. The initial agreement had specified a 35–65 percent split between farmers and the company, respectively; this was reversed in June to 65–35 because of what a district-level order described as "a mistake" in the initial MOU.[14] Precisely what kind of mistake this was, however, seems to have been deliberately unspecified. The wording was imprecise and, like many government documents, can be read in different ways. But given the competing versions of bilateral rubber cooperation described in chapter 1, it seems clear that the two versions presented in the initial versus the corrected plans—35–65 versus 65–35 percent splits—represented the very same debate about business models that was at issue at the provincial level (a concession-like "4 + 1" for the first versus a smallholder-focused "3 + 2" for the second). When provincial authorities later refused Sino-Lao's plans to work in Luang Namtha, they were likely reflecting this kind of district-level pushback. And in correcting the earlier "mistake," Vieng Phoukha authorities in fact seemed to be insisting on a "3 + 2"-type project: one based largely on farmers' own land and labor. This would have been a world apart from the tree-division model that Sino-Lao likely thought it had secured with the district.

A second major Chinese company also came up empty after courting Vieng Phoukha authorities in 2006, early 2007, or both. This effort was by the Yunnan Rubber Company, a subsidiary of Yunnan State Farms,[15] and focused on a cluster of villages in the district's southeast (map 4.1). Like Sino-Lao to the west, the company's aim was to assemble a large company plantation from territory in multiple adjacent villages, a strategy pursued by

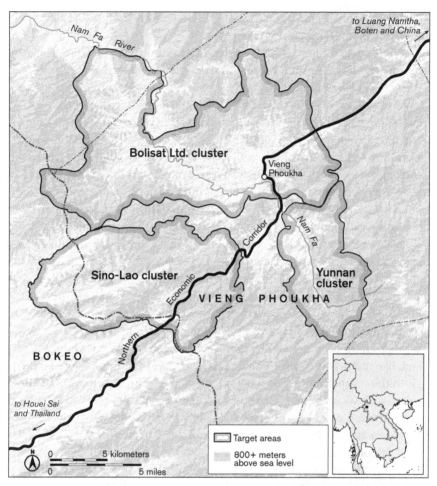

MAP 4.1   Planned target areas for Chinese rubber companies in Vieng Phoukha, c. 2006. Map by Ben Pease based on author's data.

concessionaires across the country.[16] The district technical staffer I spoke to about it, after the plan had already been rejected, described Yunnan's proposal as an attempt to build on its recent (but at the time already controversial) land concession in Namtha district, which was a multi-hundred-hectare company plantation located south of the provincial capital.[17] Like the Sino-Lao plan, Yunnan's plan for Vieng Phoukha ran afoul of local authorities because of its insistence on a company plantation rather than a contract-farming scheme. The difference here was that the district rejected the company directly rather than being preempted by the province.[18]

Thus, of the three major Chinese rubber companies with active land-finding activities in 2006 (map 4.1), only Bolisat Ltd. succeeded in developing a business operation. On one level, this was likely a function of pure economic geography. Of the three companies, Bolisat Ltd. had secured what was arguably the best cluster of target villages, since it had much more land under 800 meters in elevation and slightly better road access (via the NEC) to the Chinese border. So it is possible—and judging from Bolisat Ltd.'s operations, described below, it is indeed likely—that Sino-Lao and Yunnan judged the risk of operating in the outer reaches of Vieng Phoukha to be such that only a concession-centered operation made business sense. In fact, Bolisat Ltd. seems to have made that very same judgment: much of its latex supply would ultimately come from company plantations developed in Khet Nam Fa. But here we also need to consider the optics of enclosure. Bolisat Ltd. was constructed discursively as a *mix* of "3 + 2" and "4 + 1" operations in which the former was the norm, and the latter—taking place in only four of the company's sixteen (later expanded to twenty-two) target villages—was the exception. In framing itself as a mostly "3 + 2" project, Bolisat Ltd. differed significantly from Sino-Lao and Yunnan. In hindsight, this seems to have been a crucial move in allowing the company to get a foothold in the district.

Looking at the actual geography of enclosure that emerged, however, inverts this narrative; being mostly "3 + 2" may have been a good opening move, but it was not a long-term recipe for economic operations. As explained in chapter 1, the evolution of "contract farming"–based business models in the northwest saw the managed enclosure of the "4 + 1" model (achieved via the division of trees or land rather than latex) emerge as a response to low farmer interest in "3 + 2." In the case of Bolisat Ltd., this slippage occurred largely between 2005 and 2008, as the company pursued its "promotion" (*songserm*) efforts across its various target villages at the same time that it was also developing a "demonstration garden" (*suan sathit*) and various "4 + 1" plantations in the villages immediately surrounding its nursery operation. As the "3 + 2" efforts plateaued well below the 3,000-hectare quota listed in the company's contract, the latter continued to expand. This process was facilitated as much by local authorities as by the company; as shown in the next section, Bolisat Ltd.'s success in land-finding was largely due to the fact that it—rather than Sino-Lao or Yunnan—happened to get Khet Nam Fa as a target area.

The village heads I spoke to in 2007 and 2008 affirmed that there was relatively low farmer interest in "3 + 2": often the number of participating households was in the single digits. At the same time, they also described the parallel development of the larger company plantations in the form of both the demonstration garden near the nursery and the "4 + 1" plantations in the nearby villages of Khet Nam Fa.[19] One especially informative account came from an interview I conducted with a local official and a group of elders in the village where Bolisat Ltd. had its nursery. This took place just up the road from the site of my colleagues' and my first encounter with the company's project map, described in the book's opening sketch; part of our response to that initial bewilderment was to talk more to village-level officials and, often, other residents who happened to be around. These conversations were tricky. As scholars have noted and as I witnessed, village officials are inevitably pulled between the conflicting pressures of downward accountability to their local constituents and upward accountability to state and party officials.[20] Their responses thus tended to alternate between evasive and vague, and brutally candid. Often, prompts from the nonofficials present helped spur the emergence of crucial details.

Residents of the nursery village had had a front-row seat for Bolisat Ltd.'s operations, but had also managed to dodge the bulk of its worst enclosures. They dated the nursery's development to 2002–4, just as the NEC was getting off the ground, and the demonstration garden to the two or three years that followed (roughly 2005–8). This "garden" was in fact a large company plantation, a section of which is pictured in chapter 1 (see fig. 1.1). It straddled the boundary with the neighboring village, and in a pattern replicated across the country,[21] it had taken land from both. As compensation for the land lost to both the nursery and part of the demonstration garden, Bolisat Ltd. gave village residents three hundred rubber seedlings per household. For most households that seems to have been as far as it went; some reportedly planted the seedlings, but the active trade in seedlings in the area, coupled with the widespread lack of interest in rubber by poorer farmers (discussed above) meant that many had likely sold them. Six or seven households, in contrast, took additional seedlings from Bolisat Ltd. under the company's "3 + 2" arrangement, while about three times as many ("about twenty," I was told) purchased additional seedlings of their own to raise independently. These latter two groups were described to me as wealthier households in the village, matching the pattern of smallholder rubber development described in chapter 1. And even more tellingly for the events that followed, when the company offered the residents of the nursery village its "4 + 1" option—"if the family has only land and the company does the rest"—no one took them up on it.[22]

This story changed significantly as one moved into the neighboring villages of Khet Nam Fa. There the picture of limited enclosure, calculated compensation, and a degree of voluntary choice gave way to one of "4 + 1" plantations imposed from outside and much larger loss of land. In fact, both of these regimes reflect the notion of socially available land that I introduced in chapter 1. In the nursery village, land was *made* available by district authorities for both the nursery and part of the demonstration garden. Much of this land had already been in use; LFA zoning maps produced just a few years before Bolisat Ltd. arrived show the area that became the company's plantation as a mix of agricultural land—much of which had been sufficiently "improved" to have been demarcated cadastrally into individual farmers' plots—and, to a lesser extent, forest designated for "local use" (*pa somxai*).[23] When this land was "needed," district authorities provided it through what I have variously called "state land management" and managed enclosure. However, even while residents of the nursery village had been unable to resist the plantations' imposition in the first place—one speculated, when I asked why their village had been chosen, that someone in the village "knew someone from the district Agriculture and Forestry office"—the availability of the village's land was nonetheless fairly limited. Compensation had been provided, residents had had the option to refuse "4 + 1" plantations, and at the end of the day, the land lost to the company had numbered only in the tens of hectares.

The same was not true in Khet Nam Fa, where enclosures were in the multiple hundreds of hectares, the compensation much less, and the "4 + 1" model imposed from outside. Before examining this in detail, the next section provides crucial context by examining the history of Vieng Phoukha's western frontier. This history gave rise to the social relations that would later structure the interactions between Khet Nam Fa's residents, district authorities, and Bolisat Ltd. As the last two sections of the chapter show, the process of postwar upland reorganization that took place on the district's western frontier would create a very different model of social land availability in the years when Bolisat Ltd. came looking for land. It would be these social relations that governed the distribution of enclosure during the land-finding of the early and mid-2000s.

THE INTERNAL FRONTIER

As in Laos's central panhandle (ch. 3), state efforts to manage territory and population after 1975 in western Vieng Phoukha reflected a mix of politico-military and economic concerns. The area sat just east of the old Nam Nyu special zone (ch. 2), and following the creation of Bokeo province in 1982—by essentially splitting the former Houakhong province into southwestern and northeastern portions—western Vieng Phoukha became a sort of internal frontier space: heavily forested, lightly roaded, and targeted by a mix of pacification and forestry efforts from both sides of the new provincial border.[24] Many of the details of this history remain beyond my reach, especially during the 1980s when the area was a hot spot for what one observer characterized in 1991 as "the continuing low-level insurgency against the present government."[25] But security remained an issue into the 1990s as well, and events of this period are easier to reconstruct. The spatial dynamics of these events were nonetheless complicated by the involvement of multiple and often competing state actors, as well as by a politically diverse upland population that reflected the earlier geography of war. Unlike the model developed in chapter 3, where population management work focused on upland groups that state authorities saw as both a political and an economic threat, in western Vieng Phoukha it was not simply that forests were developed and populations corralled. Those things happened, but the pressure on forests from rival political jurisdictions, along with the imperatives of supporting the livelihood needs of those citizens who had been on the "right" side of the revolution, introduced added complexity. Security efforts thus juggled not only the problems of a waning insurgency but also the economic pressures to expand and harness the district's resource base for the benefit of both elites and at least some of its poorer citizens.

In my research, this manifested in different ways described below, but was summarized nicely in a 2007 conversation I had with a district officer I had gotten to know because of his involvement in making LFA zoning maps.[26] We were discussing the Bolisat Ltd. project, and he recounted a recent confrontation with a visiting official from Bokeo who had seen the paper version of the nursery map that I discuss in the book's opening sketch. The visiting official, with an eye to the timber in the provincial borderlands, had claimed that an unmapped area located just west of the map's westernmost village was therefore inside Bokeo. On one level, my informant admitted, this was an entirely fair reading of the map. Districts are made up of villages, after all, and a map that showed village territories on the edge of the district thus showed the edge of the district itself. But this is the problem with maps: they show a static version of territory that is, in practice, anything but. Many of the district's best forest resources, he explained to me, sat outside villages; these were "*district* forests rather than *village* forests," he emphasized. Managed village resettlement offered a way to incorporate these forests into the district, bringing "external" forest officially "in" via the creation of new borderland villages.

Explaining this required my informant to take a step back, since in the Lao context resettlement is often considered in terms of its success (or failure) in improving livelihoods, and frequently involves corralling upland populations into centralized rather than peripheral locations (as in ch. 3).[27] But resettlement here, he explained, also needed to be understood in terms of its role in serving state efforts to manage natural resources, in particular frontier forests. He gave a recent example where Vieng Phoukha had lost a chunk of territory to Na Le district because that district's governor had mobilized some of his constituents to resettle in a contested border area; this had changed the facts on the ground, so to speak, and strengthened Na Le's hand in an ongoing boundary negotiation. But this worked both ways. Vieng Phoukha's governor was, my informant explained, currently in the process of trying to do the very same thing to Long district by convincing residents from one of Vieng Phoukha's interior villages to move to the district's northern border area. This would have a twofold benefit, he explained, helping consolidate government control in a rapidly expanding part of the district while also relieving population pressure on the Nam Ha National Protected Area (which straddles much of the province's interior, covering the "Yao Mountains" mentioned in the opening sketch). With the outcome of that gambit still uncertain, my informant returned to the example of the Bolisat Ltd. map. The governor, he noted with satisfaction, had sent in a detachment of soldiers to help guard the forest against any incursion from Bokeo.[28]

Two villages on Vieng Phoukha's western edge offer a more detailed view of this intertwining of state territoriality and frontier resettlement; and in doing so, they also bring into focus the often harder-to-see *inward* displacements linked to pacification and securitization. These twin forms of state-managed resettlement—enrolling trusted populations to settle and even expand the frontier, and sending less trusted populations to the already-settled interior (map 4.2)—manifest the uneven citizenship that will ultimately lead us to Khet Nam Fa, where it will help to explain the uneven enclosures there in Bolisat Ltd.'s "4 + 1" plantation scheme.

The first village, which I will call Ban Deng, is the westernmost village in the Bolisat Ltd. project.[29] As both maps 4.1 and 4.2 show, this village exemplifies the expansive territoriality described by my informant above: its settlement, in 2003, took place after the provincial boundary had been drawn with Bokeo, and its LFA exercise seems to have conveniently extended the village well into Long district to the north, as well as slightly into Bokeo province to the west. Surveyed by district technicians (including my informant above) at over 9,000 hectares, Ban Deng is one of the two largest villages in

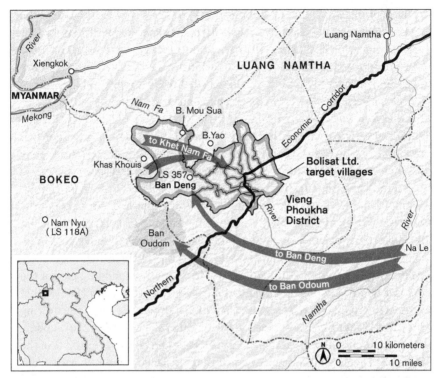

MAP 4.2 Resettlement trajectories in and out of western Vieng Phoukha. Map by Ben Pease based on author's data.

the district (by far), rivaled in area only by Ban Oudom, the second frontier village discussed below. By comparison, Vieng Phoukha's other, interior villages are, like most villages in rural Laos, much smaller, with territories in the range of hundreds to at most a few thousand hectares.[30]

Of course, lines on the map are one thing; facts on the ground are quite another. When I visited Ban Deng in late 2007, Bolisat Ltd. representatives had actually come just a week or so earlier to assess residents' interest in its "3 + 2" scheme. On the day of my visit, I spoke to a minor village official who, noting my affiliation with the National Land Management Authority, lamented that villagers were farming wherever they pleased. Little attention was being paid to taking care of the forest, he explained, and villagers' land use was expanding outward willy-nilly. Rubber exemplified this, with local interest in the crop increasing since a pair of soldiers—Ban Deng housed a large army camp—had planted a few hundred seedlings the year before.[31] The company's recent visit was attempting to capitalize on this interest, and the clear identification of the "3 + 2" scheme highlighted the lack of state effort to manage where the rubber would be planted.

This apparent disorder was also reflected in a district-government report on the LFA process from two years earlier. Despite detailing numerous aspects of the village's "progress" since its establishment in 2003, the report noted that "some of the villagers do not yet understand the Land and Forest Allocation process."[32] LFA had been conducted in 2004 and 2005, and district staff had produced a large signboard map that sat prominently in the middle of the village. Residents actually appeared to understand the exercise all too well: they had covered up precisely the pictorial parts of the map—which directed villagers where to farm and where forest was to be conserved—with posters that advocated vaccinating children.[33] The official I spoke to addressed this affront to state authority only indirectly. Despite his own misgivings about villagers' chaotic and unauthorized land use, he explained, enforcing the LFA plan depicted on the signboard was not currently a district priority.

This situation illustrates the micro-geopolitics of upland development in a few ways. The most apparent has to do with the migrants themselves, who were identified in the report mentioned above as not only being from Na Le district, but also as being members of the Khmu Rok ethnic group who had faced land shortages in their previous village.[34] These details are significant. As anthropologists Yves Goudineau and Olivier Evrard explain in their foundational work on village resettlement in Laos, the historical geography of the Cold War made the Khmu Rok (a subgroup of Khmu, and thus of the "Lao Theung" villages on display in the provincial-museum map) "a special case." Summarizing the wartime geography of southern Luang Namtha, they note that "by fighting on the winning side," the Khmu Rok populations on the east bank of the Namtha River, which runs through Na Le district, had "gained political representation at the provincial and district level," paddy fields in the provincial capital, "more schools than the right [west] bank and, finally, the chance to refuse to relocate their village[s] if a majority of the population opposed the move."[35]

Their account is doubly useful. In a general sense, Goudineau and Evrard anticipate much of the later literature on involuntary resettlement in Laos by explaining both that moving is the norm—when government officials say "move," most upland communities move—but also that there are exceptions that depend on political context. "Fighting on the winning side" had yielded resources both material and symbolic, and these came together in the power to resettle on communities' own terms rather than simply at the direction of state officials; put another way, via their role in the revolution, Khmu Rok communities in eastern Na Le had become part of the state apparatus itself, and they thus had significantly more control over their geography of (re)settlement than a number of other upland groups.

More specifically, Goudineau and Evrard explain that one implication of this ability to resist state-managed resettlement was that population pressure nonetheless accumulated in villages that chose to stay put, and that this was alleviated by periodic rural exoduses facilitated by what they called the Khmu Rok's "political integration" within the province.[36] Ban Deng appears to have been the product of precisely one such exodus. Another of my informants, who worked in Vieng Phoukha in the late 1990s, described hearing that the then-governor had been transferred to the district from Na Le in order to bring "the right kind of Khmu" to settle there.[37] Another informant, a development worker who was acutely attuned to debates within the international aid community about working in coercively resettled villages, explained that their project had initially refused to work in Ban Deng because of its recent establishment, but had subsequently elected to work there after becoming convinced that the resettlement event that established it had been completely voluntary.[38] The relatively free hand that Ban Deng's citizens had been given with respect to their extensive village territory reflected this history.

A second dimension of Ban Deng's situation is harder to see, but underpinned the village's creation in the first place: the absence of earlier settlements. Ban Deng is located directly on the site of an old CIA landing strip, one of the hundreds of STOL sites that, as described in chapter 2, helped the United States ground its version of upland territoriality in Laos in the 1960s. When US mapmaking stopped in 1975, the last generation of navigational maps created for American pilots (marked "distribution limited—destroy when no longer needed") showed three villages in the vicinity of what is now Ban Deng, plus the landing site (marked "LS 357") itself.[39] Labeled "Khas Khouis," "Ban Mou Sua," and "Ban Yao" (see map 4.2), these three villages had names directly echoing the labels ("Kui," "Muser," "Yao") used by government officials and development workers today to refer to Lahu and Iu Mien communities.[40] Equally interesting, the number and diversity of villages in the area appear to have *increased* slightly during the late 1970s and early 1980s. The Lao government's main topographic map series, issued in 1987 and produced with Soviet technical assistance in the years immediately prior, shows roughly twice as many villages in the same vicinity. The same "B. Yao" and "B. Mou Sua" appear from the earlier American map, while the earlier "Khas Khouis" has been replaced by four villages ("B. Kachoxe," "B. Chavadi," "B. Chacho," and "B. Chapa") whose names imply Lahu or Akha settlement. Near the old landing site today occupied by Ban Deng appeared the villages of "B. Namkouylave" and, nearby, "B. Kouy." Elsewhere nearby, additional villages appeared with names like "B. Kouychakhu" as well as Khmu names like "B. Phangua," "B. Hai," and "B. Tonglat," fleshing out the full spectrum of upland ethnic groups that had comprised the old Nam Nyu *maquis* (ch. 2).[41] While it is impossible for me to reconstruct the precise histories that led to their abandonment, the absence of all of these earlier villages is a key part of the frontier-settling process that followed during the late 1990s and early 2000s.

Traces of this process, however fragmentary, nonetheless appear in various sources and, as I explain below, point to the settling of Khet Nam Fa by at least some of the subpopulations who were displaced from western Vieng Phoukha. One such trace came in an interview I conducted with a development worker who lived in the district during the early 2000s, and whose work in Ban Deng and other western-district villages exposed him to stories about the area's history. Echoing the history I recounted in chapter 2 and expanding on the above reference to "the right kind of Khmu," he noted that the district had at least four old American airstrips, and that the insurgency had been active well through the 1980s and possibly into the 1990s. One clarification he added was that the insurgency had hardly been limited to the Lahu—he described it in fact as largely "Khmu-based"—and that this had led to the forced resettlement of Khmu villages out of the western zone earlier during the 1980s and early 1990s. By comparison, the displacement of the Lahu had begun later, in the late 1990s. My informant thus remained highly skeptical of any actual security threat posed by Lahu communities, but was clear nonetheless in noting its invocation as an official rationale for their repeated displacement.[42]

More traces appear in a second village, which I will call Ban Oudom, which complements the example of Ban Deng above by showing in detail how the resettlement of mistrusted groups like the Lahu intertwined with those of trusted groups like the Khmu Rok who were brought in from elsewhere. Ban Oudom has also appeared above in map 4.1 (although not by name) as the westernmost village in the planned-but-canceled Sino-Lao project. Like Ban Deng, Ban Oudom was also settled by Khmu families, as detailed below, and it seems to exemplify the timber-oriented territoriality described by my informant above. The village sits on the site of a contested "provincial production forest," and its LFA map shows a large swath of "production forest" (*pa phalit*) mapped at over 4,000 hectares—again, an incredibly large area for a single Lao village, let alone a single contiguous forest zone in a single village—and stretching well into Bokeo province.[43]

These circumstances suggest a possible reason why district authorities insisted on the "3 + 2" model for Sino-Lao and were willing to scrap the deal if they could not get it. As in Ban Deng, they were attempting to use the migrants for their own territorial ends. This would have been undercut substantially if they had turned around and started giving away the village's land to a Chinese rubber company.

I first became aware of Ban Oudom in 2007, when a district official told me that I would not be allowed to go there without special permission. I did not push it; the Sino-Lao deal had already been canceled, and I focused my fieldwork elsewhere. As the district's second focal site, however, Ban Oudom nonetheless remained on my radar. Various accounts date the village's establishment to 1999 or 2000, beginning with the arrival of a group of Khmu families from an unspecified area along the main road.[44] Troubling these accounts, however, is the presence of a group of approximately forty Lahu families that had lived in the same village site for at least ten years already (one source dates their arrival to 1986, another to 1990).[45] In my research with state officials and sources, Lahu settlement came up repeatedly as a problem. I was told multiple times by district staff-people that "Kui people don't like to live in villages," that they "prefer to go live in the forest," and that they grow opium and resist development in general.[46] A bit like the museum map in the opening sketch, Ban Oudom highlights the ambiguity and problematic nature of Lahu settlement in western Vieng Phoukha. The official establishment of the village, right around the turn of the millennium, took place despite the fact that a large group of Lahu families had already been living there for the better part of a decade.

One reason for this may have been that the Lahu presence was seen as transient. A 2004 report that I collected contains an aside that in 2001, the Lahu families that had been living there had moved "to the mountaintops in the area" but then moved back (whether voluntarily or not is unspecified) to their earlier village site later that same year, around the time the group of Khmu families mentioned above also arrived. Two years later the Lahu families moved again, this time much farther—to Sing district, in the northern part of the province—and this time clearly as part of a forced resettlement effort connected to a wider anti-opium campaign being conducted at the time across the north.[47] The 2004 report, commissioned by a donor organization that was considering funding a rural development project in Ban Oudom and was thus especially interested in issues of local food security and village relocation, noted the confluence of the removal to Sing district with the arrival of a second group of Khmu families, this time from Na Le:

Lahu people originally inhabited the area. But in December of 2003 they were moved to Muang Sing. They remained there until May of 2004 and then returned to Vieng Phoukha. In Muang Sing they had no drinking water and not enough land to plant rice. . . . They returned in two groups, one by vehicle and one walking 10 days through the mountains. Upon their return however, they found that 40+ Khmu [families] had been moved into their old site from Muang Nale in what may have been a case of ethnic nepotism. One group [of returning Lahu families] settled north of the Khmu (20–25 minutes' walk) and the other south . . . on the main road into the village. . . . A third group . . . have also settled very close to the Khmu on the east side of the village.[48]

In addition to its reference to "ethnic nepotism" of the same type elaborated above for Ban Deng, the report is notable for exemplifying the way that the micro-geopolitics of Cold War violence often haunt development reports, unacknowledged and unelaborated on the one hand but unavoidably present on the other. In describing the Lahu families' history, the report included the detail that they had moved in 1986 from an area in Bokeo called Nam Jomh, which is just south of what was, at the time, the Nam Nyu special zone. As a large group of Lahu families who had left a village cluster on the edge of a special military zone in the mid-1980s, and had moved to a remote location in the borderlands of Bokeo and Luang Namtha, these families would have been subject to the same sorts of suspicion that led to the Iu Mien's displacement to Sing district (see opening sketch), and that I elaborate below for the Lahu of Khet Nam Fa. This suspicion appears only fleetingly in the report, but it is present in both explanations of why the Lahu families were split up into three groups when they returned from the unsuccessful resettlement to Sing district. The report first references an unnamed informant who asserted, without elaboration, that "the Lahu did not want to form a large village as it may threaten the government." Later the report explains the same situation differently, claiming that upon their return to Ban Oudom, the Lahu families "did not stay together because the government said they would not accept a large 'new' Lahu village."[49] Whatever the actual reason(s), the report illustrates the official anxiety around settlement that marked subpopulations like the Lahu, slating them for displacement from areas where frontier-making depended on more trusted members of the population.

If western Vieng Phoukha illustrated a light-touch variety of population management work based on political trust and minimal enclosure, the area I have been calling Khet Nam Fa exemplified almost the polar opposite. A focal site established in the mid- to late 1990s, largely as a destination for the Lahu communities resettled from the western frontier, the Khet Nam Fa area would receive the bulk of Bolisat Ltd.'s plantations as the company's "4 + 1" operations took off in the mid- to late 2000s. By 2018 Khet Nam Fa's residents had been largely excluded from the potential forms of livelihood associated with the company's operation, whether paid rubber tapping, contract farming, or both (see ch. 1). It is thus worth examining the details of how Khet Nam Fa's land base was made available to Bolisat Ltd., since in the transition from its earlier to later years there is a noticeable shift from population management work that was aimed at incorporating Khet Nam Fa's residents into a form of permanent livelihood (however paternalistic and coercive) to a simpler, more outright land grab. Managed enclosure figures centrally throughout, but it is important to chart this shift since many of the details get lost in the blurry statistical picture of land deals that appears from farther away.

Khet Nam Fa is the official name for the group of villages that comprise the "Kui" cluster shown on the provincial-museum map. Like the Lao word *muang*, *khet* is a geographic term whose historical meaning—a localized area or zone, often within a *muang*—has been adapted to current use; *khet* refers today to a cluster of villages at the subdistrict level, where taxation and other official business is often conducted.[50] Khet Nam Fa thus refers to a group of villages located near a stretch of the Nam Fa River, which is itself a tributary of the Mekong that flows roughly northwest from Vieng Phoukha's southern uplands; then through the district capital, the villages of Khet Nam Fa and Ban Deng; and finally to its confluence with the Mekong in Long district to the northwest (see map 4.2). Khet Nam Fa, located just outside the district capital in the river's middle reach where it descends from the higher to the lower uplands, was attractive to Bolisat Ltd. for a few different reasons.

One reason is immediately apparent from map 4.1. From simply an economic-geography perspective, Bolisat Ltd.'s target region was arguably the best of the three Chinese companies that, as late as 2006, were still vying for land in the district. Combining an abundance of land under 800 meters in elevation with a proximity to the NEC via the presence of newly built feeder roads, Khet Nam Fa's location made it a good candidate for a large-scale rubber operation whose eventual output was destined for overland export to China. Khet Nam Fa thus exemplified the hinterland geography described in chapter 1: located just outside the NEC's roadside mitigation zone where land-tax certificates were issued as a nod to the risk of land grabbing, the villages of Khet Nam Fa were nonetheless well within the project's area of commercial impact. As one of the new investment projects catalyzed by the NEC road upgrade, the Bolisat Ltd. operation was precisely the sort of "subregional economic development" that regional planners and boosters were hoping for.

Another dimension of Khet Nam Fa's appeal—in this case for local officials—was its taxation potential. As noted above, some of Vieng Phoukha's agricultural lands had been cadastrally mapped before the company's arrival as part of the LFA process; these areas included lowland paddy fields, as might be expected, as well as various other forms of "improved" farmland such as fields used for annual cash crops like maize or sugarcane, or for tree crops like cardamom. But these were the exceptions that proved the rule: most of the district's land base, including the land in Khet Nam Fa, lay outside the cadastral map.

Tax officials in Vieng Phoukha divided the district's villages into those that had finance committees capable of calculating and collecting land taxes on an area basis and those that did not. Khet Nam Fa's villages all fell into the latter category. Contrary to assertions that upland areas in Laos are completely untaxed, this meant that Khet Nam Fa's agricultural lands were taxed indirectly by counting adults of working age, whom tax officials saw as a reasonable proxy for upland fields that were too difficult to locate, map, and measure.[51] While thus not entirely untaxed, the land base of villages like those in Khet Nam Fa was seen as underproductive when it came to taxation; residents were among the poorest in the district, and the per-head tax rate was indeed quite low.[52] Large-scale rubber plantations offered the opposite, in the form of both a fixed and legible crop, and a producer with the capacity to pay much more. In December 2006 Luang Namtha's provincial governor issued a rubber-tax policy that aimed to capitalize on precisely this: upon coming into production, rubber plantations over five hectares in size would be taxed six renminbi per tree per year; smaller plantations would be taxed less.[53] During my fieldwork in 2006–8, Bolisat Ltd.'s plantations in Khet Nam Fa already numbered at least a few hundred hectares, and they continued to grow through the end of the decade.[54] With their multiple hundreds of rubber trees per hectare, these plantations offered a potential tax windfall in the hundreds of thousands of dollars—far more than anything that had ever come off this land.[55]

Even still, Khet Nam Fa was hardly the only part of the district with these characteristics. A third and final piece of its "suitability" thus came via the particular sort of social land availability created by the frontier micro-geopolitics examined above. In one sense, this was a more extreme version of the land availability on display in the nursery village. As they had there, state authorities deemed the land in Khet Nam Fa to be "needed for development," and they made it available accordingly. This proceeded via a suite of practices aimed at de facto rather than legal enclosure of village lands. Following a common interpretation of Lao land law, district officials maintained that the land in Khet Nam Fa upon which Bolisat Ltd. developed its plantations "still belonged to the villages," but that since it had not been developed yet, this ownership was collective rather than individual, and was thus in need of what Laos's land laws have long referred to as "state land management."[56] This phrase appeared in the "3 + 2" policy, where it qualified the policy's apparent embrace of smallholder landownership (ch. 1). In Khet Nam Fa this qualification was even stronger, severing outright the link between villagers' power to make decisions about how their land was used on the one hand, and their formal legal ownership of it on the other. By eclipsing the former while preserving the latter in a way that was technically true yet *merely* formal, "state land management" created the conditions of possibility for Bolisat Ltd.'s "4 + 1" operation. Classifying Khet Nam Fa's former shifting-cultivation land as collective, village agricultural land, officials assigned this land to be the company's target plantation area.

In another sense, however, Khet Nam Fa's land base was not made available to Bolisat Ltd. *despite* the presence of local residents but *because* of them. Their relatively recent resettlement from the district's western frontier meant that Khet Nam Fa's residents were treated as de facto wards of the state to whom government officials and technical staff had a special obligation—however self-interested and paternalistic—when it came to livelihood development. Paternalism features widely in many development contexts, both in and out of Laos.[57] In Khet Nam Fa this took an especially exaggerated form. If residents' displacement from the frontier had been in the interest of wider security concerns, keeping them in Khet Nam Fa was seen to be part of the same suite of objectives. The managed enclosures created there were thus aimed, at least initially, at not just making land available to Bolisat Ltd., but at bringing much-needed capital to an ongoing sedentarization and livelihood (re)construction effort.

In my interviews with local officials, it quickly became clear that this effort was a fraught one. Taking land from communities that were already seen to be among the, if not *the*, poorest of the poor was both an outcome and an impression that local officials were keen to avoid. In our conversations, district agriculture and forestry officials thus echoed the "3 + 2" policy rhetoric in noting their general preference for contract farming over concessions, and they took great care to explain the "4 + 1" plantations in Khet Nam Fa as something other than the latter. In multiple accounts, their emphasis was not on land being taken but on the financial and technical resources that rubber investment was bringing to a landscape where villagers' attachment to land was already tenuous at best. One district official thus insisted to me that "rubber is helping the Kui people because it's giving them 30 percent [of the new plantation] by developing land they won't use again anyway. They go to the forest, cut a new swidden, make a new house, plant and harvest the rice, and then move on and do it all again the next year." Another official explained the situation similarly, linking the land allocation to Bolisat Ltd. to the special challenges confronting the effort to establish permanent livelihoods in Khet Nam Fa: "The reason for '4 + 1' [here, as opposed to '3 + 2' elsewhere] is because these villages are minority ethnic groups without permanent settlement—they shift from place to place, depending on their swidden farming. So according to [central] government policy and district policy to help this group have consistent villages and permanent houses, state officials asked the company to invest in these villages, specifically to plant rubber because rubber is permanent [*youn-yong*] farming."[58] It was hard to have a land grab, the rationale seemed to be, if the social link between village and land was missing in the first place.

This was certainly spin, but it was not merely that. Just as Lahu settlement had been tenuous and ambiguous on the western frontier, so it remained in Khet Nam Fa. The museum map from the chapter's opening sketch depicted Khet Nam Fa as a series of eight Lahu ("Kui") villages, all in a line and clustered closely together. Although cartographically incorrect—the cluster contains only four villages (not eight), and they are arranged around a T-junction (not a single road)—the museum map contained an important truth. Unlike the district's more widely dispersed villages of Lao Theung, Akha, and other ethnic groups, the Lahu settlements of Khet Nam Fa comprise a focal site of the sort discussed in chapter 3. As should be clear from the example of Ban Oudom above, focal sites vary significantly. Khet Nam Fa was closer to the Muang Houng variety, exemplifying the extreme structural poverty for which "focal site development" in Laos has become rightly infamous.[59] Established in the latter half of the 1990s, Khet Nam Fa was the product of resettlement efforts that, as one development worker explained in 2007, had occurred "without the full consent" of those involved and had resulted in high levels of post-resettlement mortality (with "up to

20 percent of villagers dying within the first couple of years after the move, old people and children suffering most of all"). Resettlement here, the same informant continued, was a multitemporal process, "pursued now with an avowed 'development' rationale but in the past seemingly associated more with issues of national security."[60] This was echoed in other accounts as well, such as one that described Khet Nam Fa's origins in the 1996 government effort to resettle groups of Lahu who had returned to the western frontier after the initial, earlier resettlement efforts "after the war didn't last."[61] Another of my informants, a rural development consultant with long-term experience in the area, captured this dynamic in describing one of Khet Nam Fa's settlements as "a failing village": "People don't stay there," he told me, trying to explain the extreme poverty in a part of the country that was already very poor: "They sell the rice land they receive from development projects, and they don't know how to raise the livestock [these projects] give them. The army periodically goes out to the forest, rounds them up, brings them back, and leaves—after which they trickle out again."[62]

Bolisat Ltd.'s efforts thus fit, at least initially, within a population management scheme aimed at keeping Khet Nam Fa's residents anchored in place through a mix of wage work, the provision of rubber seedlings, and a long-term plan to allocate them 30 percent (by area) of the company's plantation lands under the "4 + 1" model. This mix of land partition and wage work exemplified the "concession-like" nature of the scheme, contrasting with the "3 + 2" model in ways that exemplified my provincial informant's concern in chapter 1 that "4 + 1" was "not actually contract farming." But "4 + 1" also differed from the concession model, occupying an intermediate position on the enclosure spectrum *between* contract farming and concessions because of its planned land partition. This partial enclosure was a key piece of why tree/land division was attractive to Lao authorities throughout the northwest: it enticed companies to invest and provided wage work in the short term (like concessions); but it also offered the promise of a transition to a smallholder contract-farming model once the partition took place. Accounts of "4 + 1" that I collected in 2006–8 contained all of these elements: wage work, the provision of rubber seedlings to villagers to experiment with on their own, and the plan (still a few years away at the time) to divide the plantations into company- and villager-owned portions. While not necessarily popular—one village official complained to me at the time that "if the company is going to help the villagers, they should provide the inputs for free and villagers should get all of the proceeds from selling the product to the company"—the plantation-partition plan was well understood among village officials in Khet Nam Fa.[63] When I returned in 2018, although much had changed (see next section), this initial plan to use rubber to keep villagers in place had not been forgotten. Even as the promise of rubber-based livelihoods had all but evaporated, one village head I spoke to recalled that Bolisat Ltd. had been part of the district's opium-eradication plan, with seedlings provided "only to families who had agreed to stay in the village." He summarized the argument that villagers had heard at the time from district officials and company representatives: "If you come out of the forest and stop growing opium, you will have better livelihood options."[64]

PREVAILING INTERESTS

When I returned to Khet Nam Fa in 2018 it did not take long to see that while the so-called "4 + 1" scheme had succeeded in creating available land for Bolisat Ltd., it had not forged the working partnership between company and villagers conjured a decade earlier in so much of the development rhetoric. The enclosures begun in 2004 or so had indeed continued to expand, and what had previously been a few hundred hectares—the figures are approximate for reasons examined in chapter 5—had perhaps doubled. Lining both sides of the road through much of Khet Nam Fa, Bolisat Ltd.'s plantations consisted of the large demonstration garden described above, as well as the even larger main plantation complex near the workers' dormitory mentioned in chapter 1's opening sketch. Having matured from the terraced, newly planted hillsides shown in figure 1.1 to full-grown plantations where tapping had already begun (fig. 4.2), the operation exemplified the land's transition from shifting cultivation and subsistence farming to fixed crop and global commodity.

Yet the aspect of population management work had essentially failed. Although the land itself had been transitioned from upland rice to rubber plantation, the putative targets of the scheme—the residents of Khet Nam Fa—had been excluded from this transition rather than brought along with it. The partitions that had figured so centrally in the narration of the "4 + 1" scheme a decade earlier were nowhere in the accounts of Bolisat Ltd. that I collected in 2018. Instead, much like the "concept note" about rubber value chains mentioned at the end of chapter 1, local narratives had shifted from the nuance of a workable, best-of-both-worlds hybrid between concessions and contract farming to the simple binary of the two. District staff-people I spoke with described Bolisat Ltd.'s operation as "concession and promotion" (*sampathan kap songserm*) and clarified that Khet Nam Fa was "entirely concession" (*sampathan leui*)—a far cry from the partial enclosures conjured by earlier descriptions of "4 + 1."[65] Similarly, one of the village officials I spoke

FIGURE 4.2   Khet Nam Fa, c. 2018: rubber plantations (foreground) with upland rice fields (background).

with in Khet Nam Fa ignored the partition plans of old and instead lamented the loss of land to the company (ch. 1, opening sketch). Another, interestingly, reinterpreted the seedlings that the company had distributed a decade earlier to residents who promised to stay in the village. Rather than describe this in the terms recounted above (wage labor in the short term, plantation partition and smallholder production in the medium to long term), he recounted Bolisat Ltd.'s plantation as the result of a land sale (of seventy-plus hectares, a gross underestimate) that had been paid for with rubber seedlings. The only time a plantation partition came up was in a counterfactual, describing events that took place in a village outside Khet Nam Fa where Bolisat Ltd. had developed a "4 + 1" plantation in the years after my initial fieldwork ended. There, village residents had decided that they did not want their share of the plantation after all; two years in, and fully a year before the partition was supposed to take place, residents there had decided to sell their portion to the company.[66]

A similar trajectory of alienation (rather than incorporation) appeared in the accounts of wage work. A decade earlier, Khet Nam Fa residents had worked for the company extensively as part of the plantation-establishment process. Back in 2008, the same village official who complained about the project's lack of actual help had described his constituents' relationship to the company in language that evoked the silent compulsion of labor that had already lost its means of subsistence. Noting villagers' lack of permanent jobs, he explained that their work digging holes, planting seedlings, and weeding the new plantations entailed "working by morning to eat at night" (*ha sao kin kham*), a description that, while hardly favorable, testified to the close relationship at the time.[67]

A decade later much of this work had disappeared, seemingly because (at least in part) of a labor dispute that I was unable to get the full details of.[68] (My follow-up trip was a brief one, and since many of my best informants had left the area, my ethnographic access was not what it had been a decade earlier.) Although Khet Nam Fa residents reported still doing the occasional weeding work for Bolisat Ltd., mostly the work had gone to outsiders—the migrants who lived in the new labor dormitory mentioned above. Rather than incorporation into a new plantation regime, the major effect of the Bolisat Ltd. operation had been the further erosion of a land base that was already squeezed by a mix of resettlement, demographic change, and piecemeal land sales (on the latter, see ch. 1). Much as it had when Bolisat Ltd. arrived, upland shifting cultivation remained the precarious core of Khet Nam Fa's rural livelihoods (see fig. 4.2, horizon)—only this time with even less land.

Given this trajectory, it is essential to view Bolisat Ltd.'s activities in Khet Nam Fa not only within the state-territorial logic of trying to secure a precarious villagization, but also within the (in this case, competing) economic logic of trying to develop a viable business. Even if the company's trajectory was hardly straightforward, Bolisat Ltd. managed to address the land-access challenges that confronted Chinese companies more broadly across northwestern Laos and elsewhere.[69] In large part, this success was achieved by capitalizing on a form of social land availability that sat at the conjuncture of both a general policy preference to "stabilize" upland shifting cultivation using fixed plantation crops like rubber and, more importantly, the specific history of localized, postwar state territorialization described above. The regulatory pushback against Chinese rubber concessions meant that however tempting it may be to see the end result of company-owned plantations as simply the outcome of some initial plan, the history of actual events tells a more complex and dynamic story. Even if the "4 + 1" scheme appears in hindsight as just so much conjuring work—useful for opening the door to managed enclosure but actually unused for anything else once the land had been taken—the failure of projects like Bolisat Ltd.'s to live up to the cooperative rhetoric of the early and mid-2000s still demands explanation.

While my evidence only goes so far—I know far more about how enclosure occurred than what took place subsequently, after my main fieldwork ended—a key piece of the story involves the Chinese government's handling of opium-replacement subsidies (see ch. 1). This program is sometimes viewed as a mere sop to Chinese agribusiness, and from such a perspective, actually working *with* upland farmers in Laos and Myanmar was, despite the rhetoric, never really part of the plan. I am less cynical, for two reasons. First, some skepticism about the Chinese opium-replacement program proceeds from the apparent ecological mismatch between rubber and opium: the former grows best below about 800 meters, as noted above, while the latter is typically a "highland" crop grown above 1,000 meters. The problem with this, however, is exemplified by the case I have described above: it focuses on land rather than labor, when in fact many of the populations targeted initially by poppy-replacement projects (like the residents of Khet Nam Fa) have come *from* highland areas *to* what I have called the lower uplands. It is clear that even if resettlement was not part of the Bolisat Ltd. operations per se, local officials still very much saw the project as part of their own ongoing efforts to make a precarious resettlement work.[70]

Second, despite the opium-replacement program's management by provincial officials in Yunnan, who clearly acted with a probusiness logic, a number of scholars and practitioners have pointed out its origins in real public-health concerns about heroin use in China, and thus the plausibility that it would enable Chinese companies to manage the business risks and logistical challenges of working with poor borderland smallholders.[71] Given the program's size—between 2005 and 2015, estimates of subsidy values range in the tens of millions of dollars for both Laos and Myanmar[72]—if managed effectively, the program could conceivably have allowed the companies that received its financing, tax breaks, and import quotas to operate in ways that bent significantly to local economic needs and policy demands.[73] At a macro scale, this might have allowed for accommodations like minimum-price guarantees for latex produced under the "3 + 2" scheme, and even a more attractive version of "3 + 2" that would have taken pressure off Lao officials to find land under the "4 + 1" model. In Khet Nam Fa, a better use of subsidies might have allowed for more training and similar efforts focused on community inclusion; ongoing wage and price supports to workers and smallholders to make that inclusion more attractive; and some type of welfare provisions for food security during the period when plantations were maturing and the canopy closing over areas formerly used for upland rice.

These are, of course, hypotheticals. Even as the opium-replacement subsidies remain difficult to trace at the firm level, the enduring hardships faced by upland communities—both those like Khet Nam Fa that lost land and those (elsewhere) where contract farmers were forced to bear the full weight of low global rubber prices beginning in 2011—suggest that the program's benefits remained with the companies. (Anecdotal and official reports of resurgent opium production in the region point in a similar direction.)[74] Instead, the case of Bolisat Ltd. illustrates how micro-geopolitics created essentially one more subsidy. To the range of policy supports from the Chinese side of the border, postwar territoriality in Laos added cheap land as well.

One morning in January 2007, on a stretch of road just south of Luang Namtha's provincial capital, Sompawn Khantisouk disappeared. Khantisouk was the Lao co-owner of an internationally famous eco-lodge and trekking business. An accomplished river guide and motocross rider, he was athletic, confident, attractive: an established businessman and, though still young, an emerging civic presence. The time and place of his disappearance were publicized in the days that followed, a circular posted in shops around the provincial capital requesting the assistance of "anyone with any knowledge" of the situation. Although the flyer made no mention of how or why Khantisouk had disappeared, many people around town and, as word spread, throughout the region concluded that he had been abducted, and that his disappearance had been sanctioned, if not actually conducted, by state authorities.

Half a decade before another civic leader, Sombath Somphone, was abducted in Vientiane under similar circumstances,[75] Khantisouk's disappearance was widely read as a sort of referendum on Chinese investment and its governance in Luang Namtha. Some observers speculated that he had been "mobilizing local villagers against Chinese-sponsored rubber plantations," as one journalist put it in an article about Chinese "expansionism" in the region.[76] This was perhaps a tempting conclusion, given the widespread and often critical attention to Chinese rubber investment in the area, as well as more specific concerns in ecotourism circles about whether Luang Namtha could maintain its brand, centered on the province's reputation for untouched forests and authentic "hill tribe" culture, if the rubber boom continued.[77] As one of the most visible faces of Luang Namtha's small but robust ecotourism industry, Khantisouk and his American business partner were widely assumed to be against Chinese rubber development.

Yet in a pointed and public response to the journalist who framed Khantisouk's disappearance as a result of his upland organizing, his business partner Bill Tuffin insisted that Khantisouk "was absolutely not involved in 'mobilizing' villages against the rubber plantations." Tuffin wrote that the two of them had in fact developed a very measured position on rubber: that it "could help local farmers if it was properly planned and forest lands could be converted to rubber plantations if other forest lands were properly preserved." Instead, Tuffin argued that Khantisouk's disappearance was part of a larger process of Lao-government efforts to rein in what, in the context of this chapter, might be called active citizenship. "Sompawn's disappearance," he wrote, "coincided with a general purge of Americans and Christians in Northern Laos" during 2006 and 2007, when "close to 26 expatriates were forced to leave the area" and "several Lao [people] with close associations with Americans or Christians disappeared or were given threats they would be abducted."[78]

Tuffin's explanation for this clampdown reached into the depths of the Cold War: "The Lao People's Revolutionary Party fears peaceful evolution—the overthrow of the socialist system by peaceful means. All of the foreigners purged from Luang Namtha, Bokeo and Udomxai provinces were working with marginalized communities to give them a voice in determining their own economic future. The fact that these foreigners were giving people choices and were becoming more influential than the local governments in the economic livelihoods of these communities was the threat."[79]

This explanation is notable not just for the larger picture it paints about the wave of expulsions and disappearances, which had not been widely reported. It is also striking for the historical link it conjures between the mid-2000s and half a century earlier. The concept of "peaceful evolution" was formulated by John Foster Dulles in the 1950s, initially as a critique of the US policy of militarized containment, which had been a pillar of the so-called Truman Doctrine since the late 1940s.[80] While Dulles himself was a chief implementer of containment under President Eisenhower, he developed the idea of a "peaceful transition" or "evolution" as a more practical way to defeat communism in places like China and the Soviet Union where the United States had no intention of going to war. Dulles was confident that "Russian and Chinese Communists [were] not working for the welfare of their people" and that US support for the rule of law abroad could speed up the inevitable collapse of communism under its own weight. This theory of peaceful evolution so worried Chinese leaders in the early 1960s that Bo Yibo, a top Chinese official at the time, implicated it directly in China's split with the Soviet Union over close ties with the West, as well as with Mao's decision to launch the Cultural Revolution in 1966.[81] It is perhaps unsurprising that Lao leaders' calls for "heightened vigilance . . . on the battlefield where no gunfire can be heard" from the late 1980s (ch. 3) echo Mao's earlier calls for "heightened vigilance" against capitalist infiltration and revisionism, given that they came precisely at the moment when Lao leaders felt vulnerable to outside threats from the Western world. What is notable, however, is that two decades later these types of concerns were still visibly present.

Yet Chinese state-capitalist development has indeed brought its own forms of threat to the social stability of the Lao uplands. As the cooperative ("win-win") development envisioned by "3 + 2" rhetoric gave way to actually existing "3 + 2" projects, whose poor terms forced concession-like "4 + 1" projects to take up the slack, the management of enclosure's social distribution proved crucial. Targeting projects like Bolisat Ltd. into landscapes like Khet Nam Fa showed a certain hedging on the part of Lao officials: a hopeful optimism, perhaps, that Chinese rubber development could be used to finance permanent livelihood creation where earlier efforts had failed, but also a pragmatic limiting of the negative fallout (when such efforts of incorporation ultimately failed and produced merely a land grab) to subpopulations with limited political capital. Such a calculus is arguably the essence of government in a place and time like contemporary Laos, which exemplifies Neil Brenner and Stuart Elden's riff on Marx that "states make their own territories, not under circumstances they have chosen, but under the given and inherited circumstances with which they are confronted."[82] Littered with the remnants of American upland territoriality, and incorporated into a mode of development cooperation over which state officials have only limited control, northwestern Laos is best seen not as a space of ceded sovereignty—an anarchic space where the authority gap reigns—but as one of intense territorial politics where the legacies of Cold War violence remain all too close to the surface.

CHAPTER FIVE

Paper Landscapes

State Formation and Spatial Legibility in Postwar Laos

The understanding of the authorities and the people . . . is not deep, leading to the delay in implementation, creating opportunities for illegal land occupation and leaving the deforestation issue unaddressed in many locations.

—PRIME-MINISTERIAL "INSTRUCTION ON THE EXPANSION
OF LAND MANAGEMENT AND LAND AND FOREST
ALLOCATION," JUNE 1996

I N mid-2007 the residents of a village in southwestern Vieng Phoukha planted twenty-four thousand rubber seedlings on the hillsides behind their houses, the site of the previous season's upland rice crop. Their work, visible in panorama from the nearby NEC, was the result of a new initiative designed and promoted by the district governor. Located high in the uplands near where the road passes into Bokeo, the village had originally been part of the planned Sino-Lao rubber project. When that deal had fallen through, district authorities enrolled another company, a local sawmill, to finance a village-scale pilot scheme for rubber development. The sawmill owner had provided seedlings to the village on the same terms as Bolisat Ltd.'s "3 + 2" scheme: a 39–61 percent sharecropping split where the company provided the inputs and the villagers the labor and the land. In return, the governor had granted the sawmill owner a new logging concession in a remote part of the village, located over the hill a kilometer or so down a small dirt road.

Village authorities' explanation of the project contained many familiar tropes: the poverty alleviation and forest protection that would result from replacing shifting cultivation with permanent crops; the same strained effort I had heard elsewhere to skirt the fact that the scheme had been imposed unilaterally on the village. (The governor had "promoted" it personally, and villagers had "agreed.") More interesting, however, was the new logging concession. Exemplifying the adaptation of Lao land policy to "local interests and power struggles"[1] that we have seen before, the deal had emerged from a suite of challenges that confronted local authorities in the wake of the Sino-Lao collapse: the loss of potential rubber financing, the ongoing challenge of upland livelihoods, and growing pressure on local authorities to rein in the extractive industries on which they often relied for economic development. The collapse of the Sino-Lao deal had created both the need for an alternate source of financing and an opportunity to close the loop, so to speak, with the sawmill. By financing reforestation with rubber, village leaders explained, the sawmill was addressing its own negative impact on the forest, not to mention giving something back to the village.

This narrative was supported by a revision of the village's LFA map, which had been updated the same year (fig. 5.1). The new map showed a shuffling of land and forest categories, including most importantly the creation of a new "production forest" (the logging concession) and the reclassification of a sizable chunk of the village's "agricultural land" to "protection forest," a forest category that in some cases refers to military areas but in this case referred to watershed protection. This cartographic sleight of hand more than offset the new concession, and the revised map thus *increased* the amount of forest (on paper at least) contained in the village's territory. It had the added bonus of pushing the deforestation out of view, displacing it from the swidden fields that had previously lined the NEC (and were now a maturing rubber plantation) to the new logging area over the hill.

The sawmill scheme exemplifies two key ways that zoning maps have become important tools of population management in Laos's northwestern uplands. The first concerns the work of legitimation. As noted already, Lao officials engaged in rural development schemes often invoke the government's exclusive authority to manage or zone land (*chatsan thi din*) as outlined in the country's constitution and land laws. This is clearly at stake in the example above, where LFA seeks to draw on maps' persuasive power to assert state authority over village-scale land use. In this sense, LFA is analogous to the Bolisat Ltd. project map described in this book's introduction (and elaborated below); both use formal cartography to try to impose a particular vision—and indeed a particular spatial plan—on upland landscapes and communities.[2] These efforts are never just about maps, though. We have seen LFA maps a number of times in earlier chapters, and taken together,

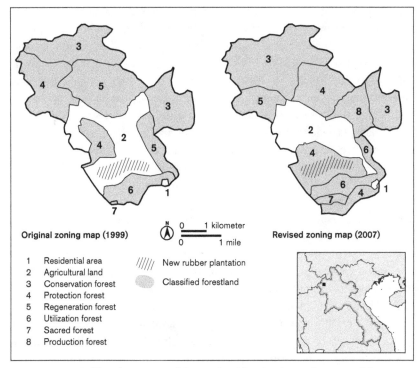

FIGURE 5.1   Rubber, logging, and forest classification in southwestern Vieng Phoukha. Maps by Ben Pease based on author's data.

their role is ambivalent at best: for every rationalization of a land grab using the tool of mapping, it is possible to find a "paper tiger" like the LFA map in Ban Deng, for instance, whose presence in the village defied rather than reinforced the dominant strand of population management work. The techniques of upland governance, after all, were developed in the 1980s, a full decade or so before the rollout of the LFA program. Zoning maps, in other words, figure into larger efforts to get upland citizens to "do as they ought," but they are hardly recipes for success in themselves. For every case where they appear as an agent of enclosure, another example testifies to the weakness of land-use interventions that are merely formal.

A second dimension of village-scale zoning work is less obvious and yet maybe even more important. This is the use of zoning maps as a political technology directed not just downward at local land users but also *upward* at central-level authorities. In recent years, "illegal" logging practices by local authorities have become a political issue in Laos on par with foreign land deals, stimulating a range of state, donor, and civil society interventions.[3]

Meanwhile, timber concessions have remained a key resource for local authorities, funding outright corruption (as is often pointed out) but also paying for local budgetary expenses like new infrastructure and salary supplements that are seen as locally legitimate, if not entirely within the letter of the law.[4] The example above shows district authorities attempting to embed an increasingly embattled status quo—the granting of a new timber concession—both within the rhetoric of economic and environmental sustainability and, more substantively, within the technical, grounded work of land-use planning and smallholder rubber development. It shows, in sum, how formal zoning has become a tool for managing not just local populations but faraway authorities as well.

The evolution of village-scale mapping in Laos exemplifies the articulation of transnational land deals and LFA in the early 2000s, as the former were on the rise and the latter was coming to a close. This is a story of localized control over the power of maps, and it ultimately helps explain the ongoing lack of central-level regulatory leverage over many rubber and other land deals *despite* the fact that village-scale LFA began as a bid to take power away from local authorities. The effort to use formalized, step-by-step mapping as a means to break local authorities' monopoly over land-use planning has received far less attention than its role in facilitating enclosure and, more generally, in what I have called population management work.[5] Yet as Peter Vandergeest points out in his foundational work on the LFA program, zoning projects need to be understood historically, as the concrete outcomes of particular conjunctures rather than an inevitably taken step on the road to state territorialization.[6] Most accounts of LFA, in contrast, do not even consider the question of timing; they take it simply as natural that Lao authorities would pursue a program like LFA because that is just what states do.[7]

My approach here focuses more explicitly on what scholars call ongoing state formation, or the struggles and fragmentations *within* the state that center on the control over spatial information as a way to control the value, or rent, that comes from land.[8] Looking at the paper landscapes created by LFA and derivative land-deal maps allows me to dig into these politics of internal regulation, which continue to plague transnational land deals more than a decade and a half after they were first officially named as a problem. This requires a lot of reading against the grain, including narratives like the epigraph above that emphasize the lack of capacity or understanding among not just local citizens but also local authorities, whose "lack of capacity" is a familiar theme in Lao (and other) development discourse.[9] In contrast, my emphasis is on elucidating the competing interests and, more specifically, the high-stakes resource politics that underlie land deals. Ultimately, this fight over regulatory authority and jurisdiction helps to explain why maps have proliferated at the local level at the same time that central-level regulatory capacity has continued to falter.

To adequately grasp the full trajectory of relevant events, we need to return (again) to Laos's market transition efforts of the late 1980s and early 1990s, and specifically to the decentralization of state control over industrial forestry. Doing so facilitates a focus on how and why information about land deals travels (or does not travel, as the case may be) through bureaucratic channels. Even as transnational land deals have become formalized on paper, this formality has not necessarily translated into legibility at the national scale. This is because of internal and ongoing state formation, which itself turns on a political economy of resource control that stems back to the late 1980s, as the Cold War was ending and the still-struggling Lao government was deciding how to recruit "investment" for purposes of national economic development. But this chapter is not merely about the weight of the past. Amid these internal struggles over legibility, we also see the emergence of *new* forms of transnational legibility, which in turn raise questions about the "global" nature of the contemporary moment.

"SOCIALIST BUSINESS ACCOUNTING" IN THE FORESTRY SECTOR

The late 1980s were a time of intense economic and political disruption. The height of neoliberalism in the United States and Britain, this was the era of perestroika and dissolution in the Soviet Union and of economic reforms across the socialist world, from those of Deng Xiaoping in China to Doi Moi in Vietnam.[10] Under Laos's New Economic Mechanism, it was the era of "stepping up population management work," "heightened vigilance," and territorial experimentation with focal sites and managed enclosure in the uplands (ch. 3). In 1986 Laos's Fourth Party Congress adopted the slogan of "everything for the socialist fatherland and for the plentiful and happy life of the people of all ethnic minorities."[11] Yet this was aspirational at best. Behind the scenes, internal communications reflected the structural difficulties inherent in the economy, from the prevalence of "backward" and "traditional" production to the increasingly predatory actions by a range of state actors whose loss of Soviet and Eastern Bloc aid meant a direct threat to their own subsistence. In 1987 a prime-ministerial "Order on the Free Market" echoed the French rhetoric of "unblocking Laos" from a century earlier (ch. 1), but pulled no punches in criticizing the heavy hand of the government's own "administration" efforts, including the disruptive "inspection of goods" and ongoing predatory interference in economic production by "provinces, districts, *tassengs* [subdistricts]," the Ministries of Defense and Interior, and various "military units, police and militia units."[12]

Amid these difficulties, central-level authorities launched a "socialist business accounting" initiative that aimed to make state-owned enterprises—at the time, the pillars of the Lao economy—more productive and accountable to market-based calculations. Piloted in 1985 and expanded in 1987, these reforms sought to replace heavy-handed administration with market-based production one enterprise at a time.[13] On one level, the statistics sounded almost impressive. By the time of a March 1988 national meeting on the topic, at least 105 provincial and 38 central-level state-owned enterprises had been "granted full autonomy"; many other businesses had "also actively made efforts to fulfill the 1987 plans" for reform.[14] Yet the transition to a "free market" was largely acknowledged as a failure. As in the above-quoted "Order on the Free Market," interference remained widespread. A 1988 reflection by Lao president Kaysone Phomvihane tried to put a positive spin on the recent "renovation and development," claiming to have "modified the attitude of Left-leaning and haste" and "stopped abolishing private and individual rights to ownership and markets." But even this public-facing account, published in the Soviet newspaper *Pravda*, acknowledged "abnormalities" in the economy that had resulted "because the production and circulation of goods had come to a halt."[15]

Forestry was the exception that proved the rule. Contra the difficulties earlier in the decade, the late 1980s are widely remembered as a boom era for the Lao timber sector due to a mix of increased "business autonomy" and rising external demand (in particular from Thailand, whose 1989 domestic logging ban helped spur exports). Lao provincial administrations, which used forestry revenues to support their long-neglected budgets, benefited significantly.[16] The transition to provincial control over SFE 1 that took place during the late 1980s and early 1990s (ch. 3) exemplified this, but Bolikhamxai was hardly unique. During this period provincial authorities across the country gained increasing control over activities like roadbuilding, logging, and sawmilling, in part owing to the creation of provincial forestry enterprises alongside and in some cases from the older SFEs.[17] A parallel dimension concerned "strategic" state enterprises like the infamous Mountainous Areas Development Company (BPKP in its Lao acronym), whose mix of military affiliation and newfound "business autonomy" made it especially powerful.[18]

Between 1987 and 1989, Lao timber exports increased to the point where they became the country's chief source of foreign exchange, accounting for roughly a third of annual exports.[19] The adoption of "market principles" was so successful that in 1988 central-level authorities issued a logging ban, and when this failed to be heeded, forestry officials attempted to at least regulate logging through the creation of a provincial quota system.[20] According to one well-placed observer, these quotas were issued, in 1990, "largely to combat the widespread overharvesting that had occurred in the late 1980s when provinces exercised almost complete control over the industry."[21]

A 1989 editorial in the Lao *People's Daily* hinted at the regulatory challenges that confronted officials in Vientiane who were increasingly realizing the unaccountable and indiscriminate nature of the logging operations they had unleashed. Targeting "those units running businesses of agricultural and forestry production"—a veiled reference to state and provincial forest enterprises, as well as strategic enterprises like the BPKP—the editorial insisted that the Ministry of Agriculture and Forestry "ha[d] the right to supervise" these units so that they could "correctly carry out their activities in accordance with the line and policy of the party and state." In the language that followed, one gets the distinct impression that there is more than just the conceptual distinction between necessary regulatory oversight and unhelpful interference that would stifle productivity: "But this does not mean that the said ministry has the right to interfere in the work of those business production units. By saying this, it does not mean that the ministry has to support or allow the said business units to carry out their businesses any way they wish. In this regard, the various business production units must also directly take responsibility over the implementation of various regulations and laws adopted by the party and the state."[22]

In such assertions of regulatory right and calls for responsible action on the part of "business production units," the multiple moving pieces of the state appear to be increasingly in conflict. In the years that followed, the nexus of extractive entrepreneurialism and local authority would only continue to snowball. In the process, it would inspire a whole policy apparatus aimed against it.

"THEN MAKE LAND MAPS": LFA AND THE PROBLEM OF LOCAL AUTHORITY

In an effort to rationalize and expand the capacity for long-term forest management, Lao officials held the country's first National Forestry Conference in May 1989. The conference set the stage for much of what would follow, including the creation of a national system of protected areas in 1993 and, in the shorter term, a series of logging bans, the first of which was issued the same year as the conference. As part of this immediate action, the conference launched an effort to address the "indiscriminate logging" of the later 1980s by "dissolving" the SFEs and associated provincial forestry enterprises. Yet despite some impressive policy language—a prime-ministerial decree ordered that logging "should only take place in inventoried production forests" and had to involve "approved economic-technical plans," "full payment of log royalties," and "compensatory tree planting"—the rationalization of the sector stumbled when the putative dissolving of the forest enterprises turned out to be simply a mix of devolution and privatization.[23] As one official source admitted years later, the lowering of accountability over the forest enterprises meant that during this period, "in many cases, Provinces harvested above the allocated plan to create additional fund[ing] for development projects, and there were many irregularities concerning log sales contracts as well as logging, grading and sales themselves."[24] A second logging ban in mid-1991 also accomplished little, as noted by the admission that the "ban" had, in fact, been little more than a slowdown, and that log *sales*—a staple of provincial operating budgets—had remained roughly the same and even increased in 1993 as supplies of "old logs" ran low and local authorities began harvesting anew.[25]

It was in this context that the LFA program was born. Initially outlined as part of the forestry-sector rationalization decreed in the wake of the first National Forestry Conference, LFA was piloted at the district scale in the early 1990s and scaled up to a nationwide program beginning in 1996. LFA is one of the most studied government land policies in contemporary Laos, and rightly so. Between the late 1990s and mid-2000s, the program oversaw village-scale zoning in roughly half of the rural villages in Laos; estimates vary—between 5,400 and 8,000 villages are reported to have received LFA implementation during this period, often in connection with foreign development projects[26]—but they collectively point to LFA's role in intensified state efforts to manage land use at the village scale.[27] As chapter 3 illustrates, LFA was hardly the beginning of such efforts; resettlement and other forms of population management work were features of upland reorganization since the late 1970s. But LFA's launch in the 1990s added a new level of intervention in village-scale agrarian affairs.[28]

Coming in the wake of the relatively ineffective forest management reforms described above, LFA also brought a more resource-intensive and micromanagerial approach to the problem of local authority. Broadcast in intent via the 1993 decree that announced LFA's scaling up to a nationwide program, the project took substantive shape in mid-1996 with the beginning of a concerted effort to formalize the practice of granting land for "development." This was an explicit play against the land-allocating pre-rogative of local officials, and it centered on a prime-ministerial decree (issued in June) and a conference (in July) that brought provincial-level officials to Vientiane for instruction.

Titled "Instruction on the expansion of land management and land and forest allocation," the decree focused on land administration broadly and was explicit about central-level intentions. It began with the epigraph above, describing "the understanding of the authorities and people" as "not deep," and thus both "creating opportunities for illegal land occupation" and "leaving the deforestation issue unaddressed in many locations."[29] Under the "activities" portion of the decree, two articles merit special attention. The first mandated the establishment of local-level committees to review all instances when "the acquisition or possession of land" by private actors had occurred "due to village administrative authorities' decision to exchange it for con-structions of public interest, such as roads, electricity, schools, hospitals, and so on." These committees were instructed to figure out whether these concessions ("exchanges") had been reasonable, and where they had not been, to withdraw part or all of the allocated land.

Second and more importantly, the decree banned local authorities from granting concessions outright in the future: "Starting from this instruction, the administrative authorities at each level shall be strictly forbidden to fur-ther exchange land for constructions."[30] In doing so, it then specified an alternative instrument for exchanging land for development that would be formalized and centrally administered: the state land concession (*sampathan thi din lat*). Focused on "building confidence in investment for land development, as well as orderliness in the Lao population's livelihood," the formalization of land-concession practices underlay an effort that would be expanded the following year in Laos's first Land Law, part of what Lao officials would eventually refer to as the transition to being a "rule-of-law state."[31] Specifically, this sought to replace the arbitrariness of local authority with a formalized mechanism grounded in the law: "State and social organizations receiving the right to use and conserve land shall not be entitled to transfer, lease, grant as concession or evaluate such land as collateral for loans. The right to use land by foreign residents, persons without nationality living in the Lao PDR, [or] aliens investing or conducting other activities shall be acknowledged by the State under the form of lawful lease or conces-sion only."[32]

The First Nationwide Review Conference on Land Management and Land-Forest Allocation was held in July 1996, and emphasized this agenda of formalization and legalization as a pathway to better governance. The conference's resolutions document emphasized the "necessity to fully continue the work of gradually putting land management into a legal framework, settling cases of illegal occupation of land, the falsification of documents, the illegal purchase/sale or occupation of state land . . . , [and] at the same time allowing the state to collect taxes and fees from land, which constitute considerable income."[33] Framing the "illegal" disposal of state land assets as something that only local authorities did was a stretch, but it was a useful simplification in that it allowed the issue to be broached and discussed didactically rather than simply ignored.[34]

After outlining various "weaknesses and shortcomings" and lamenting that the "absorption" of government policies to date was "not yet appropriately profound,"[35] the resolutions document outlined the pathway to a landscape that would be legible to regulatory oversight: "Plan for land surveying and management in order to collect data, work out management plans, and classify land types based on sectoral and regional development plans based on scientific use of land and actual local conditions. Then make land maps; particularly in the coming years the focus should be firstly on priority development areas, districts and suburban areas, which will be the basis for the delegation of management responsibility to concerned sectors as well as the allocation of land and forest to villages and families to manage and use."[36]

The document twice mentioned the goal of creating a nationwide set of fine-scale zoning maps by the year 2000, and it laid out a series of plans to facilitate central-level control over this process.[37] These plans converged on the need to reverse the existing pattern of central-level instructions going "down" to the local level but little coming back "up": in the resolutions' specification of "regional plans," it was made clear that geographically specific planning documents needed to travel *to* Vientiane for approval.[38] A newly created central-level Committee for Land Management and Land-Forest Allocation was also announced, which would oversee a series of regional pilot projects around the country.[39] Again, the message was that reforms would not just exist on paper.[40] The document promised visits from this committee "to the grassroots to direct the experimentation in some provinces or open up training on concepts, directives and various technical topics for local personnel."[41] Echoing the instructions on population management work from almost a decade earlier, it also reminded conference participants that "land management, land-forest allocation, surveys to develop land title registration, and the management of state land and housing" entailed "delicate, comprehensive work, linked to political, economic, social, environmental, and security aspects of the population."[42] As provincial officials left the conference for home, they did so with the knowledge that their independence over the disposal of land was officially a problem, and its days officially numbered.

In the half decade that followed, LFA turned into a state-territorial jugger-naut; as already noted, the program intervened in the land-use affairs of thousands of villages between the late 1990s and when it was officially sus-pended in 2003. But as LFA was taken into the field at scale, it was widely repurposed by local authorities for their own territorial ends, as in the rubber-for-logging scheme described above. As a result, LFA ended up as anything but the centralization mechanism its designers had initially envi-sioned. Upward reporting of land-use plans failed to materialize, and this caused widespread (and ongoing) challenges for large-scale projects like dams, which require locally detailed data to plan and budget resettlement infrastructure, social services, and livelihood restitution.[43] LFA maps were never collected in a centralized repository, and the summary statistics given above are basically all there is. These numbers testify to the program's proliferation, but also to its almost complete lack of success in creating the detailed spatial legibility that central-level authorities demanded of it. In summarizing and aggregating the data about how many *villages* were included in LFA, as well as in various summaries of how much of each for-est category was allocated, local officials left out what mattered most: pre-cise spatial data about what was supposed to happen *where*.

When my colleagues and I first encountered the Bolisat Ltd. project map in 2007, much of its illegibility stemmed from the fact that we had not seen the LFA maps on which it was based. In time, we discovered not only the story of uneven enclosure that underlay the map (chs. 1 and 4) but also the map's own legal-geographic origins—its cartographic genealogy, so to speak. These were, in many ways, totally different investigations. The former lay largely out in the field, in the villages shown on the map and in the various (and often place-specific, historically inflected) details of population man-agement work that facilitated the project's enclosures. The latter, on the other hand, began in the map room at the district Agriculture and Forestry office, where the original paper version of the nursery map was kept alongside the earlier generation of LFA maps. On one level, the project map (bottom of fig. 5.2, below) was of only minor help in understanding Bolisat Ltd.'s activi-ties on the ground: it represented all of the project's target villages equally, and neither its cartography nor the village-by-village statistics that accom-panied it gave any hint of why Khet Nam Fa received so much enclosure relative to the other villages. In this sense, the enclosure story was the result of digging at the reality *underneath* the map, of getting beyond the reality of equal treatment conjured on the map's surface. It was, in short, born of ignoring the map and looking elsewhere.

On another level, however, the formal geography shown on the map was far from meaningless—it just told a different piece of the story. The Bolisat Ltd. project map had been derived from the earlier generation of LFA maps created in Vieng Phoukha between 1997 and 2004 (fig. 5.2).[44] In making both generations of maps, district-government technicians had been attempting to follow various directives to create "permanent livelihoods" for upland residents. The LFA maps tried to do this by categorizing certain areas—often the most intensively or recently used shifting-cultivation areas, which forestry officials saw as the most degraded—as agriculture land (*din kasikam*), and classifying the rest of the village as various administrative forest categories. These almost always included restricted-use categories like conservation forest and watershed protection forest, as well as some form of forest for village utilization; other categories, for forest regeneration or commercial ("production") forestry, were sometimes included as well (as in the opening sketch above). This was a sort of triage: an attempt to restrict shifting cultivation into consolidated areas where it could ideally be "stabilized" through intensification, or at least corralled away from other types of (more valuable) forest. When district Agriculture and Forestry technicians made the Bolisat Ltd. project map, they followed both this same logic and this earlier geography, directing the company to target its plantation operations into areas that had been zoned for agricultural use under the LFA process. This would both this minimize the conversion of natural forest into rubber plantation and help operationalize the project-level agreements between companies and provincial officials that "the target is shifting-cultivation fallow land" (ch. 1), replacing upland cultivation with rubber at the scale of individual fields.

In the transition from individual LFA maps to the rubber-project map, we thus see a second example of how local authorities have continued to use the earlier generation of LFA data for their own state-territorial purposes. These uses differ by case and context, of course: the opening example showed a rezoning in which the earlier LFA map had been deemed to have outlived its use, while the Bolisat Ltd. case shows an example of the selective reproduction of one part of the earlier maps. But collectively, these examples contradict the position, often voiced in the international donor community, that old LFA maps have been left to rot because they are inaccurate and out of date.[45] In contrast, the examples shown here illustrate the dynamism

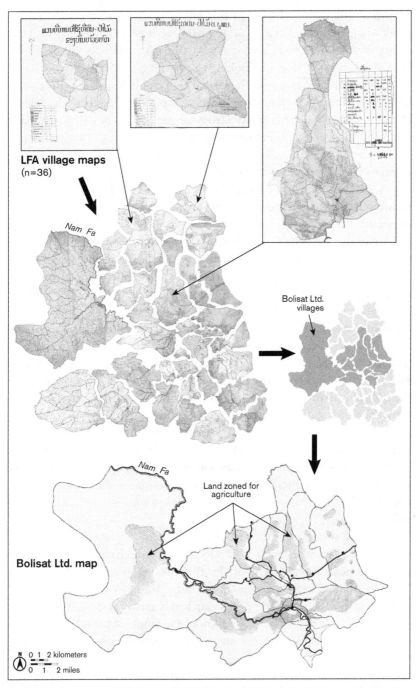

FIGURE 5.2   Cartographic genealogy of the Bolisat Ltd. map. Diagram by Ben Pease based on author's data.

and ongoing life of this earlier generation of maps. Even if they are out of date, their adaptation to changing circumstances and ongoing opportunities hardly means that they have been left to rot.

Although the distinction between Bolisat Ltd.'s "3 + 2" and "4 + 1" villages did not appear on the project map above, there is an important clue in the earlier generation of LFA maps. As a district that was both fairly small and staffed with competent technicians, Vieng Phoukha was almost fully mapped by LFA between 1997 and 2002. After they mapped the boundaries and laid down internal zoning on each village, district Agriculture and Forestry staff were faced with the question of how much additional mapping work to do in each village. They tended to distinguish between villages that had at least some upland plots that were deemed to be *individually* developed and those that did not. These two types of villages are plainly visible in the district's LFA maps; the former show the results of what district technicians described as "full" LFA—zoning plus the cadastral mapping of recognized ("allocated") individual upland plots—while the latter show the "short" version only: village zoning but no plot-level mapping. At the time, this reflected local authorities' efforts to create land-use plans that would help facilitate various land-governance goals, including agricultural intensification and sedentarization, forest triage of the sort mentioned above, and, where applicable, the taxation of "developed" land. In doing so, these efforts also operationalized the distinction between lowlands and uplands in a cartographically explicit way that created space, quite literally, for precisely the types of managed enclosures that Bolisat Ltd. and district authorities would develop in the years that followed.

In practice, this distinction was indicative rather than predictive; the key to Bolisat Ltd.'s differential geography of enclosure, as noted already, lay largely off the map. This extended to LFA as well. Perhaps unsurprisingly, the villages of Khet Nam Fa had received only the "short" version of LFA, and they were thus well positioned for their later inclusion in the "4 + 1" scheme. But a number of other villages in the project, including Ban Deng and a few of the other villages whose LFA maps are shown in figure 5.2, had also received only the "short" version of LFA; they nonetheless ended up with "3 + 2" arrangements. Still, the distinction was invoked by Bolisat Ltd. representatives to justify the project's uneven enclosures. This was laid out especially clearly by a former provincial Industry and Commerce official whom the company had hired to liaise with local officials.[46] Our interview, in late 2007, illustrated a key way that fixers like this man help companies translate their business interests into development narratives that have the trappings of legality. As he explained it, in the "3 + 2" villages, the company was working with farmers who had individual plots of land, while in the "4 + 1" villages, agricultural land was managed *collectively* and organized by the district under the state's mandate to coordinate (*chatsan*) land use. This land would thus still technically belong to the village, he explained, even as it was allocated into company-owned plantations for the next thirty years. This final qualification indicated the man's full awareness of the sleight of hand he was describing. Formally, the agricultural land allocated to Bolisat Ltd.'s plantations was still "locally owned"; substantively, as chapter 4 showed, the managed enclosures guaranteed that it was anything but.

Like the rubber-for-timber scheme profiled in the opening sketch, the "on-paper" geography of the Bolisat Ltd. project was thus formal yet flexible, capable of being manipulated to accommodate particular interests and changing circumstances while also providing an appearance of formal continuity with state-originated land-use planning and law. But despite their selectiveness and opportunism, both projects *were*, in a very real sense, a continuation of the transformation in land management begun by LFA. Long before Bolisat Ltd.'s arrival, LFA had begun creating "purified" categories of agricultural land and forest, anticipating on paper the enclosure of both forest and farmland out of a messy landscape where the two had been previously intertwined.[47] But as noted in chapter 1, LFA on its own had been largely aspirational—lines on the map, in most cases, and little more. By injecting capital in the form of hundreds of thousands of rubber seedlings and, in the years that followed, a multimillion-dollar rubber-processing facility, Bolisat Ltd. had helped to change all of this. The partnership between the company and district authorities had actually started to produce the landscape that LFA had dreamed into existence years earlier. Even if the spatial details varied, the new landscape was coming to be one where land *was* purified into distinct parcels of agriculture and forestland, where lines between state and private property existed, and where there was increasingly less space for the mixed and mobile forms of production that had predominated in the years prior.

GEOGRAPHIES OF OPACITY AND LEGIBILITY

Land deals leave extensive paper trails. While details vary by case, the rubber projects I studied exemplified the back-and-forth between processes involving various state authorities and multiple possible field locations that plantation developers traverse as they go through the land-finding process.[48] Maps like the ones shown above sit atop piles of project proposals, letters of introduction, MOUs, meeting minutes, and one-sided "agreements" (*kho toklong*) that show the backing of provincial and district governors—to name just a few of the documents involved. Yet despite all of these documents, much of the detail about the land access they have facilitated has remained illegible to central-level authorities. One of my colleagues from the NLMA once joked, in reflecting on his experience collecting land-deal information from provincial and district authorities, that despite his agency's mandate to coordinate between various ministries and administrative levels on issues of land governance, it was "policy" *not* to share documents between agencies.[49]

Often this is framed, even by local-government staff themselves, in terms of low capacity—both in making maps and in caring for them. My colleagues and I encountered this kind of dissembling in 2008, in the lead-up to viewing the cache of maps that included Vieng Phoukha's original LFA maps, the Bolisat Ltd. map, and a handful of others—including the map described in the opening sketch—that had been recently updated as part of the district's effort to formalize its ongoing forestry operations. We were told that the maps were a mess (*bo ngam*), and it was only with obvious reluctance that we were eventually allowed to examine them. Practically speaking, the maps *were* a bit of a mess, but as the examples above imply, this was not the only reason local authorities were likely reluctant to share them.

We were hardly alone. Throughout 2005, 2006, and 2007, anecdotal evidence about concessions' on-the-ground problems had been trickling into policymakers' offices in Vientiane, and this ultimately culminated in a May 2007 prime-ministerial moratorium on new agribusiness and mining concessions.[50] Yet this was merely an effort to pause the "trading of land for development" that had been ongoing for well over a decade. As one of my informants in Vientiane put it at the time, "Our central government here is very weak. We don't have the tools to check whether the provincial governors—and the provincial governments more generally—are following the national laws."[51] Another informant, also a central-government employee, explained how these problems of vertical information access created horizontal ones as well out in the field: "It's very difficult for parallel departments"—for example, a provincial Land Management Authority office and a provincial Agriculture and Forestry office—"to get information from one another at the provincial level. Usually, it has to go to the top [central level] and come back down."[52] Provincial land management officials I spoke to in Luang Namtha were experiencing this acutely in their efforts to collect specific details about land deals in the area from the provincial Finance Department. "We don't know [the details]! We don't have area statistics, we don't have maps. When a company is interested in a concession, they [go through various steps to obtain various permission documents]. These documents exist, but our office doesn't have them. Where are they? In the provincial Finance Department. But just on paper, not in the computer—and they're all mixed up [*sapson*]."[53]

Since the late 2000s, a few different efforts have aimed at assembling systematic data sets about land deals but have run into similar challenges as the 1990s-era promises to "go [down] to the grassroots" in order to improve land-use planning and governance. Researchers working with the Lao Ministry of Environment and Natural Resources on a later iteration of the NLMA inventory that had taken my colleagues and me to Vieng Phoukha echoed this sentiment in 2012 when describing the constraints on their own (ongoing) regulatory efforts: "Because state land can be granted at multiple levels and across different [sectoral] ministries within the government, land [deals] have been particularly difficult to measure and monitor. Data collection has been ad hoc in nature and transparency or dissemination of records across sectors and levels of government have been limited. As a result, aggregated data was often available from provincial or district level offices, but less on an individual project basis and often not in formats available for or compatible with other administrative areas."[54]

The distributed geography and "ad hoc nature" of land-deal data is a problem for planners as well. As explained by a researcher at the Ministry of Planning and Investment, because of the recent and significant growth of the Lao plantation sector, "specific information about the size, location and types of plantations and investors . . . remains limited and dispersed across various government agencies," and "information on projects approved and implemented at the provincial level is often not available at the national level. Total plantation investment data is [thus] not currently held by the Ministry." As a result, "the overall scope of investment in the plantation sector is unclear, which has hindered planning efforts."[55]

The common themes here—multiple land-granting authorities, limited transparency and cooperation—are not just about information. Statistical knowledge plays a key role in planning and executing large-scale projects, as noted above, but it also underlies an activity that is even more fundamental to state practice: the control over land-based taxation and, more generally, over resource rents. One reason that the timber concession featured in the chapter's opening sketch was so important to paper over was that it would have been looked at askance by central-level authorities who, as noted above, have been trying since the early 1990s to make logging more accountable to the capturing of royalties. As these efforts have become increasingly public in recent years, the magnitude of untaxed timber allocations—often by local authorities and involving special timber quotas for infrastructure or unspecified "development projects"—has been acknowledged to dwarf officially collected timber royalties by roughly an order of magnitude, leaving hundreds of millions of dollars unaccounted for.[56] A 2016 prime-ministerial order addressed to ministers and provincial governors once again forbade "the direct trade or exchange of timber for infrastructure development projects" and, just to make sure its intentions were completely clear, explicitly nullified any "previous orders, decisions, notices and legislations, including those of local authorities" that conflicted with its instructions.[57] A suite of mapping efforts by multiple government agencies, meanwhile—including revised forest categorization by the Ministry of Agriculture and Forestry; cadastral land titling under the Department of Lands; and the concession-inventory efforts by the Planning and Environment ministries quoted above—continue to gesture to both the economic stakes and the institutional scope of the issue.[58]

The question of Bolisat Ltd.'s precise plantation geography illustrates the extension of this politics of rent in the concession era, as agribusiness has emerged alongside forestry as a key economic activity. The rubber taxation policy issued by Luang Namtha's provincial governor in 2006 (ch. 4) aimed to capture a fraction of the anticipated production rents by taxing rubber trees on the basis of owners' plantation holdings: smallholders with less than one hectare would pay RMB 1 per tree per year, while larger-holders would pay RMB 3 per tree for plantations between two and six hectares, and RMB 6 per tree for plantations larger than six hectares.[59] At the time it was issued, the policy was largely hypothetical since it applied only to trees that were already being tapped; most rubber trees in the province then were still a few years away from tapping. But in the terms it set, it made explicit the stakes of the mapping that would need to be done in the coming years if the province was to realize the taxation potential of its new plantation resource.

The project map shown at the bottom of figure 5.2 is doubly interesting in this regard. On the one hand, it says very little about the company's tax burden. As a plantation-targeting map, it does not show where the company's plantations actually were; it only showed the larger area—over 9,000 hectares (compared to the company's 3,000-hectare quota)—*within* which they were supposed to be developed. Moreover, in delineating this extent, it did not distinguish between areas where the company would own the plantations directly under the "4 + 1" scheme (and thus generate tax liability for the company) versus areas where the rubber trees would be owned by smallholders working with the company as contract farmers. Since taxation rates differed according to plantation size *by owner* (rather than simply aggregate area), the map only gestured to the wide range of potential tax rents.

Thus far, these numbers have remained largely hypothetical. After global rubber prices fell in 2011, Chinese rubber companies negotiated provincial tax waivers with Luang Namtha officials—allegedly in order to keep company operations viable—and provincial authorities have reported an ongoing "reluctance" to enforce the policy.[60] Nonetheless, information about project-specific plantation areas remains closely guarded. During my 2018 revisit to Vieng Phoukha, I had an interesting interaction with government staff-people who were unable to reconcile the obvious extent of Bolisat Ltd.'s "4 + 1" plantations in Khet Nam Fa with statistics held by their office, which listed the company's plantation holdings at a mere thirty-three hectares.[61] Given the scale of the company's actual plantations—most likely in the range of 1,000–1,500 hectares—this would have translated into a few hundred thousand dollars' difference in annual tax revenues had the provincial policy been enforced.[62] Even in the policy's absence, however, the company remained wary; after registering confusion over the mismatch in the numbers, the staff-person acknowledged that the company had been reluctant to share its precise area with local officials "because they don't want to pay tax."[63]

Nevertheless, the Bolisat Ltd. map did create an important type of legibility, albeit of a different and expressly transnational sort. As noted in earlier chapters, projects like Bolisat Ltd.'s were in part financed by Chinese government subsidies that, in their stated purpose to replace opium-poppy cultivation with legal agricultural crops, articulated with and grounded the NEC's wider vision as a licit, integrated, and development-oriented transformation of the former Golden Triangle borderlands. The poppy-replacement subsidies were generous, offering reimbursement for 80–90 percent of exploration and insurance costs as well as cash payments of USD 25–70 per hectare developed, depending on crop.[64] To access these payments, however, companies were required to provide evidence of feasibility and permission such as contracts, official letters and MOUs, feasibility studies, and, yes, maps. Even if it did not show the location of Bolisat Ltd.'s actual plantations, the map shown above was a more localized version of the proposal recounted in chapter 1: it effectively said that, from the district government's perspective, providing 3,000 hectares to the company's collaborative plantation efforts "would not be a problem."

The fact that, in hindsight, this full quota seems not to have been achieved is almost beside the point. Maps are pictures that travel—"immutable mobiles" in the language of Bruno Latour. But while this traveling can be a source of power when accurate knowledge is carried across distance—in Latour's classic example, this concerns naval supremacy because one side has the foreknowledge of an area thanks to a good map[65]—the mobility can be more important than the immutability. As critical cartographers have shown, the power of maps is not merely to carry realistic representations to faraway places but to carry ideas and claims, whatever their relationship to reality.[66] Nikolas Rose, for example, describes maps as "little machine[s] for producing conviction in others,"[67] and indeed, the less the viewer knows about the area being shown, the more easily their conviction can be manipulated. Maps like Bolisat Ltd.'s would have run into problems if they had been taken too literally, and it should be no surprise that the land acquisition process itself relied on other means (ch. 4). But farther away the map would have worked like a charm, since a combination of unfamiliarity with the terrain and an interest in supporting new Chinese agribusiness made the map's potential audience unlikely to object. Like the signs that advertise Chinese poppy-replacement development projects across northern Laos (fig. 5.3), the map would have functioned—much like it did in my initial encounter—to signify approval without getting into the details.

Reading the historical literature on Laos, it can be tempting to view the persistence of local authority over the disposal of land as a direct descendant of Southeast Asian (and in particular "Tai") political geography. Martin Stuart-Fox, a prominent historian of Laos, describes Lao political culture today as the result of French, American, and then socialist rule being layered "on top of, rather than in place of, traditional Lao social and political relationships."[68] The persistence of long-held and locally oriented patron-clientelism makes provincial administrations, for Stuart-Fox, "the modern *muang*—enjoying considerable independence from the center in return for a tribute (tax) which is often [in actuality] withheld."[69] Others, too, have looked to precolonial times to explain contemporary resource politics, such as this anonymous development professional quoted in a study of timber politics in southern Laos: "In other countries, the political culture surrounding timber is often termed a 'kleptocracy.' But [here], it is more of a 'tributocracy.' The way that it is handled is very much in keeping with both the traditions of Lao politics and the long history of paying tribute to more powerful entities, be they internal or external."[70]

Without denying the clear echoes of historical *muang* politics in contemporary events, a series of distinctly contemporary processes arguably

FIGURE 5.3   Poppy-replacement project ("6,700 hectares"), Oudomxai province.

play an even more definitive role in shaping local governments' prerogatives when it comes to allocating land "for development." From the decentralization of forestry capital in the late 1980s to the distinctly modern story of postwar legacy told in chapters 2, 3, and 4, land governance in the Lao uplands must be pulled out of the mists of time and tradition in order to grasp its particular form of territoriality. Focusing on the articulation of village-scale mapping and transnational land deals, this chapter examines the way that Laos's LFA program spawned an arena of "techno-politics" that remains relevant today even as the program's heyday is in the past.[71] The ongoing politics of post–Cold War state formation figure centrally here, undermining—at least from the perspective of central-level planners and regulators—the ability to control the economic dynamism that has been unleashed at the upland frontier.

Spatial abstraction, as many scholars have noted, is fundamental to capitalist planning.[72] Yet the ways in which this occurs—the level of precision, the various actors involved, and the strength of the abstractions when it comes to the interactions between markets and law—is anything but straightforward. If transnational land deals have been embraced by governments like Laos because they offered to help strengthen their abilities to effectively govern their territories and populations, they have also articulated with ongoing struggles within the state over the ability to direct and benefit from that process. Territoriality in practice depends on how space itself is rendered calculable.[73] Part of the challenge of regulating transnational land access is thus not merely the emergence of new, cross-border legibility regimes like those created by China's opium-replacement subsidies. It is also that these emerging regimes remain hard to see, and thus difficult to govern, because of the persistent domestic-territorial politics of ongoing state formation.

Conclusion

The Politics of Spatial Transparency

A FEW months after my fieldwork ended in 2008, a striking image appeared on a widely read discussion forum in Laos. Clipped from satellite data and projected into landscape view, it showed thousands of identical rubber trees, planted in neatly contoured rows that stretched from foreground to horizon. Its title was "GoogleEarth screen capture, looking toward the Chinese border, January 2007," and it seemed to locate the viewer in northern Laos's Luang Namtha province, facing north and overlooking a vast rubber plantation.[1]

Despite sitting astride historical trade routes, Luang Namtha had long been better known for its splendid isolation: its dense forests, its abundant wildlife, its colorful "hill tribes." But times had changed. Since the early 2000s, the events recounted in chapter 1 had brought rubber to the area as the most visible example of a Chinese investment boom that extended from agribusiness and mining to tourism and casinos. The results were being written into the landscape one project at a time, as the image seemed to show. Echoing a narrative that has only continued to grow with the launch of China's Belt and Road Initiative in 2013, the screen capture resonated with emerging foreign and domestic concerns about growing Chinese influence in the country, and with growing global concerns—newly announced at the time—about the new global land grab. Part of the image's raw power was that it exemplified the trope of the "authority gap," as one journalist put it at the time, "in a growing number of areas in the country where Vientiane has effectively ceded sovereignty to Beijing."[2] Showing the Lao-China border as a mere formality, a thin line draped unconvincingly across the horizon as Chinese state plantations expanded southward, it seemed to confirm that northern Laos was indeed turning into Chinese territory.

The image turned out to be entirely false; the plantations were in Yunnan, located inside China's state-run rubber farms. (The error was the result of Google's satellite imagery being more precise than its international boundary data.) But the image was not entirely meaningless. Despite its unreality, its plausibility was perhaps even more important. Western journalists had worried since at least 2006 that Laos was "being pulled into Beijing's orbit," and since 2007 development professionals in Laos had begun to participate in the ritual of concession-area estimates that would figure centrally in the emerging global land-grab narrative.[3] The numbers were indeed growing: in the weeks after the screen capture's circulation, an estimate from the previous year of one million hectares "signed away" as concessions was increased to "between two and three million hectares—as much as 15 percent of Lao territory" in a prominent *Guardian* article.[4] Even if the landscape it showed was wrong, in evoking what one worried UNDP economist at the time called the "sovereignty implications" of Laos's concession boom,[5] it threw down a challenge to understand how transnational land deals *were* actually taking place and what their actual effects were on the ground.

In Laos's northwestern uplands, the literal transformation of "battlefields into marketplaces" helps explain how transnational land deals have overcome protective opposition to foreign land control. Until 1975, the "hot" grounding of the Cold War made the Lao uplands both a key geostrategic and human landscape for American imperialism. During the 1980s, tools of "population management work" were developed for postwar industrial forestry; these were subsequently mobilized and recombined as methods for the management of enclosure and dispossession during the concession boom of the 2000s. Yet much of this remained difficult to see, even for observers familiar with the local landscape. Obscured by internal struggles over land within the complex entity that is the Lao state, locally managed land grabs remained intertwined with the politics of ongoing state formation, and thus even more difficult to regulate effectively.

A decade or more after many of the events recounted above, this landscape continues to demand our attention. In one sense, the concession boom is more or less over. The recent update to Laos's national concession inventory, a collaboration between the University of Bern and four Lao ministries that continues the inventory effort begun almost a decade and a half earlier, has both added extensive detail and pushed the analysis of land deals' local contexts to a new level of sophistication.[6] But within this deepening knowledge, the overall numbers have roughly plateaued: the 2012 study's 1.1 million hectares, which had themselves been a downward revision from the earlier estimates cited above, remained essentially constant, while the additional research into the area "actually developed" shrank the estimate even further: "The land granted for development account[s] for 1,521 deals covering 1,008,884 ha (4 percent of Lao PDR's territory). Only 54 percent or 549,248 hectares of total areas granted for development were implemented up to the time when the inventory was conducted."[7] These are still very big numbers. But the inventory echoes a similar tapering off of the "literature rush" that occurred around the global land grab in the early 2010s.[8] Land deals and land grabs are still being investigated, but the flurry is hardly what it was.

Yet as Tania Li reminds us in a recent and powerful piece on life "after the land grab" in Indonesia's palm oil landscape, the end of the concession boom is in no way the end of the concession. Land concessions are, after all, multidecade allocations whose impacts only continue to accumulate upon one another as projects develop infrastructures of extraction, labor, and their own internal forms of (in her telling, mafia-style) governance.[9] In some ways, even, the current moment demands even more; land deals that were sensationally announced during the boom decade of the 2000s have largely gone quiet, and while some of this is due to the "great expectations" that have been unmet,[10] another source of difficulty is gaining access to the field now that the boostering has quieted down. In Cambodia, for instance, many struggles over rural land access have transitioned from fights over the initial granting of "economic land concessions" to struggles—some of which have been quite successful—against the development of the massive polygons they laid down on paper.[11] Marc Edelman makes a similar point in his 2013 critique of land-deal inventories in noting that even while concessions on paper create state-sanctioned openings for enclosure, enclosure itself requires capital, resources, and political struggle: "The almost obsessive focus on hectares," he writes, "while no doubt effective in attracting the attention of major media, foundations, policymakers and civil society organizations," leaves out a great deal: "Questions of scale do not only involve extensions of land, but also the application of capital to that land, the availability of water, and the types of accumulation and social reproduction that these factors facilitate or impede."[12]

My efforts to unpack the landscape of Chinese rubber investment in northwestern Laos probe some of the contingencies behind what Edelman calls the "messy hectares" that constitute land deals on the ground. This messiness needs to be understood not in contrast to what is written on paper, but in relation to it—and indeed as part of the process of geographic formalization that enables it. The ways that decades-old imperialism and geopolitical conflict continue to shape the uneven enclosure process should be the least surprising piece of the story. Such continuities, even if the details differ by case and context, are well established in the literature on colonial and racial capitalism, as well as the transition to the era of neoliberal globalization (and beyond) across the global South. Equally if not more important is the nexus of enclosure and legibility, that political space in which the legacies that Ann Stoler calls "imperial debris" get either (re)mobilized for political work or relegated to the past.[13] In the Lao case, the control over selective formalization and the circulation of the resulting documents allowed for a significant degree of autonomy—especially vis-à-vis regulatory oversight—even within the larger context of political-economic constraints. It thus illustrates the sort of limited power over effective sovereignty that Aihwa Ong has described as the "graduated" sovereignty exercised by weak states confronting the global economy.[14] But it shows this not through the agency of a singular state. Rather, the plans, policies, and agreements of multiple actors articulate with contingent and often only quasi-legible territorial politics to facilitate land-finding and other forms of population management at particular moments in space and time.

While the "land grab" has slowed, land-deal governance is as important as ever, and the internal struggle over land and resource rents continues. In Laos's concession-inventory update, even as the numbers have stabilized and the degree of legibility over land deals has increased, indications of ongoing state formation remain starkly on display. The authors of the inventory update discussed above repeatedly reference "a lack of clarity" in various aspects of land-deal regulation, and note both the ongoing resistance of some ministries to participate in the inventory process and "a general lack of communication between the [country's] administrative levels." This results in "information delay, if not loss" and "missing information on land deals."[15] Their call to develop a vertically integrated information management system "which is continuously fed current data by the responsible and mandated GoL agencies at different levels"[16] is, in essence, a digital-age version of the 1996 instruction to "then make land maps" and send them upward to the central level. The persistence of the same problem over the span of almost three decades illustrates the continued relevance of ongoing state formation to land-deal politics, and highlights the ongoing importance of the nexus where legibility and enclosure intersect.

COERCION AS COMPARATIVE ADVANTAGE?

It is increasingly clear that the global land rush, even if triggered by a confluence of crises and opportunities specific to the mid-to-late 2000s, is part of a larger conjuncture surrounding the destabilization of the Western-led Washington Consensus and neoliberal development era of the 1990s and early 2000s. This has significant implications for international development cooperation. Development assistance is usefully understood within the distinction between ongoing capitalist development and intentional interventions explicitly aimed at countering the worst of capitalism's social ills.[17] One problem, now widely noted, with the neoliberal policy prescriptions of the 1990s and 2000s was that they promised solutions they could not deliver—in particular, promising that global economic integration would provide not just growth, but also jobs on a large scale to citizens of the global South. As anthropologist James Ferguson notes, in response to the realization that they have effectively little to no comparative advantage in today's global economy, a number of states have begun to quietly move away from Washington Consensus–style policies of austerity and deregulation toward new types of welfarism that, even if couched in the language of neoliberalism, in fact represent experiments in social protection that are far more ambiguous, and in some cases are forthrightly progressive.[18] However, one key feature of these efforts is that they have been largely limited to countries (Mexico, Brazil, and the southern African cone, for example) where middle-income status and democratic governance coincide.

The failures of neoliberalism have been no less pronounced in the countries that have embraced transnational land deals. One way to think more broadly about the case examined in this book is that transnational land deals can be read as another type of attempted solution to the wider crisis of economic development and international aid that increasingly confronts the global South. Land deals, like neo-welfarism, also represent efforts to wrestle with what Ferguson calls "the new politics of distribution" in today's global economy, albeit in very different ways and on very different political terrains. A key difference is citizenship-in-practice—the ways social entitlements work, the limits they impose on dispossession, the claims they forge on state-managed resources in the name of social belonging and well-being. It is no coincidence, I think, that the global land rush and neo-welfarist experiments are happening at the same time but largely in different places, and that the former depends on suppressed and anemic forms of citizenship while the latter depends on active citizenship and socially supported notions of entitlement.[19] Both are wrestling with what to do at the end of the Washington Consensus, when the state is increasingly stepping back in to manage the project of economic development. But their differences are clearly stark. In examining how larger questions of national development, agrarian transition, and transnational cooperation are being addressed in one grounded case, this book contributes to a wider field of scholarship aimed at making sense of international development cooperation, whether under a "Beijing Consensus" or a model yet to be named, in the early twenty-first century.[20]

Another dimension of this concerns comparative advantage. Even if the uneven geography of enclosure is unsurprising in its rootedness in local histories of geopolitical conflict, its function requires clarification. Coercion, as Marxian scholars widely note, figures centrally in processes of enclosure and dispossession like those on display in Laos.[21] Mechanisms and degrees, however, are highly contextual; a "taking" under eminent domain is no less coercive than a state land concession, but the processes involved, including the types of compensation or restitution provided, depend heavily on the regulatory institutions within which land deals are embedded. In the transition from protective regulation to the emergence of "4 + 1" company plantations, coercion replaces regulatory pushback in a semifunctional way: it provides a very different but also effective way to manage the relationship between rural communities on the one hand, and the state and corporate actors on the other that seek to enroll them and (especially) their land into development schemes. In this sense, coercion facilitates the exploitation of social and territorial difference to navigate the challenges and openings of an increasingly difficult global economy. While there is certainly a moral critique to be made of instrumentalizing the past to facilitate coercive enclosures, there is also a historical dimension that requires us to look beyond the Lao state and to include the numerous public actors, both foreign governments and multilateral institutions, whose decisions profoundly influence Laos's room to maneuver in today's global economy. The history of the Lao uplands, and in particular the mechanisms of upland population management that span the postwar period and the concession boom of the 2000s, are especially relevant. So while we might find it reprehensible that land deals capitalize on the conflicts of the past to facilitate the enclosures of the present, we should find equally reprehensible the earlier histories (both colonial and Cold War) that gave these upland differences lasting traction. Laos's comparative advantage in the world of plantation development may be available land, but we must remember that this availability is of the social variety.

FORMALITY AND CONTESTATION

A second way of thinking more broadly about the case of northwestern Laos concerns the imbrication of transnational land deals in long-standing internal resource politics. While this book focused on Laos's particular history of local authority problems (forestry decentralization, LFA, and its continuity with more recent land deals), I suspect that these sorts of dynamics are widespread. The literature on the "resource curse," while thin and reductive in many ways, testifies to the problem of regulation and rent distribution within—and at the often blurry edges of—the state.[22] Similarly, research on transnational land access that has succeeded in interviewing state regulators has found that they themselves are often underresourced.[23] Corruption, while dominant in much of the literature, is only one dimension of the issue, and an often fuzzy one at that.[24] As important as the boundary between public and private may be, there is much at stake within the arena of intrastate politics alone. This has a few implications.

At the most basic level, approaching land deals through a lens of formality and legibility politics adds analytical depth to what many who have worked in or with government already know: that the state exists as a uniform entity only to the extent that it is strategically essentialized as such.[25] In Laos, references to "the GoL" (Government of Laos) are widespread among development practitioners, but they frequently refer to an idealized version of the state—the central government as it appears in the political theory of democratic centralism, for example, or the unified front that officials try to conjure when writing policy framed in terms of planning and implementation. "Distance" within the state, however, can be substantial, both spatially and temporally. Central-level officials pursued their quest for legibility via the LFA program but found that formalization was no fix, technical or otherwise, for addressing local authorities' reliance on land allocation for various "development projects." This situation has persisted into the present and is likely to be occurring elsewhere in corners of the global South that, like Laos, are seen to be especially "land-rich." To the extent that transnational investors are able to "forum shop" for regulatory systems and property regimes that fit their needs,[26] it is worth hypothesizing that the hinterlands of the global South that will be most sought out are not simply those with the most potentially arable land and water, but those with the most flexible options for manipulating legal land access while still working within the realm of formality. To the extent that formal landscapes remain largely illegible (whether to the public or concerned regulatory authorities), formalization politics are likely to be manipulated to instrumental ends.

Northwestern Laos's rubber boom shows that it is not formality or legibility per se that enables successful land-finding but rather the mix of flexibility, authority, and technical capacity that allows for the strategic creation or dissolving of formality *when it matters*. These are highly political issues, as the debates about land titling—both before and after the concession boom—have shown.[27] In his book *The Mystery of Capital*, the economist Hernando de Soto lauds the benefits of property formalization as a way to help the poor of the global South capitalize on the wealth that lies between their feet but to which they frequently lack legal rights. Such a recommendation has appeared with increasingly regularity in the wake of the global land rush.[28] But while de Soto insightfully describes formalization's ability to make capital "mind-friendly" by "boiling down the essentials" of property to representations "that we can easily combine, divide and mobilize,"[29] all too often, state-managed processes of formalization, like the LFA and Bolisat Ldt. maps discussed in chapter 5, are aimed at not just simplification but enclosure and dispossession.[30]

Today, as the interlocking crises of climate change, food insecurity, and deforestation dominate the global agenda, many continue to ask how much potentially "available" farmland exists within the hinterlands of the global South. While efforts have been made to quantify this "reserve" in biophysical terms, they include major caveats about the social dimensions of "suitable" or "available" land.[31] Formal geographies will likely provide the terrain upon which these types of questions will be answered, although given the asymmetrical control over the data, it is not at all obvious that they will be answered fairly or adequately. As they attempt to convince faraway planners that various land-hungry development schemes "will not be a problem," formal geographies will remain highly contestable in the landscapes where they were produced. Whether they remain shuttered away in government offices, or emerge as terrains of struggle before the next boom crop is in the ground, remains to be seen.

NOTES

FOREWORD

1 See, e.g., Borras et al., "Land Grabbing in Latin America and the Caribbean."
2 Li, *Land's End*.
3 See, e.g., Franco and Borras, "Grey Areas in Green Grabbing"; Paprocki, *Threatening Dystopias*.
4 Grandia, *Enclosed*.
5 See Beban, *Unwritten Rule*.

INTRODUCTION

1 This is a pseudonym. *Bolisat* means "private company" in Lao.
2 Turnbull, *Maps Are Territories*, 19–27.
3 Latour, *Science in Action*, 2–7.
4 See, among many others, Arezki, Deininger, and Selod, "What Drives the Global Land Rush?"; Borras et al., "Land Grabbing in Latin America"; Li, "What Is Land?"
5 Alden Wily, "Looking Back to See Forward"; Klinger and Muldavin, "New Geographies of Development"; Nyíri, "Extraterritoriality"; White et al., "The New Enclosures."
6 See, among others, De Koninck, "On the Geopolitics of Land Colonization"; Larsson, "Intertextual Relations"; Ó Tuathail, *Critical Geopolitics*; Sassen, "Land Grabs Today"; Scurrah and Hirsch, "Land and Capital across Borders."
7 Fairbairn, *Fields of Gold*.
8 Ban and Blyth, "The BRICs and the Washington Consensus"; Lee, "The Spectre of Global China"; Muldavin, "From Rural Transformation to Global Integration"; Oliveira, "Boosters, Brokers, Bureaucrats and Businessmen."

9 Borras et al., "The Rise of Flex Crops"; Holt-Giménez, Patel, and Shattuck, *Food Rebellions!*; Fairbairn, *Fields of Gold.*
10 GRAIN, "Seized!"
11 Lacey, "Across Globe, Empty Bellies Bring Rising Anger"; Holt-Giménez,
   Patel, and Shattuck, *Food Rebellions!*
12 Diouf, "The Food Crisis and the Wrong Solutions," 8.
13 GRAIN, "Seized!," annex.
14 Diouf, "TheFood Crisis and the Wrong Solutions," 8.
15 Reguly, "The Farms Race"; Rice, "Is There Such a Thing as Agro-
   Imperialism?"; Borger, "Rich Countries Launch Great Land Grab."
16 See, e.g., MacKinnon, "Resentment Rises."
17 Economist, "Outsourcing's Third Wave."
18 Branford, "Food Crisis Leading to an Unsustainable Land Grab."
19 MacKinnon, "Resentment Rises."
20 Martin Stuart-Fox, quoted in MacKinnon, "Resentment Rises."
21 Crispin, "Limits of Chinese Expansionism."
22 Paul Cohen, for example, quotes a number of foreign development
   professionals who describe the rubber boom in northern Laos in terms of
   its "lack of regulation," "'wild west' situation," the lack of nearly "any kind
   of guideline in either agricultural, environmental, or legal respects," and
   "land rights [that] are not secure, environmental assessment [that] is
   non-existent, technical extension [that] is weak, credit [that] is limited,
   regulation [that] is incomplete, and corruption [that] is rampant" (Cohen,
   "Post-Opium Scenario," 427). Also see World Bank, "Rising Global
   Interest in Farmland." I qualify the reference here to "frontier-type"
   development to exclude the excellent explanatory work (e.g., Barney,
   "Laos and the Making of a 'Relational' Resource Frontier"; Laungaramsri,
   "Frontier Capitalism"; Padwe, *Disturbed Forests, Fragmented Memories*;
   Patel and Moore, *A History of the World in Seven Cheap Things*; Tsing,
   Friction) using the concept of the frontier. Also see chapter 4.
23 Alden Wily, "Looking Back to See Forward," 763; also see Peluso and
   Vandergeest, "Genealogies of the Political Forest."
24 Alden Wily, "Looking Back," 764–66; Cotula et al., "Land Grab or
   Development Opportunity?"; De Schutter, "How Not to Think of
   Land-Grabbing."
25 Ong, "Graduated Sovereignty"; Whitington, *Anthropogenic Rivers*; also
   see below.
26 See, e.g., Borras, Fig, and Suárez, "Politics of Agrofuels"; Lavers, "'Land
   Grab' as Development Strategy?"; Lu and Schönweger, "Great Expectations"; McAlister, "Rubber, Rights and Resistance"; Li, "After the
   Land Grab."
27 Edelman, "Messy Hectares," 485.

28 Cotula et al., "Land Grab or Development Opportunity?"; Baines, "Fuel, Feed and the Corporate Restructuring"; Borras et al., "Rise of Flex Crops"; Fairbairn, *Fields of Gold*; Nyíri, "Extraterritoriality"; Wolford et al., "Governing Global Land Deals."

29 Zoomers, "Globalisation and the Foreignisation of Space."

30 Alden Wily, "Looking Back to See Forward."

31 Nyíri, "Enclaves of Improvement" and "Extraterritoriality"; Ong, "Graduated Sovereignty."

32 See, e.g., the special issue of the *Journal of Peasant Studies* introduced by White et al., "The New Enclosures."

33 Sassen, "A Savage Sorting of Winners and Losers," 26; also see Harvey, *The New Imperialism*; Marx, *Capital*; Sassen, "Land Grabs Today."

34 Sassen, "Savage Sorting," 26.

35 Ferguson, *Give a Man a Fish*, 89–90.

36 Rostow, "Stages of Economic Growth."

37 Li, "Centering Labor in the Land Grab Debate," 281; also see Davis, *Planet of Slums*; Li, "To Make Live or Let Die?"; Ferguson, *Give a Man a Fish*.

38 Diouf, "Food Crisis and the Wrong Solutions," 8.

39 For Laos, see Baird, "Land, Rubber and People" and "Turning Land into Capital"; Barney, "Ecological Knowledge and the Making of Plantation Concession Territories"; Kenney-Lazar, "Plantation Rubber, Land Grabbing and Social-Property Transformation"; Laungaramsri, "Frontier Capitalism"; Vongkhamhor et al., "Key Issues in Smallholder Rubber"; globally, see Alden Wily, "Looking Back to See Forward"; Anseeuw et al., "Creating a Public Tool"; White et al., "The New Enclosures."

40 See, e.g., Burnod, Gingembre, and Andrianirina Ratsialonana, "Competition over Authority and Access" on Madagascar, and Lee, "The Spectre of Global China" on Zambia.

41 See, e.g., Guerrero and Manji, *China's New Role in Africa*; World Bank, "Rising Global Interest in Farmland."

42 Izikowitz, *Over the Misty Mountains*; Scott, *Art of Not Being Governed*.

43 De Koninck, "The Peasantry as the Territorial Spearhead of the State"; Peluso and Vandergeest, "Genealogies of the Political Forest" and "Political Ecologies of War and Forests." This applies to the uplands of island Southeast Asia as well (see, e.g., Li, "Marginality, Power and Production"; Peluso, *Rich Forests, Poor People*; Tsing, *In the Realm of the Diamond Queen*). On landscape as a concept, see Cosgrove, *Social Formation and Symbolic Landscape*; Mitchell, *Landscape and Power*.

44 Scott, *Art of Not Being Governed*, 4; also see Jonsson, "States Lie, and Stories Are Tools"; Li, "Marginality, Power and Production"; McCoy, *Politics of Heroin*.

45 This usage follows scholarship on critical geopolitics (e.g., Agnew, *Geopolitics*; Ó Tuathail, *Critical Geopolitics*; Sneddon and Fox, "Rethinking Transboundary Waters"), as well as on the Southeast Asian uplands (e.g., De Koninck, "On the Geopolitics of Land Colonization"; Hodgdon, "Frontier Country"; Li, *Will to Improve*; Mahanty et al., "Unravelling Property Relations"; Milne, "Under the Leopard's Skin"; Peluso, "Whose Woods Are These?"; Peluso and Vandergeest, "Genealogies of the Political Forest" and "Political Ecologies of War and Forests"; Vandergeest, "Racialization and Citizenship in Thai Forest Politics"; Vandergeest and Peluso, "Territorialization and State Power in Thailand").

46 On geographers and governable space, see, e.g., Braun, "Producing Vertical Territory"; Ó Tuathail, *Critical Geopolitics*; Watts, "Resource Curse?"

47 Winichakul, *Siam Mapped*, 49 and 81–110; also see Winichakul, "The Others Within."

48 Alden Wily, "Looking Back to See Forward"; "Lavers, "'Land Grab' as Development Strategy?"; Wolford et al., "Governing Global Land Deals"; also see Klinger and Muldavin, "New Geographies of Development"; Oliveira, McKay, and Liu, "China's Belt and Road Initiative."

49 Sen and Grown, *Development, Crises and Alternative Visions*.

50 Berry, "Property, Authority and Citizenship"; Lund, *Nine-Tenths of the Law* and "Property and Citizenship"; Moore, "Crucible of Cultural Politics" and *Suffering for Territory*.

51 Mbembe, *On the Postcolony*.

52 See, e.g., Diepart and Sem, "Fragmented Territories"; Dwyer, "Micro-Geopolitics"; Li, "After the Land Grab"; Posluschny-Treuner, "Understanding Foreign Large-Scale Agricultural Investments"; Woods, "Ceasefire Capitalism." For a differently scaled but complementary approach, see Hirsch et al., *Turning Land into Capital*.

53 See, e.g., Baird, "Resistance and Contingent Contestations"; Kenney-Lazar, Suhardiman, and Dwyer, "State Spaces of Resistance"; Sikor, "Tree Plantations"; Walker, "From Covert to Overt."

54 I have found especially helpful the work of Sara Berry ("Property, Authority and Citizenship"), Hart (*Disabling Globalization*), Lund ("Property and Citizenship"), Massey (*Space, Place and Gender*), Mbembe (*On the Postcolony*), Moore (*Suffering for Territory*), Ong ("Graduated Sovereignty"), and Stoler (*Imperial Debris*).

55 Perelman, "Primitive Accumulation from Feudalism to Neoliberalism," 45–49.

56 Among others, De Angelis, "Separating the Doing and the Deed"; Harvey, *The New Imperialism*; Robinson, *Black Marxism*.

57 Blaikie and Brookfield, *Land Degradation and Society*; De Soto, *The Mystery of Capital*; Sen and Grown, *Development, Crises and Alternative Visions*.

58 Marx, *Capital*, 873.

59 See, e.g., Fairhead and Leach, "False Forest History"; Neumann, *Imposing Wilderness*.

60 Perelman, "Primitive Accumulation," 46. Other authors such as De Janvry (*The Agrarian Question and Reformism*) and Hart (*Disabling Globalization*) have discussed the same phenomenon.

61 Ong, "Graduated Sovereignty"; Robinson, *Black Marxism*; Scott, "Colonial Governmentality"; Stoler, *Imperial Debris*.

62 Edelman, "Messy Hectares"; Oya, "Methodological Reflections"; Scoones et al., "The Politics of Evidence."

63 Foucault, *Security, Territory, Population*; Hannah, *Governmentality and the Mastery of Territory*.

64 See, e.g., the case of Peter Chan, discussed at length in Dwyer, "Building the Politics Machine."

65 The mini-issue introduced by Scoones et al. ("The Politics of Evidence") brought many of these debates together.

66 Edelman, "Messy Hectares"; Scoones et al., "The Politics of Evidence."

67 I made a similar point about the politics of land-titling quantification in Cambodia in Dwyer, "The Formalization Fix."

68 Scoones et al., "The Politics of Evidence," 480–81.

69 Klinger and Muldavin, "New Geographies of Development"; Li, "After the Land Grab"; Oliveira, McKay, and Liu, "Beyond Land Grabs," 324–28; Oliveira et al., "China's Belt and Road Initiative."

70 Ferguson, *Give a Man a Fish*; Li, "To Make Live and Let Die."

71 Cotula et al., "Land Grab or Development Opportunity?"; Nyíri, "Extraterritoriality."

72 Lee, "The Spectre of Global China"; Liu, Dunford, and Gao, "Discursive Construction of the Belt and Road Initiative."

73 Lee, "The Spectre of Global China", 36.

74 On this evolving diversity, see (among others) Borras et al., "Rise of Flex Crops" and the special issue of *Globalizations* introduced by Oliveira, McKay, and Liu, "Beyond Land Grabs."

75 See, among others, Baird and Quastel, "Rescaling and Reordering Nature-Society Relations"; Goldman, *Imperial Nature*; Shoemaker and Robichaud, *Dead in the Water*; Whitington, *Anthropogenic Rivers*.

76 Cowen and Shenton, *Doctrines of Development*; Escobar, *Encountering Development*; Sachs, *The Development Dictionary*.

77 Kautsky, *The Agrarian Question*; also see Mann, *Agrarian Capitalism*; Akram-Lodhi and Kay, *Peasants and Globalization*.

78 Among published sources, McCoy, *Politics of Heroin*; Warner, *Shooting at the Moon*; and Gunn, "Resistance Coalitions" proved especially indispensable for navigating the northwest.

79 See chapter 3.

80 For Laos and its immediate surroundings, see Baird, *The Rise of the Brao*; Diana, "Roses and Rifles"; High, *Fields of Desire and Projectland*; Padwe, *Disturbed Forests, Fragmented Memories*; Pholsena, *Post-War Laos*; Singh, *Natural Potency and Political Power*; and Turner, *Red Stamps and Gold Stars*.

81 For a comparable approach, see Whitington, *Anthropogenic Rivers*.

1. WHERE THE RUBBER MEETS THE ROAD

Epigraph: Chinese rubber company, project proposal document for Luang Namtha Province, 2005, pp. 3–4 (author's data).

1 Author interviews, July 2018; also see Shi, "Rubber Boom in Luang Namtha" and Thongmanivong et al., "Concession or Cooperation?"

2 Shi, "Rubber Boom" and "Rubber Boom in Luang Namtha: Seven Years Later"; Dwyer, "Trying to Follow the Money"; Su, "Nontraditional Security"; Hett et al., *Land Leases and Concessions in the Lao PDR*.

3 Wolford et al., "Governing Global Land Deals," 190–91; see, e.g., World Bank, "Rising Global Interest."

4 Dean, *Brazil and the Struggle for Rubber*.

5 Xu, "The Political, Social, and Ecological Transformation of a Landscape," 254, 256.

6 Chanthavong et al., "Rubber Institutions in Ban Hat Nyao"; Sturgeon et al., "Enclosing Ethnic Minorities," 65.

7 Shi, "Rubber Boom," 17.

8 Scott, *Seeing Like a State* and *Art of Not Being Governed*.

9 Bryant, *The Political Ecology of Forestry in Burma*; Izikowitz, *Over the Misty Mountains*; Lu, "Tapping into Rubber"; Manivong and Cramb, "Economics of Smallholder Rubber"; Peluso, *Rich Forests, Poor People*; Scott, *Art of Not Being Governed*; Sturgeon, "Governing Minorities and Development"; Stuart-Fox, "The French in Laos"; Tsing, *In the Realm of the Diamond Queen*; Vandergeest, "Land to Some Tillers."

10 McCoy, *Politics of Heroin*; Scott, *Art of Not Being Governed*; Sturgeon et al., "Enclosing Ethnic Minorities."

11 Baird and Shoemaker, "Unsettling Experiences"; Chamberlain, "Participatory Poverty Assessment"; Rigg, *Living with Transition*; Vandergeest, "Land to Some Tillers"; also see chapter 5.

12 Manivong and Cramb, "Economics of Smallholder Rubber"; Chanthavong et al., "Rubber Institutions in Ban Hat Nyao"; Sturgeon, "Governing Ethnic Minorities."

13 Alton, Blum, and Sannanikone, "Para Rubber in Northern Laos."

14 Chanthavong et al., "Rubber Institutions in Ban Hat Nyao."

15 Lu, "Tapping into Rubber."

16 Sturgeon et al., "Enclosing Ethnic Minorities," 63.

17 Nathan Associates, "Preparing the Northern Economic Corridor," ch. 5, p. 36 (pagination repeats by chapter).

18 This $400 figure comes from an interview with a provincial official (June 2007); also see details below in table 1.1.

19 "Documents on Sino-Lao Cooperation Signed," *People's Daily*; Shi, "Rubber Boom," 25.

20 Chinese rubber company, project proposal document for Luang Namtha province, 2005, pp. 3–4 (author's data).

21 Ohmae, *The End of the Nation State*; Ong, "Graduated Sovereignty"; Walker, "Regional Trade in Northwestern Laos."

22 ADB, "Technical Assistance for the Chiang Rai-Kunming Road Improvement," 1, 2.

23 Gupta and Ferguson, "Beyond 'Culture'"; Harvey and Knox, *Roads*.

24 Garnier, *Travels in Cambodia and Part of Laos*, 269. This section draws on ideas developed at greater length in Dwyer, "Upland Geopolitics: Finding Zomia in Northern Laos c. 1875."

25 Garnier, *Travels*, 293, 294; cf. Scott, *Art of Not Being Governed*.

26 Walker, *Legend of the Golden Boat*.

27 Garnier, *Travels*, 294.

28 Ivarsson, *Creating Laos*.

29 Garnier, *Travels*, 295.

30 Brocheux and Hémery, *Indochina*; Evans, *A Short History of Laos*; McCarthy, *Surveying and Exploring in Siam*; Winichakul, *Siam Mapped*.

31 Stuart-Fox, "The French in Laos."

32 Ivarsson, *Creating Laos*.

33 Gunn, *Rebellion in Laos*; Ivarsson, *Creating Laos*; Stuart-Fox, "The French in Laos."

34 Miller, *China's Asian Dream*.

35 Hirsch, "Globalisation, Regionalisation and Local Voices." On the NEC in the BRI, see Dwyer, "'They Will Not Automatically Benefit,'" 103.

36 Dheeraprasart, *After the Logging Ban*; Hirsch, "Globalisation, Regionalisation and Local Voices"; Innes-Brown and Valencia, "Thailand's Resource Diplomacy."

37 Jerndal and Rigg, "From Buffer State to Crossroads State."

38 Walker, *Legend of the Golden Boat* and "Regional Trade."

39 Dwyer, "'They Will Not Automatically Benefit'"; Walker, "Regional Trade in Northwestern Laos"; for details, see ADB, "Technical Assistance"; SEI and ADB, "Strategic Environmental Framework for the Greater Mekong Subregion," 36.

40 ADB, "Technical Assistance," 2.

41 ADB, "Proposed Grant Assistance," 8–9.

42 Project document, cooperative rubber development project, Luang Namtha, August 2000 (author's data); Shi, "Rubber Boom," 25.

43 Project document, cooperative rubber development project, Luang Namtha, January 2001 (author's data).

44 The most famous statement of these is the "Five Principles of Peaceful Coexistence" outlined in the Sino-Indian Agreement of 1954.

45 See, among others, Barney and Souksakoun, "Credit Crunch"; IMF, "Lao People's Democratic Republic"; Stuart-Fox, "Laos"; Su, "Rescaling the Chinese State."

46 Alton, Blum, and Sannanikone, "Para Rubber in Northern Laos," 97; also see Shi, "Rubber Boom," 25.

47 See Lu, "Tapping into Rubber"; Lu and Schönweger, "Great Expectations"; and Shi, "Rubber Boom" on Chinese rubber companies in northern Laos; this matches the wider push for concessions across Laos documented in, among others, Baird, "Land, Rubber and People" and "Turning Land into Capital, Turning People into Labor"; Barney, "Power, Progress and Impoverishment" and "Laos and the Making of a 'Relational' Resource Frontier"; Kenney-Lazar, "Plantation Rubber" and "Governing Dispossession"; Laungaramsri, "Frontier Capitalism"; and Suhardiman et al., "Revealing the Hidden Effects of Land Grabbing."

48 Cover letter, February 2005, Lao Ministry of Agriculture and Forestry (author's data).

49 Draft Plan for Cooperation in Rubber Planting between Lao PDR and the PR China, 2005–2007, pp. 1–2 (author's data).

50 The Draft Plan specifies 667 and 2,667 hectares per year of company and smallholder plantation, respectively, in each of the three provinces (pp. 6–7).

51 Project proposal document for Luang Namtha province, May 2005, pp. 3–4 (author's data).

52 Project proposal document for Luang Namtha province, May 2005, p. 4 (author's data).

53 Shi, "Summary and Analysis."

54 Manivong and Cramb, "Economics of Smallholder Rubber."

55 See, e.g., Brechin, *Imperial San Francisco*; Harvey and Knox, *Roads*; Tsing, *Friction*.

56 Harvey, "The Spatial Fix"; Glassman, "Primitive Accumulation" and *Bounding the Mekong*.

57 Clark, Fox, and Treakle, *Demanding Accountability*.

58 Himberg, "Comparative Review"; for more detail, see Dwyer, "'They Will Not Automatically Benefit.'"

59 World Bank, "Operation Manual on OP 4.12."
60 Nathan Associates, "Preparing the Northern Economic Corridor," ch. 2, p. 6 (emphasis added).
61 ADB, "Report and Recommendation," 32.
62 Chamberlain, "Participatory Poverty Assessment."
63 Nathan Associates, "Preparing the Northern Economic Corridor," ch. 6, pp. 7–8.
64 Nathan Associates, "Preparing the Northern Economic Corridor," ch. 5, p. 36.
65 ADB, "Social Action Plan," 22.
66 In addition to the documents cited, this section is based on conversations in late 2006 and early 2007 with development practitioners working on both of the schemes described below.
67 Lyttleton, "Build It and They Will Come," 19.
68 ADB, "Report and Recommendation," 32; ADB, "Social Action Plan," 8.
69 Nathan Associates, "Preparing the Northern Economic Corridor," ch. 6, p. 8.
70 The lack of security offered by the tax documents was also reflected by the fact that many of them covered parcels within twenty-five meters of the road's centerline, which is the extent of the state's right-of-way along national roads. These parcels, while eligible for tax collection, would thus be legally prohibited from being converted to titles at any point in the future (see, e.g., Dwyer, "'They Will Not Automatically Benefit,'" fig. 3).
71 Fieldwork notes, November 2006.
72 The full listing is given in Nathan Associates, "Preparing the Northern Economic Corridor," ch. 6, pp. 41–44.
73 Nathan Associates, "Preparing the Northern Economic Corridor," ch. 5, p. 25.
74 Nathan Associates, "Preparing the Northern Economic Corridor," ch. 5, p. 69. The Nathan study also referred (incorrectly, given subsequent events) to an unspecified future "loan to continue on" from the nine-village pilot, presumably aimed at the other villages in the corridor (ch. 6, 24; also see ch. 5, 69, ch. 6, 24–25; and ADB, "Proposed Grant Assistance").
75 Fieldwork notes, November 2006.
76 Nathan Associates, "Preparing the Northern Economic Corridor," ch. 4, p. 55. My reasoning here is based on the work of Brent Flyvbjerg and colleagues, who note the prevalence of highly optimistic estimates of benefits and costs in the infrastructure planning process (often bordering on "delusion and deception"), as well as the direct link between the magnitude of these estimates and projects' estimated internal rates of return (Flyvbjerg, Bruzelius, and Rothengatter, *Megaprojects and Risk*;

Flyvbjerg, Garbuio, and Lovallo, "Delusion and Deception"; Flyvbjerg and Sunstein, "Principle of the Malevolent Hiding Hand").

77 Fieldwork notes, November 2006; government interviews, December 2007.

78 ADB, "Project Data Sheet for 'Lao People's Democratic Republic: Sustainable Agroforestry Systems for Livelihood Enhancement of the Rural Poor.'"

79 See sources in n. 47 above, especially Barney, "Laos and the Making of a 'Relational' Resource Frontier"; also see Schönweger et al., *Concessions and Leases in the Lao PDR*; Kenney-Lazar, Suhardiman, and Dwyer, "State Spaces of Resistance."

80 On some of the more bureaucratic details, see GTZ, "Study No. 4"; Schönweger et al., *Concessions and Leases*; Lu and Schönweger, "Great Expectations." I return to the politics of paperwork in the land-finding process in chapter 5.

81 Interviews and field notes, late 2006 and 2007.

82 Interview and field notes, Vieng Phoukha, December 2007.

83 Author's comparison of location with local LFA map.

84 Interviews, Vieng Phoukha, April, June, and December 2007.

85 Interview, July 2007.

86 Vongkhamor et al., "Key Issues in Smallholder Rubber," 39 (lightly edited for flow).

87 Minutes of the meeting about Chinese cooperative rubber planting between Luang Namtha, Oudomxai, and Bokeo provinces, October 10, 2005, authorized by the governor of Luang Namtha; article 2.2 (author's data).

88 This was clear from fieldwork interviews in which local authorities and government technical staff would refer to rubber investment as being "3 + 2" or a similar variant like "cooperation with people" or "promotion" (*songserm*); it is also clear from contemporary published sources like Vongkhamor et al., "Key Issues" and Shi, "Rubber Boom."

89 Baird, "Laos, Rubber and People"; Dwyer, "Turning Land into Capital"; "Authority Voices Concern" and "Govt Suspends Land Concessions," *Vientiane Times*.

90 Interview, December 2007. For other examples of Chinese companies tapping into Lao networks, see Lyttleton et al., "Watermelons, Bars and Trucks"; Friis and Nielsen, "Small-Scale Land Acquisitions."

91 Alton, Blum, and Sannanikone, "Para Rubber in Northern Laos"; Manivong and Cramb, "Economics of Smallholder Rubber"; Shi, "Rubber Boom"; interviews, July 2018.

92 These include the sources in the previous note, as well as Diana, "Roses and Rifles"; Kenney-Lazar, "Rubber Production in Northern Laos"; and Lu, "Rubber's Reach."

93　Interviews, December 2007, with village heads and provincial-level technical staff. This was confirmed in July 2018 interviews, where informants discussed "3 + 2" as the clearly suboptimal arrangement compared to independent production.

94　Shi, "Rubber Boom," 25.

95　Thongmanivong et al., "Concession or Cooperation?," 47.

96　Hett et al., *Land Leases and Concessions in the Lao PDR*; Shi, "Rubber Boom"; Vongvisouk and Dwyer, "After the Boom."

97　Shi, "Rubber Boom," 42.

98　Interview, June 2007; Shi, "Rubber Boom," 46.

99　Schönweger et al., *Concessions and Leases*, 10 and 20.

100　Vongvisouk and Dwyer, "After the Boom."

101　Luang Namtha Provincial Agriculture and Forestry Office, "Rubber Value Chain Concept of Luang Namtha Province (2013–25)," August 2013, unofficial translation (author's data), p. 3.

102　"Rubber Value Chain Concept" (above, n. 101), pp. 2 and 11. Also see Shi, "Rubber Boom in Luang Namtha: Seven Years Later."

103　Barney, "Laos and the Making of a 'Relational' Resource Frontier," 150.

104　Lu, "Rubber's Reach"; Lu and Schönweger, "Great Expectations."

105　This distinction between public and hidden transcripts comes from Scott, *Domination and the Arts of Resistance.*

106　Lu, "Tapping into Rubber"; Shi, "Rubber Boom"; Su, "Nontraditional Security."

107　Kramer and Woods, "Financing Dispossession"; on Thailand, see Alton, Blum, and Sannanikone, "Para Rubber in Northern Laos" and Shattuck, "Risky Subjects"; on Malaysia, see Sutton, "Agribusiness on a Grand Scale."

108　Shi, "Rubber Boom"; Su, "Nontraditional Security," 79.

109　Liu and Dunford, "Inclusive Globalization."

110　Kramer and Woods, "Financing Dispossession"; Lu, "Tapping into Rubber" and "Rubber's Reach"; Su, "Nontraditional Security."

111　Guo, "Towards Resolution," 52.

112　Baird, "Turning Land into Capital, Turning People into Labor"; Barney, "Laos and the Making of a 'Relational' Resource Frontier"; Kenney-Lazar, "Governing Dispossession"; Kenney-Lazar, Suhardiman, and Dwyer, "State Spaces of Resistance"; Laungaramsri, "Frontier Capitalism"; Suhardiman et al., "Revealing the Hidden Effects of Land Grabbing."

113　Ducourtieux, Laffort, and Sacklokham, "Land Policy and Farming Practices in Laos," 507.

114　Glassman, *Bounding the Mekong*; Hirsch, "Globalisation, Regionalisation and Local Voices."

2. A REAL COUNTRY?

Epigraph: Quoted in Deitchman, *The Best-Laid Schemes*, 33.

1 Blaufarb, "Organizing and Managing Unconventional War in Laos." On RAND in Southeast Asia more broadly, see Elliott, *RAND in Southeast Asia*.

2 Blaufarb, *The Counterinsurgency Era*.

3 Blaufarb, "Unconventional War in Laos," v and 32.

4 Blaufarb, "Unconventional War," 2.

5 Kong Le's coup and associated events are discussed in numerous sources; see, among others, Evans, *A Short History of Laos*; Stuart-Fox, *A History of Laos*.

6 Blaufarb, "Unconventional War," v.

7 Blaufarb, "Unconventional War," 2–3.

8 See, e.g., Henry Kissinger's elaboration of the claim, made in the days after the US withdrawal from Afghanistan in August 2021, that "Afghanistan has never been a modern state" (Kissinger, "Why America Failed in Afghanistan").

9 Blaufarb, "Unconventional War," 32; also see Kurlantzick, *A Great Place to Have a War*; McCoy, *Politics of Heroin*; Warner, *Shooting at the Moon*.

10 See, e.g., Kurlantzick, *A Great Place to Have a War*; Warner, *Shooting at the Moon*.

11 Izikowitz, *Over the Misty Mountains*; Kunstadter, Chapman, and Sabhasri, *Farmers in the Forest*.

12 For a recent take on this, see Gordillo, "Terrain as Insurgent Weapon."

13 Scott, *Art of Not Being Governed*, 4 and 20.

14 Examples abound, and often focus on the mix of infrastructuring and land zoning that seeks to render space abstract and governable; see, e.g., Brechin, *Imperial San Francisco*; Cronon, *Nature's Metropolis*; Vandergeest and Peluso, "Territorialization and State Power in Thailand."

15 Stuart-Fox, "The French in Laos," 133 and 136. Also see Ivarsson (*Creating Laos*) on both "the stereotypical dichotomy" of French Indochina— the racialized distinction "between the dynamic and industrious Vietnamese [and] the decadent and lazy Lao" (104)—and the relatively late French efforts (in the 1930s) to encourage emerging ideas of Lao nationalism (ch. 4).

16 Warner, *Shooting at the Moon*; also see Branfman, *Voices from the Plain of Jars*.

17 González, "Human Terrain"; Bryan and Wood, *Weaponizing Maps*; Gordillo, "Terrain as Insurgent Weapon."

18 Given the scope and concerns of the book, my focus is on the lasting impact within Laos. But as recent scholarship emphasizes, this statement

applies as well to the effects of Laos's secret war on the CIA more broadly, including most famously its activities in Afghanistan before and during the "global war on terror" (Coll, *Ghost Wars*; Kurlantzick, *A Great Place to Have a War*; Mamdani, *Good Muslim, Bad Muslim*; Mazzetti, *Way of the Knife*).

19 Sassen, "Land Grabs Today" and "Savage Sorting"; Nyíri, "Enclaves of Improvement" and "Extraterritoriality"; see introduction.

20 British Pathé News archive, https://www.britishpathe.com/video /president-kennedy-talks-on-laos.

21 Clausewitz, *On War*.

22 Prados, *Vietnam*, 13–19.

23 The political entity of South Vietnam—and the implied one of North Vietnam—grew out of Washington's support for Ngo Din Diem's scrapping of the plan, outlined in the 1954 Geneva Accords after the French defeat at Dien Bien Phu, to hold nationwide elections in Vietnam within two years. Contrary to Diem's and Washington's interpretation, the 1954 agreements did not create two sovereign nations of North and South Vietnam; rather, they created "regroupment zones" in northern and southern Vietnam (and northern and southern Laos) for the various sides, an arrangement that Washington read as a giveaway to the communists (Prados, *Vietnam*, 26–38).

24 Prados, *Vietnam*, 26–38.

25 Conboy and Morrison, *Shadow War*; Gilkey, "Laos"; Halpern, "Economic Development and American Aid in Laos"; Stuart-Fox, *A History of Laos*. For a comparison of the strategic-hamlet programs in both countries, see Phillips, *Why Vietnam Matters*; on the issue of regular military capacity, see Prados, *Vietnam* on South Vietnam and Conboy and Morrison, *Shadow War* and Warner, *Shooting at the Moon* on Laos; on urban corruption in wartime Laos, see Gilkey, "Laos" and Stuart-Fox, *A History of Laos*.

26 Warner, *Shooting at the Moon*, 7.

27 Gilkey, "Laos," 92.

28 Rist, *The History of Development*, 80–92.

29 Greenstein and Immerman, "Letter to the Editor," 363.

30 Blaufarb, "Unconventional War in Laos," 5.

31 Conboy and Morrison, *Shadow War*; Jonsson, "War's Ontogeny"; Kurlantzick, *A Great Place to Have a War*.

32 Conboy and Morrison, *Shadow War*, 6; Warner, *Shooting at the Moon*.

33 Trinquier, *Modern Warfare*.

34 Fall, "Introduction," x.

35 Fall, "Introduction," xiv. The term *maquis* (bush) seems to have originated in the Free French (guerrilla) resistance set up during the Second World War.

36 Conboy and Morrison, *Shadow War*, 59–60.

37 Warner, *Shooting at the Moon*; Conboy and Morrison, *Shadow War*.
38 Blaufarb, "Unconventional War," viii.
39 Blaufarb, "Unconventional War," 52–53; Robbins, *Air America*; Warner, *Shooting at the Moon*.
40 Blaufarb, "Unconventional War," 6.
41 Conboy and Morrison, *Shadow War*, 90–91.
42 Nam Nyu is the English-language rendering of the contemporary Lao spelling. In many English-language historical sources it is spelled Nam Yu (e.g., Warner, *Shooting at the Moon*) or Nam Lieu (e.g., Morrow, "CIA's Spy Teams inside Red China").
43 Lintner, *Burma in Revolt*, 57–58.
44 Lintner, *Burma in Revolt*; McCoy, *Politics of Heroin*.
45 McCoy, *Politics of Heroin*, 306.
46 Warner, *Shooting at the Moon*; McCoy, *Politics of Heroin*.
47 McCoy, *Politics of Heroin*; Warner, *Shooting at the Moon*.
48 Jonsson, "War's Ontogeny," 131–32.
49 Gunn, *Rebellion in Laos*, 74.
50 Gunn, *Rebellion in Laos*, 61.
51 Taxes were calculated in cash and could be paid in kind via opium or corvée labor; see Stuart-Fox, *A History of Laos* and Gunn, *Rebellion in Laos*, which also discuss upland insurrections during the colonial period. Jonsson wrote: "Some of my contacts recall the hardship of French colonial taxation, when many Iu Mien were forced to sell off children in order to pay" ("War's Ontogeny," 139).
52 Gunn, *Rebellion in Laos*; Stuart-Fox, *A History of Laos*.
53 Jonsson, "War's Ontogeny"; McCoy, *Politics of Heroin*.
54 Brocheux and Hémery, *Indochina*; Gunn, *Rebellion in Laos*.
55 McCoy, *Politics of Heroin*, 132.
56 Jonsson ("War's Ontogeny", 127) describes how allegiance and leadership hardened in times of war, and in this setting in particular, because of the control that authorities like Chao Mai and Chao La wielded over refugee processing and relief services.
57 Evans, *Politics of Ritual and Remembrance*; Dwyer, "Upland Geopolitics."
58 Warner, *Shooting at the Moon*, 126.
59 McCoy, *Politics of Heroin*, 335–49. Unless otherwise indicated, my information about Nam Nyu's espionage program and Young's family history comes from McCoy, who interviewed Young in 1971. Roger Warner, who also interviewed Young, confirms the basic outline of events, if not the precise details, related here (Warner, *Shooting at the Moon*).
60 McCoy, *Politics of Heroin*; also see Shackley and Finney, *Spymaster*, 191–2.
61 The first front was the Korean War, which started in 1950 as well.

62 McCoy, *Politics of Heroin*, 339.

63 Theodore Shackley, CIA station chief in Vientiane in 1967, gave the following tallies for "irregular" forces in Laos in 1967 (from Shackley and Finney, *Spymaster*, 157):

Long [Ch]eng (north)	21,741
Nam [Ny]u (northwest)	6,843
Pakse (south)	4,232
Savannakhet (central)	3,535
Luang Prabang (north central)	2,502
Total	38,853

64 McCoy, *Politics of Heroin*, 336.

65 Air America's *Facilities Data* (Texas Tech archives); US Defense Mapping Agency Topographic Center, Washington, DC, compiled 1975, map series 1501, 3rd ed., 1:250,000 scale (accessed via https://911gfx.nexus.net/sea-ao .html).

66 McCoy, *Politics of Heroin*; Robbins, *Air America*; Warner, *Shooting at the Moon*.

67 Blaufarb, "Unconventional War," 6.

68 Blaufarb, "Unconventional War," 32.

69 Warner, *Shooting at the Moon*, 352.

70 Branfman, *Voices from the Plain of Jars*, 1972; Warner, *Shooting at the Moon*.

71 Blaufarb, "Unconventional War," 50. These ranged between a high of 14,181 in January 1970 and a low of 3,567 in September 1970. Only seven of twenty-three months shown had fewer than 10,000 sorties.

72 Blaufarb, "Unconventional War," 51.

73 Blaufarb, "Unconventional War," 33.

74 Blaufarb, "Unconventional War," 33 (emphasis in original).

75 Johnson, "War's Ontogeny"; Prados, *Vietnam*.

76 Phillips, *Why Vietnam Matters*.

77 Phillips argues that even though the US government espoused nation-building, Americans in Laos were not actually doing much of it in the late 1950s. Despite being inspired by what he called "the Magsaysay experience" in the Philippines, Phillips describes his naive disappointment when he was received as a "spook" in Laos, and his efforts in May 1958 to "create a link [between villages and] the Lao government and thus forestall a [communist] election landslide" were hamstrung

less by conditions on the ground than by opposition within the American aid community. When, later, a "crash village-aid program, using mainly air drops of construction materials and tools" did actually get off the ground, the whole thing lasted a month and reached about a thousand rural villages. "Nothing on this scale had ever happened before in Laos" (*Why Vietnam Matters*, 95–96).

78 Blaufarb, "Unconventional War," 2.

79 See, e.g., Gunn, *Rebellion in Laos*; Ivarsson, *Creating Laos*; Stuart-Fox, *A History of Laos*.

80 Blaufarb, "Unconventional War," 2.

81 Blaufarb, "Unconventional War," v–vi.

82 Godley and St. Goar, "The Chinese Road in Northwest Laos," 291.

83 Godley and St. Goar, "Chinese Road," 291.

84 Godley and St. Goar, "Chinese Road," 285.

85 Godley and St. Goar, "Chinese Road," 285.

86 Godley and St. Goar, "Chinese Road," 285.

87 CIA, "Central Intelligence Bulletin," June 3, 1965 (p. 6); CIA Directorate of Intelligence, "Developments in Indochina," [precise date illegible] May 1973 (p. 6). Accessed via CIA Records Search Tool archives, College Park, MD, May 2012 (hereafter CREST).

88 CIA Office of Current Intelligence, "Weekly summary," December 3, 1965, p. 10 (accessed via CREST archives).

89 Godley and St. Goar, "Chinese Road," 292.

90 Godley and St. Goar, "Chinese Road," 286 and 294.

91 Godley and St. Goar, "Chinese Road," 294.

92 See, e.g., Stern, "Deeper CIA Role in Laos Revealed" (accessed via CREST archives).

93 "Laos: April 1971" (the Symington Committee investigation by Lowenstein and Moose), as read into the *Congressional Record* (p. S 12966) by Senator William Fulbright on June 7, 1971 (accessed via CREST archives).

94 Godley and St. Goar, "Chinese Road," 307–8.

95 CIA Directorate of Intelligence, "Developments in Indochina," May 1973, p. 7 (accessed via CREST archives).

96 Evans, "Introduction," 1 (all quotes in this paragraph).

97 Dommen, *Conflict in Laos*; Fall, *Anatomy of a Crisis*. Fall is well-known for his analysis of American "overreach" during the "Laotian crisis," which Dommen—famous for characterizing Laos as the geostrategic "keystone of Indochina"—witnessed firsthand (Evans, *A Short History of Laos*, 116).

98 Fall, "Introduction."

99 Phillips, *Why Vietnam Matters*, 95–96.

100 Halpern, *Aspects of Village Life.*
101 Halpern, "Economic Development and American Aid in Laos," 153.
102 Halpern, "Economic Development"; also see Gilkey, "Laos."
103 Halpern, "Economic Development," 168–70.
104 Halpern, "Economic Development," 171.
105 Evans, "Introduction," 1.
106 Deitchman, *The Best-Laid Schemes.* Project Camelot's widely assumed regional target was Latin America, and its downfall shares some similarities with the more recent controversy over the so-called Bowman Expeditions (see Bryan and Wood, *Weaponizing Maps*).
107 Deitchman, *Best-Laid Schemes*, 23–24.
108 Deitchman, *Best-Laid Schemes*; Elliott, *RAND in Southeast Asia*; Klare, *War without End*; Wakin, *Anthropology Goes to War.*
109 For example: responding to a 1962 National Security Action Memorandum (NSAM 162, Development of U.S. and Indigenous Police, Paramilitary and Military Resources, https://www.jfklibrary.org/asset-viewer /archives/JFKNSF/337/JFKNSF-337-001), the CIA's Geography Division undertook what its acting chief described as "a broad project . . . which is intended to study 11 critical countries to identify minority groups having an exploitable paramilitary potential" ("Geography Division support for CIA Counterinsurgency Action," July 12, 1962, accessed via CREST online: https://www.cia.gov/library/readingroom/docs/CIA -RDP80B01083A000100100030-1.pdf). More generally, see Kurlantzick, *A Great Place to Have a War*, 1–2.
110 Wakin, *Anthropology Goes to War*, 57.

3. THE GEOGRAPHY OF SECURITY

Epigraph: Thongphachanh and Birgegard, "Muong Paksane Regional Development Study," 23.
  1 All quotes in this paragraph from "Instruction on stepping up population management work, issued by the Lao PDR's Council of Ministers and signed by Nouhak Phoumsavan, vice chairman of the council," February 1, 1988; translated by the United States' Foreign Broadcast Information Service (hereafter FBIS). Texas Tech University Vietnam Center and Archives, Vietnam Veterans Association Project—Laos; box 30, folder 4; accessed March 11, 2009.
  2 Quoted in Scott, "Colonial Governmentality," 202; also see Foucault, *Discipline and Punish* and *Security, Territory, Population.*
  3 Stuart-Fox, *A History of Laos.*
  4 Stuart-Fox, *A History of Laos.*
  5 Gunn, "Resistance Coalitions in Laos."

6   "Instruction . . ." (n. 1).

7   Evrard and Goudineau, "Planned Resettlement"; Rigg, *Living with Transition*.

8   Stuart-Fox, "The French in Laos," 134.

9   National Geographic Service of Viet-Nam, "Economic map of Indochina."

10 US Army, "Army Service Forces Manual," 28.

11 USAID, "Termination Report, Laos," 184, 225, 326, and 341–43.

12 Persson, "Forestry in Laos," 52–53.

13 Goppers and Bergström, "Elephants Don't Rust," 11–12.

14 I reproduce Persson's map below as part of map 3.1, but omit the following data (from Persson, "Forestry in Laos," 38) about "development partners":

SFE	AREA ALLOCATED	PARTNER
SFE 1	530,000 ha	Sweden
SFE 2	not fixed	Vietnam
SFE 3	420,000 ha	Sweden (originally Hungary)
SFE 4	460,000 ha	USSR
SFE 5	not fixed	Bulgaria
SFE 6	not fixed	Czech.
SFE 7	not fixed	—
SFE 8	not fixed	(IBRD)
SFE 9	420,000 ha	ADB

15 Goppers and Bergström, "Elephants Don't Rust."

16 Goppers and Bergström, "Elephants Don't Rust," 11.

17 Goppers and Bergström, "Elephants Don't Rust," 10.

18 Goppers and Bergström, "Elephants Don't Rust," 9–10.

19 Goppers and Bergström, "Elephants Don't Rust."

20 Thongphachanh and Birgegard, "Muong Paksane Regional Development Study," v.

21 Thongphachanh and Birgegard, "Muong Paksane Regional Development Study," 20 (emphasis in original).

22 Thongphachanh and Birgegard, "Muong Paksane Regional Development Study," 3.

23 Thongphachanh and Birgegard, "Muong Paksane Regional Development Study," 3.

24 USAID, "Termination Report, Laos," 184–85.

25 Thongphachanh and Birgegard, "Muong Paksane Regional Development Study," 3–4 and 11–12. This landscape was hardly unique in Southeast Asia; see Kunstadter, Chapman, and Sabhasri, *Farmers in the Forest* for other examples of shifting cultivation being taken up by economically and politically displaced populations who had not traditionally practiced it.

26 Thongphachanh and Birgegard, "Muong Paksane Regional Development Study," 2–4.

27 Thongphachanh and Birgegard, "Muong Paksane Regional Development Study," 11–12.

28 Thongphachanh and Birgegard, "Muong Paksane Regional Development Study," 20.

29 Thongphachanh and Birgegard, "Muong Paksane Regional Development Study," 20.

30 Goppers and Bergström, "Elephants Don't Rust."

31 Marx, *Capital*, 875.

32 Thongphachanh and Birgegard, "Muong Paksane Regional Development Study," 29.

33 Even in the mid-1980s, Sweden was sensitive to accusations of forced labor in its aid projects in Vietnam and Laos. Although it denied these in the latter, it took them seriously and deemed them worthy of rebuttal (see Goppers and Bergström, "Elephants Don't Rust," 37–39).

34 Foucault, *Security, Territory, Population*.

35 Elden, "Governmentality"; Huxley, "Geographies of Governmentality"; Scott, "Colonial Governmentality."

36 Foucault, *Discipline and Punish*; Scott, *Seeing Like a State*.

37 Foucault, *Security, Territory, Population*; also see Heilbroner, *The Worldly Philosophers*.

38 Foucault, *Security, Territory, Population*; Patterson, *Slavery and Social Death*.

39 STOL site locations have been sourced from the US Defense Mapping Agency Topographic Center, Washington, DC, compiled 1975, map series 1501, 3rd ed., 1:250,000 scale; accessed online via Jim Henthorn's excellent map collection for Laos (https://911gfx.nexus.net/laos.html).

40 Goppers and Bergström, "Elephants Don't Rust"; Hansson, "Swedish Correspondent Views Problems with Aid Project"; Trankell, *On the Road in Laos*.

41 Goppers and Bergström, "Elephants Don't Rust," 29.

42 Ferguson, *The Anti-Politics Machine*; Li, *The Will to Improve*.

43 Evans, *A Short History of Laos*; Stuart-Fox, *A History of Laos*.

44 Hansson, "Swedish Correspondent Views Problems with Aid Project" (translated by FBIS).

45 "Vietnam's Rebellious 'Colony,'" *Far Eastern Economic Review*. In his *Short History of Laos*, Grant Evans makes this point more broadly. Describing "Vietnam's *mission civilatrice*" in the early postwar years, he gestures to the hypocrisy that was plainly visible to many Lao citizens: "The major role played by the Vietnamese communists at key levels of the state appeared to contradict Lao People's Revolutionary Party claims to have fought against the Royal Lao Government for 'true independence,' against the 'new colonialism' it said the old government was part of. To many Lao, the new regime seemed equally part of a 'new colonial' system, especially following the signing of the 20-year treaty between the two countries" (189).

46 Thongphachanh and Birgegard, "Muong Paksane Regional Development Study," 23.

47 Thongphachanh and Birgegard, "Muong Paksane Regional Development Study," 23.

48 High, "'Join Together, Work Together'"; also see GTZ, "Study No. 11," 18.

49 Thongphachanh and Birgegard, "Muong Paksane Regional Development Study," 23.

50 Thongphachanh and Birgegard, "Muong Paksane Regional Development Study," 27 and 43.

51 Cullather, *The Hungry World*, 159–79; Phillips, *Why Vietnam Matters*.

52 Thongphachanh and Birgegard, "Muong Paksane Regional Development Study," 29.

53 Dove, "Living Rubber, Dead Land."

54 Thongphachanh and Birgegard, "Muong Paksane Regional Development Study," 23 and 29.

55 Trankell, *On the Road in Laos*, vii.

56 Trankell, *On the Road in Laos*, 80–81.

57 Trankell, *On the Road in Laos*, 17.

58 Trankell, *On the Road in Laos*, 17 and 65.

59 Bolikhamxai Provincial Authority, "Bolikhamxai Province Socio-Economic Profile," 18.

60 Trankell, *On the Road in Laos*, 17.

61 Thongphachanh and Birgegard, "Muong Paksane Regional Development Study," 2.

62 Thongphachanh and Birgegard, "Muong Paksane Regional Development Study," 38.

63 Thongphachanh and Birgegard, "Muong Paksane Regional Development Study," 38 (emphasis in original).

64 Thongphachanh and Birgegard, "Muong Paksane Regional Development Study," 39.

65 Thongphachanh and Birgegard, "Muong Paksane Regional Development Study," 80–84.

66 Thongphachanh and Birgegard, "Muong Paksane Regional Development Study," 32.

67 See Baird and Shoemaker, "Unsettling Experiences," 875.

68 The Bolikhamxai authorities are quoting the "Official Government Document" presented at the May 1998 Sixth Roundtable Follow-up Meeting on the National Rural Development Program, a process mandated by a Geneva Roundtable meeting with international donors in June 1997.

69 Bolikhamxai Provincial Authority, "Bolikhamxai Province Socio-Economic Profile" (subsection "Bolikhan District Profile," pp. 18, 19, 21). The document refers to the combined areas of Muang Houng and Muang Bo, an adjacent area just to the west, as a single focal site named "Pha Muang"; to reduce confusion, I refer to both areas collectively as Muang Houng.

70 Bolikhamxai Provincial Authority, "Bolikhamxai Province Socio-Economic Profile" (subsection "Bolikhan District Profile," p. 20).

71 Bolikhamxai Provincial Authority, "Bolikhamxai Province Socio-Economic Profile," 17–18.

72 Bolikhamxai Provincial Authority, "Bolikhamxai Province Socio-Economic Profile," 17–18.

73 Messerli et al., *Socio-Economic Atlas of the Lao PDR*, 131–35.

74 On the Paksan Regional Project, see Goppers and Bergström, "Elephants Don't Rust," 29; on SFE devolution, see chapter 5.

75 Bolikhamxai Provincial Authority, "Bolikhamxai Province Socio-Economic Profile" (subsection "Bolikhan District Profile," p. 2); Hodgdon, "No Success Like Failure." (See especially Hodgdon's map on p. 39; Muang Houng sits in the white space between provincial forestry areas 34 and 36. A "provincial land use planning map" included in MCTPC and IUCN's "Bolikhamxai Province Environmental Inventory" [32] shows this same geography, but not as clearly.)

76 Bolikhamxai Provincial Authority, "Bolikhamxai Province Socio-Economic Profile" (subsection "Bolikhan District Profile," p. 10).

77 Foucault, *Security, Territory, Population*, 43–44.

78 Evrard and Goudineau, "Planned Resettlement"; Rigg, *Living with Transition*.

79 Baird and Shoemaker, "Unsettling Experiences"; Barney, "Laos and the Making of a 'Relational' Resource Frontier"; Evrard and Goudineau, "Planned Resettlement"; Rigg, *Living with Transition*; Vandergeest, "Land to Some Tillers"; also see chapters 1 and 5.

80 Lao radio, September 7, 1988, "Heighten Vigilance against Enemies' New Schemes"; translation by FBIS.

81 Lao radio, September 7, 1988, "Heighten Vigilance against Enemies' New Schemes"; translation by FBIS.

82 Lao radio, April 1, 1989, "The Open-Door Policy Is Linked to the Maintenance of Internal Security"; translation by FBIS.

4. MICRO-GEOPOLITICS

Epigraph: Mbembe, *On the Postcolony*, 88.

1 The Lao National Tourism Authority describes the museum this way on its website: "The provincial museum has a variety of artifacts made by Luang Namtha's multi-ethnic people. Of particular interest is the extensive collection of indigenous clothing as well as many agricultural tools and household implements used in daily life. The museum has an excellent collection of Buddha images, bronze drums, ceramics and textiles. Also of interest are the traditional hand-made weapons on display that were once used for hunting and national defense." http://www.tourismlaos.org/web/show_content.php?contID=42 (accessed December 1, 2011).

2 Anderson, *Imagined Communities*, ch. 10; also see Cohn, "The Census, Social Structure and Objectification"; Hannah, *Governmentality and the Mastery of Territory*; Scott, *Seeing like a State*.

3 Izikowitz, *Over the Misty Mountains*, 74–75, 95–102; also see Hanks and Hanks, "Ethnographic Notes on Northern Thailand"; Schliesinger, *Ethnic Groups of Laos*; Young, "Hill Tribes of Northern Thailand." My use of ethnic-group terminology in this paragraph follows the English-language labels on the map. A number of these names ("Lao Theung," "Yao," "Kui") are exonyms, labels used by state authorities that differ from the labels that groups use to refer to themselves (autonyms). As elaborated below, "Kui" (like "Muser," in ch. 1) refers to Lahu, while "Yao" refers to Iu Mien.

4 Key sources include Action Contra le Faim, "Summary of Reports on Resettlement"; Baird and Shoemaker, "Unsettling Experiences"; Chamberlain, "Participatory Poverty Assessment"; Ducourtieux, Laffort, and Sacklokham, "Land Policy"; Evrard and Goudineau, "Planned Resettlement"; Ireson and Ireson, "Ethnicity and Development"; and Vandergeest, "Land to Some Tillers."

5 Rigg, *Living with Transition*, 126.

6 Vandergeest, "Land to Some Tillers," 52.

7 The dynamics described below are similar to those described in postwar upland Vietnam by Andrew Hardy (*Red Hills*) and Rodolphe De Koninck ("Geopolitics of Land Colonization" and "Peasantry as the Territorial Spearhead of the State").

8   Robinson, *Racial Capitalism*; Ong, "Graduated Sovereignty."
9   Particularly important to my thinking have been De Koninck's land-centric approach to geopolitics (cited above, n. 7); the work of Robinson and Ong (cited above, n. 8); and Stoler (*Imperial Debris*) on the ways that racialized forms of social difference continue to facilitate capitalist accumulation.
10 Marx, *Capital*, ch. 1. Marx's critique of the commodity fetish, focusing on the need to uncover the social relations that underpin the *production* of commodities, has much similarity to Foucault's approach to power described here.
11 Foucault, *"Society Must Be Defended,"* 28, 30.
12 Ferguson, *The Anti-Politics Machine*; Rigg, *Living with Transition*; see, e.g., Chamberlain, "Participatory Poverty Assessment"; Cohen, "Post-Opium Scenario." Also see ch. 5.
13 Foucault, *"Society Must Be Defended,"* 30.
14 Fieldwork notes, April 2007.
15 Shi, "Rubber Boom."
16 See, e.g., Barney, "Power, Progress and Impoverishment"; Hunt, "Planta-tions, Deforestation and Forest Sector Aid Interventions"; Laungaramsri, "Frontier Capitalism"; Obein, "Assessment."
17 This was the concession in Ban Sopdut; see Shi, "Rubber Boom," 30. For more on Yunnan Rubber, also see Lu, "Tapping into Rubber"; Lu and Schönweger, "Great Expectations."
18 Fieldwork notes, June 2007.
19 Village-head survey and key informant interviews in twelve Vieng Phoukha villages, December 2007 and January 2008.
20 Whitington, "Beleaguered Village Leader"; also see Baird, "Rubber, Land and People"; Laungaramsri, "Frontier Capitalism."
21 Hunt, "Plantations, Deforestation and Forest Sector Aid Interventions."
22 Village interview, December 2007.
23 This is clear from the LFA map of the village, both the signboard version posted in the village itself (photographed June 2007 by the author, map dated "year 1999–2000") and the paper version held in the local district Agriculture and Forestry office (author's data).
24 Hodgdon, "No Success like Failure," 39; Walker, *Legend of the Golden Boat*, 20–23, 57–62.
25 Ireson and Ireson, "Ethnicity and Development," 933; also see Goudineau and Evrard, "Resettlement," vol. 2; Gunn, "Resistance Coalitions."
26 Fieldwork notes, December 2007.
27 What he was explaining is more along the lines of how state-managed resettlement worked in upland Vietnam (Hardy, *Red Hills*; De Koninck, "Theory and Practice").

28 Fieldwork notes, December 2007. I had heard about one of these other district-level boundary negotiations and village movements from another informant almost a year earlier (fieldwork notes, November 2006).

29 This is a pseudonym, meaning "Red Village," which I use to note the parallels to Andrew Hardy's work on upland Vietnam (Hardy, *Red Hills*).

30 Author's data: Vieng Phoukha district LFA statistics (detailed, 2005); Luang Namtha provincial LFA statistics (summary); cf. Barney, "Grounding Global Forest Economies," 289 (~1,800 ha); Thongmanivong et al., "Concession or Cooperation?," 33 (826 ha); Hunt, "Plantations, Deforestation and Forest Sector Aid Interventions," 138 (435 ha) and 141 (~3,000 ha).

31 Fieldwork notes, December 2007.

32 Summary of Land and Forest Allocation 2004–5 in Ban [Deng], Vieng Phoukha Agriculture and Forestry Office (author's data).

33 An image of this appears in Dwyer, "Micro-Geopolitics," 392.

34 Summary (above, n. 32).

35 Goudineau and Evrard, "Resettlement," vol. 2, 23 and 26. Goudineau and Evrard use the terminology of *left bank* and *right bank*, which correspond roughly to the Namtha's east and west banks, respectively; the river flows first south and then southwest (see map 4.2).

36 Goudineau and Evrard, "Resettlement," vol. 2, 23.

37 Fieldwork interview, 2007.

38 Fieldwork interview, July 2007. On debates about resettlement in Laos, see Baird and Shoemaker, "Unsettling Experiences"; Evrard and Goudineau, "Planned Resettlement."

39 US Defense Mapping Agency Topographic Center, Washington, DC, compiled 1975, map series 1501, 3rd ed., 1:250,000 scale, sheet NF 47–16 ("Luang-Namtha, Laos; Thailand; Burma").

40 In addition to these examples, compare Ban Na Woua, an Iu Mien village discussed by McCoy (*Politics of Heroin*, 336) that appears on the US map and has since disappeared.

41 Lao PDR 1987 topographic map series (based on 1986 aerial imagery), National Geographic Department, Lao PDR, sheets F-47 xxix and F-47 xxxv (author's data). Compare "Laos population and ethnic groups," 2005 census (available on Laofab.org).

42 Fieldwork interview, July 2007.

43 Hodgdon, "No Success like Failure," 39 (plus geo-referencing by the author); village LFA map (author's data).

44 Village Histories Survey, 2006 (author's data, anonymized); Siphavanh et al., "Main Causes of High Repetition Rate," 12.

45 Village Histories (above, n. 44); Survey of [details removed] Villages in Vieng Phoukha District, Luang Namtha Province, 2004 (author's data, anonymized).

46 Fieldwork notes, 2007, 2008.

47 On the latter, see Lyttleton, "Relative Pleasures"; Lyttleton et al., "Watermelons, Bars and Trucks"; UNODC, "Laos Opium Survey."

48 Survey (above, n. 45), p. 47.

49 Survey (above, n. 45), pp. 17, 47.

50 There is a longer history here of the official dissolution of the older *tasseng* (subdistrict) administrative level in 1991 owing to its perceived threats to central-state power and its subsequent reconstitution (still for political and administrative purposes) as first the *khet* ("area" or "zone") and, more recently, the village group or cluster (*kum-ban*). For a partial elaboration, see Stuart-Fox, "The Political Culture of Corruption"; Foppes, "Knowledge Capitalization."

51 Fieldwork interviews, June 2007 and December 2007. On the narrative that the uplands are untaxed, see Dwyer, "Building the Politics Machine," 314–21.

52 Fieldwork interviews, June 2007 and December 2007.

53 Shi, "Rubber Boom," 14.

54 Plantation area numbers are difficult statistics for reasons discussed briefly in chapter 1 and elaborated in chapter 5. A development project report from early 2007 described Bolisat Ltd.'s plantation in one part of Khet Nam Fa as "a 500 hectare rubber concession" (Project report [details removed] 2007, p. 6). Plantation ages reported during 2018 fieldwork as well as a key informant (anonymous pers. comm., 2018) imply continued planting in the company's plantations throughout the latter 2000s.

55 At prevailing assumptions, a 1,000-hectare plantation would have owed (conservatively assuming 400 trees per hectare; MAF and Sino-Lao assumed 495—see ch. 1) roughly $300,000 per year once tapping began. While actual taxation rates seem not to have materialized anywhere near this rate (see Hett et al., *Land Leases and Concessions*, 110, 114, 122), the tax-based logic of replacing upland swidden fields with corporate rubber plantations would nonetheless have been significant.

56 "Landownership: Land of the Lao PDR is under the ownership of the national community as prescribed in Article 17 of the Constitution *in which the State is charged with the centralized and uniform management* [of land] throughout the country" (2003 Land Law, article 3, emphasis added).

57 For Laos, see Baird and Shoemaker, "Unsettling Experiences"; Chamberlain, "Participatory Poverty Assessment"; Laungaramsri, "Frontier Capitalism"; Vandergeest, "Land to Some Tillers," among many others. Nonetheless, this is hardly one-sided; there is much give-and-take, as is clear from literature on land politics in general, and resistance in particular, in authoritarian countries; see, e.g., Walker, "From Covert to

Overt" on China; Sikor, "Tree Plantations" on Vietnam; and Baird, "Resistance and Contingent Contestations"; Kenney-Lazar, Suhardiman, and Dwyer, "State Spaces of Resistance"; and McAllister, "Rubber, Rights and Resistance" on Laos.

58 Interviews, December 2007.

59 Baird and Shoemaker, "Unsettling Experiences"; Chamberlain, "Participatory Poverty Assessment"; Daviau, "Resettlement in Long District" and "Update 2003"; Ducourtieux, Laffort, and Sacklokham, "Land Policy"; Lyttleton et al., "Watermelons, Bars and Trucks."

60 Project report, 2007 (author's data, anonymized); quotes are from pp. 5 and 6.

61 Report on Resettlement in Vieng Phoukha District, Luang Namtha Province 2004 (author's data, anonymized), pp. 2–3.

62 Interview, February 2008.

63 Interviews with village heads in Khet Nam Fa, December 2008.

64 Interview, July 2018.

65 Interviews, July 2018.

66 Interviews, July 2018.

67 Village interview, December 2008 (cf. Marx, *Capital*, 874).

68 Interview, July 2018. One informant reported a not-insignificant figure of 90 million Lao kip (about $10,000) in unpaid wages from planting work, saying that the company had asked villagers to wait until tapping began. While impossible to verify, this figure is not unrealistic given the size of the plantation (a few hundred hectares, with roughly 400–500 trees per hectare and piecework rates in the range of a few hundred kip per tree).

69 Lu and Schönweger, "Great Expectations"; also see Kenney-Lazar, "Governing Dispossession."

70 Dwyer, "Micro-Geopolitics"; Juliet Lu makes a similar point on the resettlement-based logic of China's opium-replacement program; see Lu, "Tapping into Rubber," 742.

71 Jie, "China: Facilitating Cooperation"; Kramer and Woods, "Financing Dispossession."

72 Dwyer, "Trying to Follow the Money"; Shi, "Rubber Boom"; Su, "Nontraditional Security."

73 My language here draws explicitly on C. K. Lee's concept of encompassing accumulation, which the author uses to describe Chinese capital's effectiveness at accommodating host-country political and economic demands, especially when that capital is state-owned (Lee, "Spectre of Global China," 36).

74 UNODC, "Southeast Asia Opium Survey"; interview, July 2018.

75 Creak, "Laos in 2013," 152–55.

76 Crispin, "Limits of Chinese Expansionism." The article, which raised "questions about how far China has gone to manage its investment image," intimated that the Chinese government had been involved as well.

77 See, e.g., Schipani, "Ecotourism as an Alternative to Upland Rubber."

78 Tuffin, "Letter Re: Shawn Crispin's 'The Limits of Chinese Expansionism.'"

79 Tuffin, "Letter."

80 Dulles, *War or Peace.*

81 Zhai, "1959: Preventing Peaceful Evolution."

82 Brenner and Elden, "Henri Lefebvre on State, Space, Territory," 367.

5. PAPER LANDSCAPES

1 Ducourtieux, Laffort, and Sacklokham, "Land Policy," 507 (quoted in ch. 1).

2 Rose, *Property and Persuasion*; Wood, Fels, and Krygier, *Rethinking the Power of Maps.*

3 EIA and Telapak, "Borderlines"; Hodgdon, "No Success like Failure" and "Frontier Country"; "Poor Accounting Hollows Out Timber Revenues," *Vientiane Times.*

4 Baird, "Quotas"; Stuart-Fox, "Political Culture of Corruption"; Walker, *Legend of the Golden Boat.*

5 See, e.g., Barney, "Power, Progress, and Impoverishment"; Ducourtieux, Laffort, and Sacklokham, "Land Policy"; Evrard and Goudineau, "Planned Resettlement"; Lestrelin, Castella, and Bourgoin, "Territorialising Sustainable Development"; and Vandergeest, "Land to Some Tillers." Important exceptions that this chapter builds on include Baird and Shoemaker, "Unsettling Experiences"; Chamberlain, "Participatory Poverty Assessment"; and LCG, "Existing Land Tenure and Forest Lands Study."

6 Vandergeest, "Land to Some Tillers," 48.

7 Baird and Shoemaker ("Unsettling Experiences," 873) are an important exception here in that they connect the rise of LFA to the Tropical Forestry Action Plan process launched by the World Bank in the late 1980s. This is true but hardly the whole story; while LFA did emerge in the wake of Laos's TFAP process, as this chapter shows, there is much more to it than the impetus of foreign donors and lenders.

8 Eilenberg, *At the Edges of States*; Kain and Baigent, *Cadastral Map in the Service of the State*; Mitchell, *Rule of Experts*, 80–119; Scott, *Seeing like a State*, 11–52.

9 Rigg, *Living with Transition*, 101; also see West, "We Are Here to Build Your Capacity." For examples of the "policy implementation gap," an

important variant on the undercapacity narrative in Laos, see Chamberlain, "Participatory Poverty Assessment"; MAF, "Forestry Strategy 2020."

10 Evans, *A Short History of Laos*; Goldman, *Imperial Nature*; Mongkhonvilay, "Agriculture and Environment under the New Economic Policy"; Rigg, *Living with Transition*; Stuart-Fox, *A History of Laos*; Than and Tan, *Laos' Dilemmas and Options*; UNDP, "National Human Development Report"; Walker, *Legend of the Golden Boat.*

11 Texas Tech University Vietnam Center and Archives, Vietnam Veterans Association Project—Laos; box 30, folder 2; accessed March 11, 2009. From an unattributed English-language document ("Present Situation in Laos, February 1987") found with missionary materials.

12 Texas Tech Archives (above): *Vientiane Pasason*, "Order on the Free Market" (August 6, 1987; translated by FBIS).

13 Texas Tech Archives (above): *Vientiane Pasason*, "The Posts and Telecommunications Company and the Bridge and Road Company Change to Businesses" (May 18, 1987; translated by FBIS); *Vientiane Pasason*, "State Publishing House Attains Business Autonomy" (August 24, 1987; translated by FBIS); Lao Radio, "Development Company Granted Autonomy" (December 1, 1987; translated by FBIS).

14 These were given as fourteen enterprises under the Ministry of Transport and Post, eight each under Industry and Handicraft and Agriculture and Forestry, six under Construction, and one each under Health and Interior. At the provincial level, the figures were seventy-one in Vientiane, fourteen in Champasak, thirteen in Savannakhet, and eight in Luang Prabang (Texas Tech Archives [above]: Lao Radio, "Report on Production Increases by Chairman of the State Planning Committee Sali Vongkhamsao," March 5, 1988; translated by FBIS).

15 Texas Tech Archives (above): Kaysone Phomvihane, "Renovation and Development," *Pravda* (1988; translated by FBIS).

16 Baird, "Quotas"; MAF, "Forestry Strategy 2020"; Walker, *Legend of the Golden Boat.*

17 Anonymous, "Aspects of Forestry Management"; Hodgdon, "No Success like Failure" and "Frontier Country"; MAF, "Forestry Strategy 2020."

18 Stuart-Fox, "Political Culture of Corruption," 61; Walker, *Legend of the Golden Boat*, 178.

19 Ireson and Ireson, "Ethnicity and Development," 930.

20 Texas Tech Archives (above): *Vientiane Mai*, "Before a Forest Is Cleared" (August 24, 1988; translated by FBIS under the title "Rationale for, Exceptions to Logging Export Ban Discussed").

21 Anonymous, "Aspects of Forestry Management," 7.

22 Texas Tech Archives (above): *Vientiane Pasason*, "Turn All Activities into the New Management Mechanism" (March 29, 1989; translated by FBIS).

23 MAF, "Forestry Strategy 2020," 4; the quoted language refers to Prime Ministerial Decree no. 117 of October 1989.

24 MAF, "Forestry Strategy 2020," 5–6.

25 The Ministry of Agriculture and Forestry's "Forestry Strategy 2020" acknowledged this cryptically: "The [1991] logging ban was well implemented, causing log production in 1992 to fall to half of that of the previous years, with much of the remaining production coming from old logs or trees felled in the previous years. In 1993, however, log production increased dramatically to levels in excess of those recorded before the ban in 1991" (p. 6).

26 In 1999 Nathan Badenoch, then with the World Resources Institute, reported that "8,000 villages out of a total of 20,000 have participated in land allocation, and the number is expected to reach 12,000 in 1999" (Badenoch, "Watershed Management and Upland Development," 6). Five years later, a German development assistance report cited government estimates that between 1995 and 2003, "district agricultural and forestry staff ha[d] conducted LUP/LA [Land-Use Planning/Land Allocation, the formal name in English for LFA] activities in a total of 5,400 villages in all provinces," and that this represented "approximately half" of the nation's total villages (GTZ, "Study on Land Allocation," vi, 1, 12). Not only do these figures differ substantially but they also come from very different baselines, with GTZ's total number of villages just over half of Badenoch's (10,800 versus 20,000). Research on "internal resettlement" in Laos by Chamberlain ("Participatory Poverty Assessment"), Evrard and Goudineau ("Planned Resettlement"), Lyttleton et al. ("Watermelons, Bars and Trucks"), Baird and Shoemaker ("Unsettling Experiences"), and others highlights the fact that LFA was frequently used in combination with involuntary village resettlement, often involving the consolidation of rural villages. This helps explain why, despite very different sets of numbers, there is widespread belief that LFA took place in roughly half the villages in the country.

27 See, e.g., Baird and Shoemaker, "Unsettling Experiences"; Chamberlain, "Participatory Poverty Assessment"; Ducourtieux, Laffort, and Sacklokham, "Land Policy"; Evrard and Goudineau, "Planned Resettlement"; Vandergeest, "Land to Some Tillers."

28 Barney, "Power, Progress, and Impoverishment"; Lestrelin, Castella, and Bourgoin, "Territorialising Sustainable Development"; Rigg, *Living with Transition*.

29 Prime Ministerial Decree no. 03, "Instruction on the expansion of land management and land and forest allocation" (June 25, 1996); the passages quoted here are based on two unsourced translations (author's data).

30 Decree no. 03, article 5.

31 Decree no. 03, article 6. On the plan to transition to a "rule-of-law" state, see Dwyer, Ingalls, and Baird, "The Security Exception"; MoJ, "Legal Sector Master Plan"; Wong, "In the Space between Words and Meaning."

32 Decree no. 03, article 6.

33 Resolutions of the First Nationwide Review Conference on Land Management and Land-Forest Allocation (July 19, 1996), unsourced translation found in the International Union of the Conservation of Nature (IUCN) library, Vientiane (author's data), p. 2.

34 Through the 1990s, ad hoc timber allocations for both high-level private individuals and specific holes in the state budget were a recurrent theme in the forestry sector (Anonymous, "Aspects of Forestry Management"); and well into the 2000s, the allocation of land and resources in return for "national revolutionary tasks" remained such a problem that a six-page decree "on Implementation of Privileges towards Persons with Outstanding Performance and Good Contribution to National Revolutionary Tasks" (Prime Ministerial Decree no. 343, November 2007) was deemed necessary (GTZ, "Study No. 12," 72–77).

35 Resolutions (above, n. 33), p. 3.

36 Resolutions (above, n. 33), pp. 4–5 (English corrected from original translation).

37 Resolutions (above, n. 33), pp. 5, 6.

38 Resolutions (above, n. 33), p. 5.

39 These were named as Luang Prabang, Vientiane, Savannakhet, and Champasak provinces.

40 Resolutions (above, n. 33), p. 5.

41 Resolutions (above, n. 33), p. 8.

42 Resolutions (above, n. 33), p. 6.

43 See, among others, Baird and Barney, "Political Ecology of Cross-Sectoral Cumulative Impacts"; Barney, "Power, Progress, and Impoverishment" and "Laos and the Making of a 'Relational' Resource Frontier"; Blake and Barney, "Structural Injustice, Slow Violence?"; Boer et al., *The Mekong*.

44 Statistics on LFA implementation, Vieng Phoukha, undated (author's data, collected 2007). For more detail on the cartographic genealogy described in this section, see Dwyer, "Building the Politics Machine," 323–26.

45 The following example is from a German land-sector report:

> In general there is poor registration and management of land allocation data at district level. Copies of [plot-scale land certificates] and land use maps are stored in district agricultural offices without any specific protection or classification. Hardly any of the data has been registered in computerized files. This entails a high risk that within

the next years all relevant data form the LUP/LA [LFA] activities will disappear. . . . [In the cases observed, LFA] documents and maps were in most cases either incomplete or lost altogether. There is no systematic record system in place at [district Agriculture and Forestry offices] to check that all relevant documents elaborated during LUP/LA [LFA] are kept according to a filing system. (GTZ, "Study on Land Allocation," 18, 39)

46 Interview in company's Luang Namtha office, December 2007.

47 The concept of purification in this sense of the term is from Latour, *We Have Never Been Modern*.

48 Also see, among others, Laungaramsri, "Frontier Capitalism"; Lu and Schönweger, "Great Expectations."

49 Fieldwork notes, June 2007.

50 See, among others, Baird, "Land, Rubber and People"; Dwyer, "Turning Land into Capital"; Kenney-Lazar, "Plantation Rubber."

51 Fieldwork notes, May 2007.

52 Fieldwork notes, June 2007.

53 Fieldwork notes, June 2007.

54 Schönweger et al., *Concessions and Leases*, 19.

55 Voladet, "Sustainable Development in the Plantation Industry," vii.

56 "Poor Accounting," *Vientiane Times*.

57 Order no. 15/PM, "On Strengthening Strictness of Timber Harvest Management and Inspection, Timber Transport and Business," Vientiane Municipality (unsourced unofficial translation; author's data).

58 Dwyer, "Land and Forest Tenure"; Hett et al., *Land Leases and Concessions*.

59 Shi, "Rubber Boom," 14.

60 Dwyer and Vongvisouk, "Long Land Grab"; anonymous pers. comm., July 2018.

61 Fieldwork notes, July 2018. The statistics in question were dated 2017.

62 This figure is based on the area estimate reported in chapter 1, combined with a conservative assumption of four hundred rubber trees per hectare (see ch. 1).

63 Fieldwork notes, July 2018. Such reticence is not limited to local governments. The update to the 2012 concession inventory discussed above notes the extensive slippage between the areas allocated to various land deals on paper and the areas actually developed in the field (Hett et al., *Land Leases and Concessions*, 24–25, 47–50). While the results vary widely by context (not surprisingly), it is telling that the maps in the published version show only the initial plan ("area granted") rather than what has actually occurred.

64 Shi, "Rubber Boom," 27 (original figures in renminbi).

65 Latour, *Science in Action*, 219–25; also see Turnbull, *Maps Are Territories*.
66 Harley, *The New Nature of Maps*; Pickles, *A History of Spaces*.
67 Rose, *Powers of Freedom*, 39.
68 Stuart-Fox, "Political Culture of Corruption," 66.
69 Stuart-Fox, "On the Writing of Lao History," 14.
70 Quoted in Hodgdon, "Frontier Country," 63.
71 Mitchell, *Rule of Experts*.
72 Brenner and Elden, "Henri Lefebvre on State, Space, Territory"; Lefebvre, *The Production of Space*.
73 Elden, "Missing the Point," 8.

CONCLUSION

1   Image available in Dwyer, "Building the Politics Machine," 310; original available at http://www.laofab.org/document/view/263.
2   Crispin, "Limits of Chinese Expansionism," quoted in introduction.
3   Fullbrook, "Beijing Pulls Laos into Its Orbit"; also see Gray, "China Farms the World"; McCartan, "China Rubber Demand Stretches Laos"; Schuettler, "Laos Faces Thorny Land Issues."
4   Hanssen, "Lao Land Concessions"; MacKinnon, "Resentment Rises." Over the years that followed, these estimates would include 3.5 million hectares "and growing" (Glofcheski, "Turning Land into Capital," 7), and five million hectares, over 20 percent of Laos's national territory (Wellmann, "Discussion Paper").
5   Glofcheski, "Turning Land into Capital," 7.
6   Hett et al., *Land Leases and Concessions*.
7   Hett et al., *Land Leases and Concessions*, xiv; cf. Schönweger et al., *Concessions and Leases*, 20. Also see GTZ, "Study No. 4."
8   Oya, "Methodological Reflections," 503.
9   Li, "After the Land Grab."
10 Lu and Schönweger, "Great Expectations."
11 Dwyer, Polack, and So, "'Better-Practice' Concessions?"
12 Edelman, "Messy Hectares," 497.
13 Stoler, *Imperial Debris*.
14 Ong, "Graduated Sovereignty"; also see introduction.
15 Hett et al., *Land Leases and Concessions*, 120–22.
16 Hett et al., *Land Leases and Concessions*, 122.
17 Cowen and Shenton, *Doctrines of Development*; also see Bebbington, "NGOs and Uneven Development"; Biddulph "Tenure Security Interventions"; Hart, *Disabling Globalization*; Polanyi, *Great Transformation*.
18 Ferguson, *Give a Man a Fish*.

19 These politics of uneven citizenship appear in the literature on the global land rush in, among other places, Colombia (Ballvé, "Everyday State Formation"), Myanmar (Woods, "Ceasefire Capitalism"), Cambodia (Biddulph, "Geographies of Evasion"; Work, "'There Was So Much'"), Ethiopia (Lavers, "'Land Grab' as Development Strategy?"; Posluschny-Treuner, "Understanding Foreign Large-Scale Agricultural Investments"), and Mozambique (Borras, Fig, and Suárez, "Politics of Agrofuels").

20 On the Beijing Consensus, see Ramo, "The Beijing Consensus"; Klinger and Muldavin, "New Geographies of Development." Also see Nyíri, "Enclaves of Improvement" and "Extraterritoriality."

21 De Angelis, "Separating the Doing and the Deed"; Harvey, New Imperialism; Marx, Capital, 873; Perelman, "Primitive Accumulation."

22 See, e.g., Eilenberg, At the Edges of States; Watts, "Resource Curse?"

23 Cotula et al., "Land Grab or Development Opportunity?"; NLMA and FER, "Summary Report"; NLMA and GTZ, "Findings."

24 Baird, "Quotas"; Stuart-Fox, "Political Culture of Corruption."

25 Abrams, "Notes on the Difficulty of Studying the State"; Foucault, "Governmentality."

26 Benda-Beckmann, "Forum Shopping"; Sikor and Lund, "Access and Property."

27 Dwyer, "Formalization Fix."

28 See, e.g., FAO et al., "Principles for Responsible Agricultural Investment."

29 De Soto, Mystery of Capital, 219; cf. Latour, Science in Action.

30 In addition to the material presented here, see Kain and Baigent, Cadastral Map in the Service of the State; Scott, Seeing like a State and Art of Not Being Governed.

31 E.g., Fischer et al., "Global Agro-Ecological Assessment," 80.

BIBLIOGRAPHY

Abrams, Philip. "Notes on the Difficulty of Studying the State." *Journal of Historical Sociology* 1, no. 1 (March 1988): 58–89. https://doi.org/10.1111/j .1467-6443.1988.tb00004.x.

Action Contra le Faim. "Summary of Reports on Resettlement." Vientiane: Action Contra le Faim, 2004.

ADB. "Greater Mekong Subregion Atlas of the Environment." Bangkok: ADB Core Environment Program, 2004. http://www.gms-eoc.org/resources /greater-mekong-subregion-atlas-of-the-environment.

———. "Proposed Grant Assistance (Financed by the Japan Fund for Poverty Reduction) to the Lao People's Democratic Republic for Sustainable Agroforestry Systems for Livelihood Enhancement of the Rural Poor. JFPR: 37650-02." Manila: Asian Development Bank, 2004. https://www.adb.org /sites/default/files/project-document/69544/jfpr-lao-37650-02.pdf.

———. "Project Data Sheet for 'Lao People's Democratic Republic: Sustainable Agroforestry Systems for Livelihood Enhancement of the Rural Poor.' Sovereign (Public) Project No. 37650-022." n.d. https://www.adb.org /projects/37650-022/main#project-pds.

———. "Report and Recommendation of the President to the Board of Directors on a Proposed Loan to the Lao PDR for the Greater Mekong Subregion: Northern Economic Corridor Project. RRP: Lao 34321." Manila: Asian Development Bank, 2002.

———. "Social Action Plan, Greater Mekong Subregion: Northern Economic Corridor Project in the Lao PDR." Manila: Asian Development Bank, 2002.

———. "Technical Assistance for the Chiang Rai-Kunming Road Improvement via Lao PDR Project. Report TAR: STU 30004." Manila: Asian Development Bank, February 1997. https://www.adb.org/sites/default/files/project -document/72434/30004-stu-tar.pdf.

Agnew, John A. *Geopolitics: Re-Visioning World Politics.* New York: Routledge, 1999.

Akram-Lodhi, Haroon, and Cristobal Kay, eds. *Peasants and Globalization: Political Economy, Rural Transformation and the Agrarian Question.* New York: Routledge, 2009.

Alden Wily, Liz. "Looking Back to See Forward: The Legal Niceties of Land Theft in Land Rushes." *Journal of Peasant Studies* 39, no. 3–4 (July 2012): 751–75. https://doi.org/10.1080/03066150.2012.674033.

Alton, C., D. Blum, and S. Sannanikone. "Para Rubber in Northern Laos: The Case of Luangnamtha." Vientiane: German Technical Cooperation (GTZ), 2005.

Anderson, Benedict R. O'G. *Imagined Communities: Reflections on the Origin and Spread of Nationalism.* New York: Verso, 1991.Anonymous. "Aspects of Forestry Management in the Lao PDR." Amsterdam: Tropical Rainforest Programme, 2000.

Anseeuw, Ward, Jann Lay, Peter Messerli, Markus Giger, and Michael Taylor. "Creating a Public Tool to Assess and Promote Transparency in Global Land Deals: The Experience of the Land Matrix." *Journal of Peasant Studies* 40, no. 3 (May 2013): 521–30. https://doi.org/10.1080/03066150.2013.803071.

Arezki, Rabah, Klaus Deininger, and Harris Selod. "What Drives the Global Land Rush?" IMF Working Paper WP/11/251. Washington, DC: International Monetary Fund, 2011.

"Authority Voices Concern over Land Concessions." *Vientiane Times*, May 8, 2007.

Badenoch, N. "Watershed Management and Upland Development in Lao PDR: A Synthesis of Policy Issues." Washington, DC: World Resources Institute, 1999.

Baines, Joseph. "Fuel, Feed and the Corporate Restructuring of the Food Regime." *Journal of Peasant Studies* 42, no. 2 (March 2015): 295–321. https://doi.org/10.1080/03066150.2014.970534.

Baird, Ian G. "Land, Rubber and People: Rapid Agrarian Changes and Responses in Southern Laos." *Journal of Lao Studies* 1, no. 1 (2010): 1–47.

———. "Quotas, Powers, Patronage and Illegal Rent-Seeking: The Political Economy of Logging and the Timber Trade in Southern Laos." Washington, DC: Forest Trends, 2010.

———. "Resistance and Contingent Contestations to Large-Scale Land Concessions in Southern Laos and Northeastern Cambodia." *Land* 6, no. 1 (February 2017): 16. https://doi.org/10.3390/land6010016.

———. *Rise of the Brao. Ethnic Minorities in Northeastern Cambodia during Vietnamese Occupation.* Madison: University of Wisconsin Press, 2020.

———. "Turning Land into Capital, Turning People into Labor: Primitive Accumulation and the Arrival of Large-Scale Economic Land Concessions in the Lao People's Democratic Republic." *New Proposals: Journal of Marxism and Interdisciplinary Inquiry* 5, no. 1 (2011): 10–26.

Baird, Ian G., and Keith Barney. "The Political Ecology of Cross-Sectoral Cumulative Impacts: Modern Landscapes, Large Hydropower Dams and Industrial Tree Plantations in Laos and Cambodia." *Journal of Peasant Studies* 44, no. 4 (July 2017): 769–95. https://doi.org/10.1080/03066150.2017.1289921.

Baird, Ian G., and Noah Quastel. "Rescaling and Reordering Nature–Society Relations: The Nam Theun 2 Hydropower Dam and Laos–Thailand Electricity Networks." *Annals of the Association of American Geographers* 105, no. 6 (November 2015): 1221–39. https://doi.org/10.1080/00045608.2015.1064511.

Baird, Ian G., and Bruce Shoemaker. "Unsettling Experiences: Internal Resettlement and International Aid Agencies in Laos." *Development and Change* 38, no. 5 (2007): 865–88.

Ballvé, Teo. "Everyday State Formation: Territory, Decentralization, and the Narco Landgrab in Colombia." *Environment and Planning D: Society and Space* 30, no. 4 (August 2012): 603–22. https://doi.org/10.1068/d4611.

Ban, Cornel, and Mark Blyth. "The BRICs and the Washington Consensus: An Introduction." *Review of International Political Economy* 20, no. 2 (April 2013): 241–55. https://doi.org/10.1080/09692290.2013.779374.

Barney, Keith. "China and the Production of Forestlands in Laos: A Political Ecology of Transnational Enclosure." In *Taking Southeast Asia to Market: Commodities, Nature, and People in the Neoliberal Age*, edited by Joseph Nevins and Nancy Lee Peluso, 91–107. Ithaca, NY: Cornell University Press, 2008.

———. "Ecological Knowledge and the Making of Plantation Concession Territories in Southern Laos." *Conservation and Society* 12, no. 4 (October 2014): 352. https://doi.org/10.4103/0972-4923.155579.

———. "Grounding Global Forest Economies: Resource Governance and Commodity Power in Rural Laos." PhD diss., York University, 2011.

———. "Laos and the Making of a 'Relational' Resource Frontier." *Geographical Journal* 175, no. 2 (June 2009): 146–59. https://doi.org/10.1111/j.1475-4959.2009.00323.x.

———. "Power, Progress and Impoverishment: Plantations, Hydropower, Ecological Change and Community Transformation in Hinboun District, Lao PDR." Toronto: York University Center for Asian Research, 2007.

Barney, Keith, and Kanya Souksakoun. "Credit Crunch: Chinese Infrastructure Lending and Lao Sovereign Debt." *Asia & the Pacific Policy Studies* 8, no. 1 (2021): 94–113. https://doi.org/10.1002/app5.318.

Beban, Alice. *Unwritten Rule: State-Making through Land Reform in Cambodia.* Ithaca, NY: Cornell University Press, 2021.

Bebbington, Anthony. "NGOs and Uneven Development: Geographies of Development Intervention." *Progress in Human Geography* 28, no. 6 (December 2004): 725–45. https://doi.org/10.1191/0309132504ph5160a.

Benda-Beckmann, Keebet von. "Forum Shopping and Shopping Forums: Dispute Processing in a Minangkabau Village in West Sumatra." *Journal of Legal Pluralism and Unofficial Law* 13, no. 19 (1981): 117–59.

Berry, Sara. "Property, Authority and Citizenship: Land Claims, Politics and the Dynamics of Social Division in West Africa." *Development and Change* 40, no. 1 (2009): 23–45. https://doi.org/10.1111/j.1467-7660.2009.01504.x.

Biddulph, Robin. "Geographies of Evasion: The Development Industry and Property Rights Interventions in Early 21st-Century Cambodia." PhD diss., University of Gothenburg, 2010.

———. "Tenure Security Interventions in Cambodia: Testing Bebbington's Approach to Development Geography." *Geografiska Annaler: Series B, Human Geography* 93, no. 3 (September 2011): 223–36. https://doi.org/10.1111/j.1468-0467.2011.00374.x.

Blaikie, Piers, and Harold Brookfield. *Land Degradation and Society.* London: Methuen, 1987.

Blake, David J. H., and Keith Barney. "Structural Injustice, Slow Violence? The Political Ecology of a 'Best Practice' Hydropower Dam in Lao PDR." *Journal of Contemporary Asia* 48, no. 5 (October 2018): 808–34. https://doi.org/10.1080/00472336.2018.1482560.

Blaufarb, Douglas S. *The Counterinsurgency Era: U.S. Doctrine and Performance, 1950 to the Present.* New York: Free Press, 1977.

———. "Organizing and Managing Unconventional War in Laos, 1962-1970. A Report Prepared for the Advanced Research Projects Agency (R-919-ARPA; Approved for Public Release 5 August 1997)." Santa Monica, CA: RAND Corporation, 1972.

Boer, Ben, Philip Hirsch, Fleur Johns, Ben Saul, and Natalia Scurrah. *The Mekong: A Socio-Legal Approach to River Basin Development.* New York: Routledge, 2016.

Bolikhamxai Provincial Authority. "Bolikhamxai Province Socio-Economic Profile, with Emphasis on District Development." Paksan: State Planning Committee and UNDP (Project Lao/98/G81), 2000.

Borger, Julian. "Rich Countries Launch Great Land Grab to Safeguard Food Supply." *Guardian*, November 22, 2008.

Borras, Saturnino M., David Fig, and Sofía Monsalve Suárez. "The Politics of Agrofuels and Mega-Land and Water Deals: Insights from the ProCana Case, Mozambique." *Review of African Political Economy* 38, no. 128 (June 2011): 215–34. https://doi.org/10.1080/03056244.2011.582758.

Borras, Saturnino M., Jennifer C. Franco, Sergio Gomez, Cristobal Kay, and Max Spoor. "Land Grabbing in Latin America and the Caribbean." *Journal of Peasant Studies* 39, no. 3–4 (2012): 845–72. https://doi.org/10.1080 /03066150.2012.679931.

Borras, Saturnino M., Jennifer C. Franco, S. Ryan Isakson, Les Levidow, and Pietje Vervest. "The Rise of Flex Crops and Commodities: Implications for Research." *Journal of Peasant Studies* 43, no. 1 (January 2016): 93–115. https://doi.org/10.1080/03066150.2015.1036417.

Branfman, Fred. *Voices from the Plain of Jars: Life under an Air War*. New York: Harper & Row, 1972.

Branford, Sue. "Food Crisis Leading to an Unsustainable Land Grab." *Guardian*, November 22, 2008.

Braun, Bruce. "Producing Vertical Territory: Geology and Governmentality in Late Victorian Canada." *Ecumene* 7, no. 1 (January 2000): 7–46. https://doi .org/10.1177/096746608000700102.

Brechin, Gray A. *Imperial San Francisco: Urban Power, Earthly Ruin*. Berkeley: University of California Press, 1999.

Brenner, Neil, and Stuart Elden. "Henri Lefebvre on State, Space, Territory." *International Political Sociology* 3, no. 4 (December 2009): 353–77. https://doi.org/10.1111/j.1749-5687.2009.00081.x.

Brocheux, Pierre, and Daniel Hémery. *Indochina: An Ambiguous Colonization, 1858–1954*. Berkeley: University of California Press, 2009.

Bryan, Joe, and Denis Wood. *Weaponizing Maps: Indigenous Peoples and Counterinsurgency in the Americas*. New York: Guildford, 2015.

Bryant, Raymond L. *The Political Ecology of Forestry in Burma, 1824–1994*. Honolulu: University of Hawai'i Press, 1997.

Burnod, Perrine, Mathilde Gingembre, and Rivo Andrianirina Ratsialonana. "Competition over Authority and Access: International Land Deals in Madagascar." *Development and Change* 44, no. 2 (March 2013): 357–79. https://doi.org/10.1111/dech.12015.

Chamberlain, Jim. "Participatory Poverty Assessment, Lao PDR." Manila: Asian Development Bank, 2001.

Chanthavong, Nitkham, Khamsing Xayleuxong, Somneuk Chitpanya, Nathan Badenoch, and Thongsavanh Keonakhone. "Rubber Institutions in Ban Hat

Nyao: Managing Trees, Markets and Producers." URDP Field Report no. 0903. Vientiane: Lao National Agricuture and Forestry Research Institute (NAFRI), 2009.

Clark, Dana, Jonathan Fox, and Kay Treakle. *Demanding Accountability: Civil-Society Claims and the World Bank Inspection Panel*. Lanham, MD: Rowman & Littlefield, 2004.

Clausewitz, Carl von. *On War—Volume 1*. Translated by Col. J. J. Graham. London: Kegan Paul, Trench, Trubner, 1918.

Cohen, Paul T. "The Post-Opium Scenario and Rubber in Northern Laos: Alternative Western and Chinese Models of Development." *International Journal of Drug Policy* 20, no. 5 (September 2009): 424–30. https://doi.org /10.1016/j.drugpo.2008.12.005.

Cohn, Bernard. "The Census, Social Structure and Objectification in South Asia." In *An Anthropologist among the Historians and Other Essays*, edited by Bernard Cohn, 224–54. Delhi: Oxford University Press, 1987.

Coll, Steve. *Ghost Wars: The Secret History of the CIA, Afghanistan, and Bin Laden, from the Soviet Invasion to September 10, 2001*. London: Penguin Books, 2005.

Conboy, Kenneth J., and James Morrison. *Shadow War: The CIA's Secret War in Laos*. Boulder, CO: Paladin, 1995.

Cosgrove, Denis E. *Social Formation and Symbolic Landscape*. London: Croom Helm, 1984.

Cotula, Lorenzo, Sonja Vermeulen, Rebecca Leonard, and James Keeley. "Land Grab or Development Opportunity? Agricultural Investment and International Land Deals in Africa." London: IIED, FAO, and IFAD, 2009.

Cowen, Michael, and Robert W. Shenton. *Doctrines of Development*. London: Routledge, 1996.

Creak, Simon. "Laos in 2013: International Controversies, Economic Concerns and the Post-Socialist Rhetoric of Rule." *Southeast Asian Affairs* (2014): 151–71.

Crispin, Shawn. "The Limits of Chinese Expansionism." *Asia Times Online*, December 23, 2010.

Cronon, William. *Nature's Metropolis: Chicago and the Great West*. New York: W. W. Norton, 1991.

Cullather, Nick. *The Hungry World: America's Cold War Battle against Poverty in Asia*. Cambridge, MA: Harvard University Press, 2013.

Daviau, Steeve. "Resettlement in Long District, Louang Namtha Province." Vientiane: Action Contra le Faim, 2001.

———. "Resettlement in Long District, Louang Namtha Province: Update 2003." Vientiane: Action Contra le Faim, 2003.

Davis, Mike. *Planet of Slums*. London: Verso, 2005.

De Angelis, Massimo. "Separating the Doing and the Deed: Capital and the Continuous Character of Enclosures." *Historical Materialism* 12, no. 2 (January 2004): 57–87. https://doi.org/10.1163/1569206041551609.

De Janvry, Alain. *The Agrarian Question and Reformism in Latin America*. Baltimore: Johns Hopkins University Press, 1981.

De Koninck, Rodolphe. "On the Geopolitics of Land Colonization: Order and Disorder on the Frontiers of Vietnam and Indonesia." *Moussons* 9–10 (2006): 33–59.

———. "The Peasantry as the Territorial Spearhead of the State in Southeast Asia: The Case of Vietnam." *Sojourn: Journal of Social Issues in Southeast Asia* 11, no. 2 (1996): 231–58.

———. "The Theory and Practice of Frontier Development: Vietnam's Contribution." *Asia Pacific Viewpoint* 41, no. 1 (2000): 7–21. https://doi.org/10.1111/1467-8373.00103.

De Schutter, Olivier. "How Not to Think of Land-Grabbing: Three Critiques of Large-Scale Investments in Farmland." *Journal of Peasant Studies* 38, no. 2 (2011), 249–279.

de Soto, Hernando. *The Mystery of Capital: Why Capitalism Triumphs in the West and Fails Everywhere Else*. New York: Basic Books, 2000.

Dean, Warren. *Brazil and the Struggle for Rubber: A Study in Environmental History*. Cambridge: Cambridge University Press, 1987.

Deitchman, Seymour J. *The Best-Laid Schemes: A Tale of Social Research and Bureaucracy*. Cambridge, MA: MIT Press, 1976.

Dheeraprasart, V. *After the Logging Ban: The Politics of Forest Management in Thailand*. Bangkok: Foundation for Ecological Recovery, 2005.

Diana, Antonella. "Roses and Rifles: Experiments of Governing on the China-Laos Frontier." PhD diss., Australian National University, 2009.

Diepart, Jean-Christophe, and Thol Sem. "Fragmented Territories: Incomplete Enclosures and Agrarian Change on the Agricultural Frontier of Samlaut District, North-West Cambodia." *Journal of Agrarian Change* 18, no. 1 (2018): 156–77. http://onlinelibrary.wiley.com/doi/10.1111/joac.12155/full.

Diouf, J. "The Food Crisis and the Wrong Solutions." *Kommunikation Global/Global Perspectives: The Bumpy Road to Accra*, August 2008, p. 8.

"Documents on Sino-Lao Cooperation Signed." *People's Daily*, November 12, 2000.

Dommen, Arthur J. *Conflict in Laos: The Politics of Neutralization*. New York: Praeger, 1964.

Dove, Michael R. "Living Rubber, Dead Land, and Persisting Systems in Borneo: Indigenous Representation of Sustainability." *Bijdragen Tot de Taal-, Land- En Volkenkunde* 154, no. 1 (1998): 20–54.

Ducourtieux, Olivier, Jean-Richard Laffort, and Silinthone Sacklokham. "Land Policy and Farming Practices in Laos." *Development and Change* 36, no. 3 (May 2005): 499–526. https://doi.org/10.1111/j.0012-155X.2005 .00421.x.

Dulles, John Foster. *War or Peace.* London: Harrap, 1950.

Dwyer, Michael B. "Building the Politics Machine: Tools for 'Resolving' the Global Land Grab." *Development and Change* 44, no. 2 (March 2013): 309–33. https://doi.org/10.1111/dech.12014.

———. "The Formalization Fix? Land Titling, Land Concessions and the Politics of Spatial Transparency in Cambodia." *Journal of Peasant Studies* 42, no. 5 (September 2015): 903–28. https://doi.org/10.1080/03066150.2014 .994510.

———. "Land and Forest Tenure in Laos: Baseline Overview 2016 with Options for Community Participation in Forest Management." UN-REDD Programme (FAO, UNDP, and UNEP), 2017.

———. "Micro-Geopolitics: Capitalising Security in Laos's Golden Quadrangle." *Geopolitics* 19, no. 2 (April 2014): 377–405. https://doi.org/10.1080 /14650045.2013.780033.

———. "'They Will Not Automatically Benefit': The Politics of Infrastructure Development in Laos's Northern Economic Corridor." *Political Geography* 78 (April 2020): 102–118. https://doi.org/10.1016/j.polgeo.2019.102118.

———. "Trying to Follow the Money: Possibilities and Limits of Investor Transparency in Southeast Asia's Rush for 'Available' Land." CIFOR Working Paper 177. Bogor, Indonesia: Center for International Forestry Research (CIFOR), 2015.

———. "Turning Land into Capital: A Review of Recent Research on Land Concessions for Investment in Lao PDR." Vientiane: Land Issues Working Group, 2007.

———. "Upland Geopolitics: Finding Zomia in Northern Laos c. 1875." *Journal of Lao Studies*, Special Issue 3 (2016): 37–57.

Dwyer, Michael B., Micah L. Ingalls, and Ian G. Baird. "The Security Exception: Development and Militarization in Laos's Protected Areas." *Geoforum* 69 (2016): 207–17.

Dwyer, Michael B., Emily Polack, and Sokbunthoeun So. "'Better-Practice' Concessions? Some Lessons from Cambodia's Leopard Skin Landscape." *International Development Policy/ Revue Internationale de Politique de Développement* 6 (2015). https://poldev.revues.org/2046.

Dwyer, Michael, and Thoumthone Vongvisouk. "The Long Land Grab: Market-Assisted Enclosure on the China-Lao Rubber Frontier." *Territory, Politics, Governance* 7, no. 1 (January 2019): 96–114. https://doi.org/10.1080 /21622671.2017.1371635.

"Economic Map of Indochina." Hanoi: Geographical Service of Indochina, 1937. https://gallica.bnf.fr/ark:/12148/btv1b53121256z.

Economist. "Outsourcing's Third Wave." *The Economist*, May 21, 2009.

Edelman, Marc. "Messy Hectares: Questions about the Epistemology of Land Grabbing Data." *Journal of Peasant Studies* 40, no. 3 (May 2013): 485–501. https://doi.org/10.1080/03066150.2013.801340.

Eilenberg, Michael. *At the Edges of States: Dynamics of State Formation in the Indonesian Borderlands*. Leiden: KITLV, 2012.

Elden, Stuart. "Governmentality." In *Dictionary of Human Geography*, 5th ed., edited by Derek Gregory, Ron Johnson, Geraldine Pratt, Michael J. Watts, and Sarah Wattmore, 000–000. Chichester, West Sussex, UK: Wiley-Blackwell, 2009.

———. "Missing the Point: Globalization, Deterritorialization and the Space of the World." *Transactions of the Institute of British Geographers* 30, no. 1 (March 2005): 8–19. https://doi.org/10.1111/j.1475-5661.2005.00148.x.

Elliott, Duong Van Mai. *RAND in Southeast Asia: A History of the Vietnam War Era*. Santa Monica, CA: RAND Corporation, 2010. http://public.eblib .com/choice/publicfullrecord.aspx?p=3031586.

Environmental Investigations Agency (EIA) and Telapak. "Borderlines: Vietnam's Booming Furniture Industry and Timber Smuggling in the Mekong Region." London: EIA and Telapak, 2008.

Escobar, Arturo. *Encountering Development: The Making and Unmaking of the Third World*. Princeton, NJ: Princeton University Press, 1995.

Evans, Grant, "Introduction: What Is Lao Culture and Society?" In *Laos: Culture and Society*, edited by Grant Evans, 1–34. Chiang Mai, Thailand: Silkworm Books, 1999.

———. *The Politics of Ritual and Remembrance: Laos since 1975*. Honolulu: University of Hawai'i Press, 1998.

———. *A Short History of Laos: The Land in Between*. Crows Nest, Australia: Allen & Unwin, 2002.

Evrard, Olivier, and Yves Goudineau. "Planned Resettlement, Unexpected Migrations and Cultural Trauma in Laos." *Development and Change* 35, no. 5 (November 2004): 937–62. https://doi.org/10.1111/j.1467-7660.2004 .00387.x.

Fairbairn, Madeleine. *Fields of Gold: Financing the Global Land Rush*. Ithaca, NY: Cornell University Press, 2020.

Fairhead, James, and Melissa Leach. "False Forest History, Complicit Social Analysis: Rethinking Some West African Environmental Narratives." *World Development* 23, no. 6 (June 1995): 1023–35. https://doi.org/10.1016/0305-750X(95)00026-9.

Fall, Bernard B. *Anatomy of a Crisis: The Laotian Crisis of 1960-1961.* Garden City, NY: Doubleday, 1969.

———. "Introduction: A Portrait of the 'Centurion.'" In Roger Trinquier, *Modern Warfare: A French View of Counterinsurgency,* vii–xviii. New York: Praeger, 1964.

FAO, IFAD, UNCTAD, and World Bank. "Principles for Responsible Agricultural Investment That Respects Rights, Livelihoods and Resources (Extended Version): A Discussion Note to Contribute to an Ongoing Global Dialogue." Rome: FAO, IFAD, UNCTAD, and the World Bank Group, January 25, 2010.

Ferguson, James. *The Anti-Politics Machine: "Development," Depoliticization, and Bureaucratic Power in Lesotho.* Minneapolis: University of Minnesota Press, 1994.

———. *Give a Man a Fish: Reflections on the New Politics of Distribution.* Durham, NC: Duke University Press, 2015.

Fischer, Gunther, Harrij van Velthuizen, Mahendra Shah, and Freddy Nachtergaele. "Global Agro-Ecological Assessment for Agriculture in the 21st Century: Methodology and Results." Laxenburg, Austria: International Institute for Applied Systems Analysis and UN Food and Agriculture Organization, 2002.

Flyvbjerg, Bent, Nils Bruzelius, and Werner Rothengatter. *Megaprojects and Risk: An Anatomy of Ambition.* Cambridge: Cambridge University Press, 2003.

Flyvbjerg, Bent, Massimo Garbuio, and Dan Lovallo. "Delusion and Deception in Large Infrastructure Projects: Two Models for Explaining and Preventing Executive Disaster." *California Management Review* 51, no. 2 (2009): 170–94.

Flyvbjerg, Bent, and Cass R. Sunstein. "The Principle of the Malevolent Hiding Hand; or, the Planning Fallacy Writ Large." *Social Research: An International Quarterly* 83, no. 4 (2016): 979–1004.

Foppes, Joost. "Knowledge Capitalization: Agriculture and Forestry Development at 'Kum Ban' Village Cluster Level in Lao PDR." Vientiane: Lao Extension for Agriculture Project (LEAP), 2008.

Foucault, Michel. *Discipline and Punish: The Birth of the Prison.* New York: Vintage, 1995.

———. "Governmentality." In *The Foucault Effect: Studies in Governmentality*, edited by Graham Burchell, Colin Gordon, and Peter Miller, 87–104. Chicago: University of Chicago Press, 1991.

———. *Security, Territory, Population: Lectures at the Collège de France, 1977–1978*. New York: Picador, 2009.

———. *"Society Must Be Defended": Lectures at the Collège de France 1975–76*. London: Penguin Books, 2004.

Franco, Jennifer, and Saturnino M. Borras. "Grey Areas in Green Grabbing: Subtle and Indirect Interconnections between Climate Change Politics and Land Grabs and Their Implications for Research." *Land Use Policy* 84 (2019):192–99.

Friis, Cecilie, and Jonas Østergaard Nielsen. "Small-Scale Land Acquisitions, Large-Scale Implications: Exploring the Case of Chinese Banana Investments in Northern Laos." *Land Use Policy* 57 (November 2016): 117–29. https://doi.org/10.1016/j.landusepol.2016.05.028.

Fullbrook, David. "Beijing Pulls Laos into Its Orbit." *Asia Times Online*, October 25, 2006.

Garnier, Francis. *Travels in Cambodia and Part of Laos: The Mekong Exploration Commission Report (1866–1868)*. Vol. 1. Edited by Walter E. J. Tips. Bangkok: White Lotus, 1996.

Gilkey, Robert. "Laos: Politics, Elections and Foreign Aid." *Far Eastern Survey* 27 (1958): 89–94.

Glassman, Jim. *Bounding the Mekong: The Asian Development Bank, China, and Thailand*. Honolulu: University of Hawai'i Press, 2010.

———. "Primitive Accumulation, Accumulation by Dispossession, Accumulation by 'Extra-Economic' Means." *Progress in Human Geography* 30, no. 5 (October 2006): 608–25. https://doi.org/10.1177/03091325060 70172.

Glofcheski, Robert. "Turning Land into Capital: Maximizing the Benefits for Lao PDR, Some International Perspectives." Paper presented at the Land Conference, National Land Management Authority, Vientiane, October 5, 2010.

Godley, G. McMurtrie, and Jinny St. Goar. "The Chinese Road in Northwest Laos 1961–73: An American Perspective." In *Laos: Beyond the Revolution*, edited by Joseph Jermiah Zasloff and Leonard Unger, 285–314. Houndmills, Basingstoke, UK: Macmillan, 1991.

Goldman, Michael. *Imperial Nature: The World Bank and Struggles for Justice in the Age of Globalization*. Yale Agrarian Studies. New Haven, CT: Yale University Press, 2005.

González, Roberto J. "'Human Terrain.'" *Anthropology Today* 24, no. 1 (2008): 21–26. https://doi.org/10.1111/j.1467-8322.2008.00561.x.

Goppers, Karlis, and Sven Bo Bergström. "Elephants Don't Rust: An Evaluation of SIDA-Supported Forestry Development and Forestry Industry in Laos." Stockholm: Swedish International Development Authority, 1986.

Gordillo, Gastón. "Terrain as Insurgent Weapon: An Affective Geometry of Warfare in the Mountains of Afghanistan." *Political Geography* 64 (May 2018): 53–62. https://doi.org/10.1016/j.polgeo.2018.03.001.

Goudineau, Yves, and Olivier Evrard. "Resettlement and Social Characteristics of New Villages." Vol 1. "Main Report." Vientiane: UNESCO and UNDP, 1997.

———. "Resettlement and Social Characteristics of New Villages." Vol 2. "Provincial Reports." Vientiane: UNESCO and UNDP, 1997.

"Govt Suspends Land Concessions." *Vientiane Times*, May 9, 2007.

GRAIN. "Seized! The 2008 Land Grab for Food and Financial Security." GRAIN, October 24, 2008. https://grain.org/article/entries/93-seized-the-2008-landgrab-for-food-and-financial-security.

———. "Seized! The 2008 Land Grab for Food and Financial Security, Annex." GRAIN, 2008. https://grain.org/media/BAhbBlsHOgZmSSI3MjAxMS8wN i8zMC8xNl8wMV8zNF8oMTNfbGFuZGdyYWJfMjAwOF9lbl9hhbm-5leC5wZGYGOgZFVA/landgrab-2008-en-annex.pdf.

Grandia, Liza. *Enclosed: Conservation, Cattle, and Commerce among the Q'eqchi' Maya Lowlanders.* Seattle: University of Washington Press, 2012.

Gray, Denis. "China Farms the World to Feed a Ravenous Economy." Associated Press, May 4, 2008.

Greenstein, Fred I., and Richard H. Immerman. "Letter to the Editor." *Journal of American History* 80, no. 1 (1993): 362–63. https://doi.org/10.2307/2080047.

GTZ. "Study No. 4: State Land Leases and Concessions in Lao PDR. Land Policy Study under the Second Lao Land Titling Project (LLTP II)." Vientiane: German Technical Cooperation (GTZ), 2006.

———. "Study No. 7: Land Consolidation in Lao PDR. Land Policy Study under the Second Lao Land Titling Project (LLTP II)." Vientiane: German Technical Cooperation (GTZ), 2007.

———. "Study No. 9: Land Conflict in Lao PDR. Land Policy Study under the Second Lao Land Titling Project (LLTP II)." Vientiane: German Technical Cooperation (GTZ), 2007.

———. "Study No. 11: Expropriation and Compensation in Lao PDR. Land Policy Study under the Second Lao Land Titling Project (LLTP II)." Vientiane: German Technical Cooperation (GTZ), 2007.

———. "Study No. 12: State Land Inventory and Management. Land Policy Study under the Second Lao Land Titling Project (LLTP II)." Vientiane: German Technical Cooperation (GTZ), 2008.

———. "Study on Land Allocation to Individual Households in Rural Areas of Lao PDR." Vientiane: German Technical Cooperation (GTZ), 2004.

Guerrero, Dorothy-Grace, and Firoze Manji, eds. *China's New Role in Africa and the South: A Search for a New Perspective.* Oxford: Fahamu, 2008.

Gunn, Geoffrey C. *Rebellion in Laos: Peasants and Politics in a Colonial Backwater.* Bangkok: White Lotus, 1990.

———. "Resistance Coalitions in Laos." *Asian Survey* 23, no. 3 (1983): 316–40. https://doi.org/10.2307/2644276.

Guo, Xiaolin. "Towards Resolution: China in the Myanmar Issue." Central Asia-Caucasus Institute and Silk Road Studies Program, Johns Hopkins University-SAIS and Uppsala University, 2007.

Gupta, Akhil, and James Ferguson. "Beyond 'Culture': Space, Identity, and the Politics of Difference." *Cultural Anthropology* 7, no. 1 (1992): 6–23.

Halpern, Joel Martin. *Aspects of Village Life and Culture Change in Laos.* New York: Council on Economic and Cultural Affairs, 1958.

———. "Economic Development and American Aid in Laos." *Practical Anthropology* 6, no. 4 (1959): 151–71.

Hanks, Lucien M., and Jane Richardson Hanks. "Ethnographic Notes on Northern Thailand." Ithaca, NY: Southeast Asia Program, Cornell University, 1965.

Hannah, Matthew G. *Governmentality and the Mastery of Territory in Nineteenth-Century America.* Cambridge Studies in Historical Geography 32. Cambridge: Cambridge University Press, 2000.

Hanssen, Cor. "Lao Land Concessions: Development for the People?" Paper presented at the International Conference on Poverty Reduction and Forests, Bangkok, September 3–7, 2007.

Hansson, Tom. "Swedish Correspondent Views Problems with Aid Project." *Svenska Dagbladet,* May 2, 1987.

Hardy, Andrew. *Red Hills: Migrants and the State in the Highlands of Vietnam.* Honolulu: University of Hawai'i Press, 2003.

Harley, J. B. *The New Nature of Maps: Essays in the History of Cartography.* Edited by Paul Laxton. Baltimore: Johns Hopkins University Press, 2001.

Hart, Gillian Patricia. *Disabling Globalization: Places of Power in Post-Apartheid South Africa.* Pietermaritzburg, South Africa: University of Natal Press, 2002.

Harvey, David. *The New Imperialism.* New York: Oxford University Press, 2003.

———. "The Spatial Fix: Hegel, Von Thunen, and Marx." *Antipode* 13, no. 3 (1981): 1–12. https://doi.org/10.1111/j.1467-8330.1981.tb00312.x.

Harvey, Penelope, and Hannah Knox. *Roads: An Anthropology of Infrastructure and Expertise.* Ithaca, NY: Cornell University Press, 2015.

Hecht, Susanna, and Alexander Cockburn. *The Fate of the Forest: Developers, Destroyers, and Defenders of the Amazon.* Updated ed. Chicago: University of Chicago Press, 2011.

Heilbroner, Robert L. *The Worldly Philosophers: The Lives, Times, and Ideas of the Great Economic Thinkers.* Rev. 7th ed. New York: Simon & Schuster, 1999.

Hett, Cornelia, Vong Nanhthavong, Savanh Hanephom, Anongsone Phommachanh, Boungnong Sidavong, Ketkeo Phouangphet, Juliet Lu et al. *Land Leases and Concessions in the Lao PDR: A Characterization of Investments in Land and Their Impacts.* Bern: Bern Open Publishing, 2020. https://boris.unibe.ch/133115.

High, Holly. *Fields of Desire: Poverty and Policy in Laos.* Singapore: NUS Press, 2014.

———. "'Join Together, Work Together, for the Common Good—Solidarity': Village Formation Processes in the Rural South of Laos." *Sojourn: Journal of Social Issues in Southeast Asia* 21, no. 1 (2006): 22–45.

———. *Projectland: Life in a Lao Socialist Model Village.* Honolulu: University of Hawai'i Press, 2021.

Himberg, Harvey. "Comparative Review of Multilateral Development Bank Safeguard Systems: Main Report and Annexes." Consultant Report to the World Bank, 2015. https://consultations.worldbank.org/Data/hub/files /consultationtemplate/ review-and-update-world-bank-safeguard-policies /en/related/mdb_sa feguard_comparison_main_report_and_annexes_may _2015.pdf.

Hirsch, Philip. "Globalisation, Regionalisation and Local Voices: The Asian Development Bank and Rescaled Politics of Environment in the Mekong Region." *Singapore Journal of Tropical Geography* 22, no. 3 (2001): 237–51. https://doi.org/10.1111/1467-9493.00108.

Hirsch, Philip, Kevin Woods, Natalia Scurrah, and Michael B. Dwyer, eds. *Turning Land into Capital: Development and Dispossession in the Mekong Region.* Seattle: University of Washington Press, 2022.

Hodgdon, B. "Frontier Country." *Kyoto Journal* 69 (2008): 58–65.

———. "No Success like Failure: Policy versus Reality in the Lao Forestry Sector." *Watershed* 12, no. 1 (July 2006–February 2007): 37–46.

Holt-Giménez, Eric, Raj Patel, and Annie Shattuck. *Food Rebellions!: Crisis and the Hunger for Justice.* Cape Town; Oakland, CA; Boston: Pambazuka; Food First Books; Grassroots International, 2009.

Hunt, Glenn. "Plantations, Deforestation and Forest Sector Aid Interventions: An Analysis of Japanese Plantations as Foreign Direct Investment in Central Lao PDR." MA thesis, Macquarie University, 2011.

Huxley, Margo. "Geographies of Governmentality." In *Space, Knowledge and Power: Foucault and Geography*, edited by Jeremy Crampton and Stuart Elden, 185–204. London: Ashgate, 2007.

IMF. "Lao People's Democratic Republic: Staff Report for the 2016 Article IV Consultation: Debt Sustainability Analysis." International Monetary Fund, 2017. https://www.imf.org/external/pubs/ft/dsa/pdf/2017/dsacr1753.pdf.

Innes-Brown, M., and M. J. Valencia. "Thailand's Resource Diplomacy in Indochina and Myanmar." *Contemporary Southeast Asia* 14 (1993): 332–51.

Ireson, Carol J., and W. Randall Ireson. "Ethnicity and Development in Laos." *Asian Survey* 31, no. 10 (1991): 929–37.

Ivarsson, Søren. *Creating Laos: The Making of a Lao Space between Indochina and Siam, 1860–1945*. Copenhagen: NIAS, 2008.

Izikowitz, Karl Gustav. *Over the Misty Mountain: A Journey from Tonkin to the Lamet in Laos*. Bangkok: White Lotus, 2004. https://catalog.hathitrust.org/Record/005674226.

Jerndal, Randi, and Jonathan Rigg. "From Buffer State to Crossroads State." In *Laos: Culture and Society*, edited by Grant Evans, 35–60. Chiang Mai, Thailand: Silkworm Books, 1999.

Jie, Liu. "China: Facilitating Cooperation and Striving to Build a Brand New Harmonious Drugless Golden Triangle." In *Collected Papers from a Regional Seminar* [held in Chiang Mai, Thailand, December 15–17, 2008] *on Sustaining Opium Reduction in Southeast Asia: Sharing Experiences on Alternative Development and Beyond*, 25–34. United Nations Office on Drugs and Crime, 2008.

Johnson, Wray R. *Vietnam and American Doctrine for Small Wars*. Chiang Mai, Thailand: Silkworm Books, 2000.

Jonsson, Hjorleifur. "States Lie, and Stories Are Tools: Following Up on Zomia." *Bijdragen Tot de Taal-, Land- En Volkenkunde* 167, no. 1 (2011): 92–95.

———. "War's Ontogeny: Militias and Ethnic Boundaries in Laos and Exile." *Southeast Asian Studies* 47, no. 2 (2009): 125–49.

Kain, Roger J. P., and Elizabeth Baigent. *The Cadastral Map in the Service of the State: History of Property Mapping*. Chicago: University of Chicago Press, 1992.

Kautsky, Karl. *The Agrarian Question*. Vol. 1. London: Zwan, 1988.

Kenney-Lazar, Miles. "Governing Dispossession: Relational Land Grabbing in Laos." *Annals of the American Association of Geographers* 108, no. 3 (May 2018): 679–94. https://doi.org/10.1080/24694452.2017.1373627.

———. "Plantation Rubber, Land Grabbing and Social-Property Transformation in Southern Laos." *Journal of Peasant Studies* 39, no. 3–4 (July 2012): 1017–37. https://doi.org/10.1080/03066150.2012.674942.

———. "Rubber Production in Northern Laos: Geographies of Growth and Contractual Diversity." Field Report, 2009.

Kenney-Lazar, Miles, Diana Suhardiman, and Michael B. Dwyer. "State Spaces of Resistance: Industrial Tree Plantations and the Struggle for Land in Laos." *Antipode* 50, no. 5 (November 2018): 1290–1310. https://doi.org/10.1111/anti.12391.

Kissinger, Henry. "Why America Failed in Afghanistan." *The Economist*, August 25, 2021.

Klare, Michael T. *War without End: American Planning for the Next Vietnams.* New York: Alfred A. Knopf, 1972.

Klinger, Julie Michelle, and Joshua S. S. Muldavin. "New Geographies of Development: Grounding China's Global Integration." *Territory, Politics, Governance* 7, no. 1 (January 2019): 1–21. https://doi.org/10.1080/21622671.2018.1559757.

Kramer, Tom, and Kevin Woods. *Financing Dispossession: China's Opium Substitution Programme in Northern Burma.* Drugs and Democracy Program. Amsterdam: Transnational Institute, 2012.

Kunstadter, Peter, E. C. Chapman, and Sanga Sabhasri, eds. *Farmers in the Forest: Economic Development and Marginal Agriculture in Northern Thailand.* Honolulu: University of Hawai'i Press, 1978.

Kurlantzick, Joshua. *A Great Place to Have a War: America in Laos and the Birth of a Military CIA.* New York: Simon & Schuster, 2016.

Lacey, Marc. "Across Globe, Empty Bellies Bring Rising Anger." *New York Times*, April 18, 2008.

Larsson, Tomas. "Intertextual Relations: The Geopolitics of Land Rights in Thailand." *Political Geography* 26, no. 7 (September 2007): 775–803. https://doi.org/10.1016/j.polgeo.2007.05.003.

Latour, Bruno. *Science in Action: How to Follow Scientists and Engineers through Society.* Cambridge, MA: Harvard University Press, 1987.

———. *We Have Never Been Modern.* Cambridge, MA: Harvard University Press, 1993.

Laungaramsri, Pinkaew. "Frontier Capitalism and the Expansion of Rubber Plantations in Southern Laos." *Journal of Southeast Asian Studies* 43, no. 3 (2012): 463–77.

Lavers, Tom. "'Land Grab' as Development Strategy? The Political Economy of Agricultural Investment in Ethiopia." *Journal of Peasant Studies* 39, no. 1 (January 2012): 105–32. https://doi.org/10.1080/03066150.2011.652091.

LCG (Lao Consulting Group). "Existing Land Tenure and Forest Lands Study: Land Titling (Project IDA Loan CR 2832 LA)." Vientiane: Lao Ministry of Finance, Department of Lands, 2002.

Lee, Ching Kwan. "The Spectre of Global China." *New Left Review* 2, no. 89 (2014): 28–65.

Lefebvre, Henri. *The Production of Space*. Oxford, UK: Blackwell, 1991.

Lestrelin, Guillaume, Jean-Christophe Castella, and Jeremy Bourgoin. "Territorialising Sustainable Development: The Politics of Land-Use Planning in Laos." *Journal of Contemporary Asia* 42, no. 4 (2012): 581–602.

Li, Tania Murray. "After the Land Grab: Infrastructural Violence and the 'Mafia System' in Indonesia's Oil Palm Plantation Zones." *Geoforum* 96 (November 2018): 328–37. https://doi.org/10.1016/j.geoforum.2017.10.012.

———. "Centering Labor in the Land Grab Debate." *Journal of Peasant Studies* 38, no. 2 (March 2011): 281–98. https://doi.org/10.1080/03066150.2011.559009.

———. *Land's End: Capitalist Relations on an Indigenous Frontier*. Durham, NC: Duke University Press, 2014.

———. "Marginality, Power and Production: Analysing Upland Transformations." In *Transforming the Indonesian Uplands: Marginality, Power and Production*, edited by Tania Murray Li, 1–46. Amsterdam: Harwood Academic, 1999.

———. "To Make Live or Let Die? Rural Dispossession and the Protection of Surplus Populations." *Antipode* 41, no. s1 (2010): 66–93. https://doi.org/10.1111/j.1467-8330.2009.00717.x.

———. "What Is Land? Assembling a Resource for Global Investment." *Transactions of the Institute of British Geographers* 39, no. 4 (2014): 589–602. https://doi.org/10.1111/tran.12065.

———. *The Will to Improve: Governmentality, Development, and the Practice of Politics*. Durham, NC: Duke University Press, 2007.

Lintner, Bertil. *Burma in Revolt: Opium and Insurgency since 1948*. Boulder, CO: Westview; Bangkok, Thailand: White Lotus, 1994.

Liu, Weidong, and Michael Dunford. "Inclusive Globalization: Unpacking China's Belt and Road Initiative." *Area Development and Policy* 1, no. 3 (November 2016): 323–40. https://doi.org/10.1080/23792949.2016.1232598.

Lu, Juliet. "Rubber's Reach: Chinese Land Investments and State Territorialization in the Sino-Lao Borderlands." PhD diss., University of California, Berkeley, 2020. (ProQuest ID: Lu_berkeley_0028E_19993. Merritt ID: ark:/13030/m5bs486x.)

———. "Tapping into Rubber: China's Opium Replacement Program and Rubber Production in Laos." *Journal of Peasant Studies* 44, no. 4 (June 2017): 726–47. https://doi.org/10.1080/03066150.2017.1314268.

Lu, Juliet, and Oliver Schönweger. "Great Expectations: Chinese Investment in Laos and the Myth of Empty Land." *Territory, Politics, Governance* 7, no. 1 (January 2019): 61–78. https://doi.org/10.1080/21622671.2017.1360195.

Lund, Christian. *Nine-Tenths of the Law: Enduring Dispossession in Indonesia.* New Haven, CT: Yale University Press, 2021.

———. "Property and Citizenship: Conceptually Connecting Land Rights and Belonging in Africa." *Africa Spectrum* 46, no. 3 (March 2012): 71–75.

Lyttleton, Chris. "Build It and They Will Come: Lessons from the Northern Economic Corridor: Mitigating HIV and Other Diseases." Manila: Asian Development Bank, 2009.

———. "Relative Pleasures: Drugs, Development and Modern Dependencies in Asia's Golden Triangle." *Development and Change* 35, no. 5 (November 2004): 909–35. https://doi.org/10.1111/j.1467-7660.2004.00386.x.

Lyttleton, Chris, Houmphanh Rattanavong, Paul Cohen, Bouakham Thongkhamhane, and Souriyanh Sisaengrat. "Watermelons, Bars and Trucks: Dangerous Intersections in Northwest Lao PDR: An Ethnographic Study of Social Change and Health Vulnerability along the Road through Muang Sing and Muang Long." Vientiane and Sydney: Lao Institute for Cultural Research of Laos and Macquarie University, 2004.

MacKinnon, Ian. "The Resentment Rises as Villagers Are Stripped of Holdings and Livelihood." *Guardian*, November 22, 2008.

MAF. "Forestry Strategy 2020 for the Lao People's Democratic Republic." Vientiane: Lao Ministry of Agriculture and Forestry, 2005.

Mahanty, Sango, Wolfram Dressler, Sarah Milne, and Colin Filer. "Unravelling Property Relations around Forest Carbon." *Singapore Journal of Tropical Geography* 34, no. 2 (2013): 188–205. https://doi.org/10.1111/sjtg.12024.

Mamdani, Mahmood. *Good Muslim, Bad Muslim: America, the Cold War and the Roots of Terror.* New York: Doubleday, 2005.

Manivong, Vongpaphane, and Robert A. Cramb. "Economics of Smallholder Rubber Expansion in Northern Laos." *Agroforestry Systems* 74, no. 2 (May 2008): 113. https://doi.org/10.1007/s10457-008-9136-3.

Mann, Susan. *Agrarian Capitalism in Theory and Practice.* Chapel Hill: University of North Carolina Press, 1990.

Marx, Karl. *Capital: A Critique of Political Economy.* Vol. 1. London: Pelican Books, 1976.

Massey, Doreen. *Space, Place and Gender*. Minneapolis: University of Minnesota Press, 1994.

Mazzetti, Mark. *The Way of the Knife: The CIA, a Secret Army, and a War at the Ends of the Earth*. New York: Penguin Books, 2014.

Mbembe, Achille. *On the Postcolony*. Studies on the History of Society and Culture 41. Berkeley: University of California Press, 2001.

McAllister, Karen E. "Rubber, Rights and Resistance: The Evolution of Local Struggles against a Chinese Rubber Concession in Northern Laos." *Journal of Peasant Studies* 42, no. 3–4 (July 2015): 817–37. https://doi.org/10.1080 /03066150.2015.1036418.

McCartan, Brian. "China Rubber Demand Stretches Laos." *Asia Times Online*, December 19, 2007.

McCarthy, James. *Surveying and Exploring in Siam*. London: J. Murray, 1900. http://catalog.hathitrust.org/Record/100344941.

McCoy, Alfred W. *The Politics of Heroin: CIA Complicity in the Global Drug Trade: Afghanistan, Southeast Asia, Central America, Colombia*. Chicago: Lawrence Hill Books, 2003.

MCTPC and IUCN. "Bolikhamxai Province Environmental Inventory." Vientiane: Ministry of Communication, Transport, Post and Construction, IUCN—the World Conservation Union, and the Swedish International Development Cooperation Agency, 2000.

Messerli, Peter, Andreas Heinimann, Michael Epprecht, Phonesaly Souksavath, Thiraka Chanthalanouvong, and Nicholas Minot, eds. *Socio-Economic Atlas of the Lao PDR: An Analysis Based on the 2005 Population and Housing Census*. Geographica Bernensia. Bern: Swiss National Center of Competence in Research (NCCR) North-South, University of Bern, 2008.

Miller, Tom. *China's Asian Dream: Empire Building along the New Silk Road*. London: Zed Books, 2017.

Milne, Sarah. "Under the Leopard's Skin: Land Commodification and the Dilemmas of Indigenous Communal Title in Upland Cambodia." *Asia Pacific Viewpoint* 54, no. 3 (2013): 323–39. https://doi.org/10.1111/apv.12027.

Mitchell, Timothy. *Rule of Experts: Egypt, Techno-Politics, Modernity*. Berkeley: University of California Press, 2002.

Mitchell, W. J. Thomas. *Landscape and Power*. Chicago: University of Chicago Press, 1994.

MoJ. "Legal Sector Master Plan." Vientiane: Ministry of Justice of Lao PDR, 2009.

Mongkhonvilay, S. "Agriculture and Environment under the New Economic Policy of the Lao People's Democratic Republic." In *Environment, Natural*

Resources, and the Future Development of Laos and Vietnam: Papers from
a Seminar, edited by N. Manh Hung, N. L. Jamieson, and A. T. Rambo,
27–44. Arlington, VA: Indochina Institute of George Mason University
and Environment and Policy Institute of the East-West Center, 1991.

Moore, Donald S. "The Crucible of Cultural Politics: Reworking 'Development' in Zimbabwe's Eastern Highlands." *American Ethnologist* 26, no. 3
(August 1999): 654–89. https://doi.org/10.1525/ae.1999.26.3.654.

——. *Suffering for Territory: Race, Place, and Power in Zimbabwe*. Durham,
NC: Duke University Press, 2005. http://www.h-net.org/review/hrev-aofos5
-aa.Morrow, Michael. "CIA's Spy Teams inside Red China." *San Francisco
Chronicle*, September 4, 1970.

Muldavin, Joshua. "From Rural Transformation to Global Integration:
Comparative Analyses of the Environmental Dimensions of China's Rise."
Eurasian Geography and Economics 54, no. 3 (June 2013): 259–79. https://
doi.org/10.1080/15387216.2013.849522.

National Geographic Service of Viet-Nam. "Economic Map of Indochina."
1937.

Nathan Associates. "Preparing the Northern Economic Corridor, Final Report
(vol. 1): Main Text, T.A. No. 3817—Lao." Nathan Associates Inc., CPCS
Upham Corporation, and Communication Design and Research Institute,
Lao PDR, 2003.

Neumann, Roderick P. *Imposing Wilderness: Struggles over Livelihood and
Nature Preservation in Africa*. Berkeley: University of California Press,
1998.

NLMA and FER. "Summary Report: Research Evaluation of Economic, Social,
and Ecological Implications of the Programme for Commercial Tree
Plantations: Case Study of Rubber in the South of Laos PDR." Vientiane
and Bangkok: National Land Management Authority (NLMA) and
Foundation for Ecological Recovery (FER), 2009.

NLMA and GTZ. "Findings of the State Land Concession and Lease Inventory
Project in Pilot of Vientiane Province, Phase II." Vientiane: National Land
Management Authority (NLMA) and German Technical Assistance
(GTZ), 2009.

Nyíri, Pál. "Enclaves of Improvement: Sovereignty and Developmentalism in
the Special Zones of the China-Lao Borderlands." *Comparative Studies in
Society and History* 54, no. 3 (July 2012): 533–62. https://doi.org/10.1017
/S0010417512000229.

——. "Extraterritoriality: Foreign Concessions: The Past and Future of a
Form of Shared Sovereignty." Inaugural Oration at Amsterdam's Free

University, November 19, 2009. http://www.espacestemps.net
/document7952.html.

Ó Tuathail, Gearóid. *Critical Geopolitics: The Politics of Writing Global Political Space*. Minneapolis: University of Minnesota Press, 1996.

Obein, F. "Assessment of the Environmental and Social Impacts Created by the VLRC Industrial Rubber Plantation and Proposed Environmental and Social Plans, Final Report." Vientiane: Earth Systems Lao, 2007.

Ohmae, Kenichi. *The End of the Nation State: The Rise of Regional Economies*. New York: Simon & Schuster, 1995.

Oliveira, Gustavo de L. T. "Boosters, Brokers, Bureaucrats and Businessmen: Assembling Chinese Capital with Brazilian Agribusiness." *Territory, Politics, Governance* 7, no. 1 (January 2019): 22–41. https://doi.org/10.1080 /21622671.2017.1374205.

Oliveira, Gustavo de L. T., Ben M. McKay, and Juan Liu. "Beyond Land Grabs: New Insights on Land Struggles and Global Agrarian Change." *Globalizations* 18, no. 3 (April 2021): 321–38. https://doi.org/10.1080/14747731.2020 .1843842.

Oliveira, Gustavo de L. T., Galen Murton, Alessandro Rippa, Tyler Harlan, and Yang Yang. "China's Belt and Road Initiative: Views from the Ground." *Political Geography* 82 (October 2020): 102225. https://doi.org/10.1016/j .polgeo.2020.102225.

Ong, Aihwa. "Graduated Sovereignty in South-East Asia." *Theory, Culture & Society* 17, no. 4 (2000): 55–75.

Oya, Carlos. "Methodological Reflections on 'Land Grab' Databases and the 'Land Grab' Literature 'Rush.'" *Journal of Peasant Studies* 40, no. 3 (May 2013): 503–20. https://doi.org/10.1080/03066150.2013.799465.

Padwe, Jonathan. *Disturbed Forests, Fragmented Memories: Jarai and Other Lives in the Cambodian Highlands*. Seattle: University of Washington Press, 2020.

Paprocki, Kasia. 2020. *Threatening Dystopias: The Global Politics of Climate Change Adaptation in Bangladesh*. Ithaca, NY: Cornell University Press.

Patel, Raj, and Jason W. Moore. *A History of the World in Seven Cheap Things: A Guide to Capitalism, Nature, and the Future of the Planet*. Berkeley: University of California Press, 2018.

Patterson, Orlando. *Slavery and Social Death: A Comparative Study, with a New Preface*. Cambridge, MA: Harvard University Press, 2018.

Peluso, Nancy Lee. *Rich Forests, Poor People: Resource Control and Resistance in Java*. Berkeley: University of California Press, 1994.

———. "Whose Woods Are These? Counter-Mapping Forest Territories in Kalimantan, Indonesia." *Antipode* 27, no. 4 (October 1995): 383–406. https://doi.org/10.1111/j.1467-8330.1995.tb00286.x.

Peluso, Nancy Lee, and Christian Lund. "New Frontiers of Land Control: Introduction." *Journal of Peasant Studies* 38, no. 4 (October 2011): 667–81. https://doi.org/10.1080/03066150.2011.607692.

Peluso, Nancy Lee, and Peter Vandergeest. "Genealogies of the Political Forest and Customary Rights in Indonesia, Malaysia, and Thailand." *Journal of Asian Studies* 60, no. 3 (2001): 761–812.

———. "Political Ecologies of War and Forests: Counterinsurgencies and the Making of National Natures." *Annals of the Association of American Geographers* 101, no. 3 (April 2011): 587–608. https://doi.org/10.1080/00045608.2011.560064.

Perelman, Michael. "Primitive Accumulation from Feudalism to Neoliberalism." *Capitalism Nature Socialism* 18, no. 2 (June 2007): 44–61. https://doi.org/10.1080/10455750701366410.

Persson, R. "Forestry in Laos." Vientiane: Self-published, 1983.

Phillips, Rufus. *Why Vietnam Matters: An Eyewitness Account of Lessons Not Learned.* Annapolis, MD: Naval Institute Press, 2008.

Pholsena, Vatthana. *Post-War Laos: The Politics of Culture, History, and Identity.* Ithaca, NY: Cornell University Press, 2006.

Pickles, John. *A History of Spaces: Cartographic Reason, Mapping and the Geo-Coded World.* New York: Routledge, 2004.

Polanyi, Karl. *The Great Transformation: The Political and Economic Origins of Our Time.* Boston: Beacon, 1944.

"Poor Accounting Hollows Out Timber Revenues." *Vientiane Times*, July 8, 2015.

Posluschny-Treuner, Myra. "Understanding Foreign Large-Scale Agricultural Investments in Ethiopia." PhD diss., University of Basel, 2017.

Prados, John. *Vietnam: The History of an Unwinnable War, 1945–1975.* Lawrence: University Press of Kansas, 2009.

Ramo, Joshua Cooper. "The Beijing Consensus." London: Foreign Policy Centre, 2004. http://fpc.org.uk/fsblob/244.pdf.

Reguly, E. "The Farms Race." *Globe and Mail*, January 30, 2009.

Rice, Andrew. "Is There Such a Thing as Agro-Imperialism?" *New York Times*, November 16, 2009. http://www.nytimes.com/2009/11/22/magazine/22land-t.html.

Rigg, Jonathan. *Living with Transition in Laos: Market Integration in Southeast Asia.* New York: Routledge, 2005.

Rist, Gilbert. *The History of Development: From Western Origins to Global Faith*. London: Zed Books, 2008.

Robbins, Christopher. *Air America*. New York: Putnam, 1979.

Robinson, Cedric J. *Black Marxism*. Rev. and updated 3rd ed. *The Making of the Black Radical Tradition*. Chapel Hill: University of North Carolina Press, 1983.

Rose, Carol M. *Property and Persuasion: Essays on the History, Theory, and Rhetoric of Ownership*. Boulder, CO: Westview, 1994.

Rose, Nikolas S. *Powers of Freedom: Reframing Political Thought*. Cambridge: Cambridge University Press, 1999.

Rostow, W. W. "The Stages of Economic Growth." *Economic History Review* 12, no. 1 (1959): 1–16. https://doi.org/10.2307/2591077.

Sachs, Wolfgang. *The Development Dictionary: A Guide to Knowledge as Power*. London: Zed Books, 1992.

Sassen, Saskia. "Land Grabs Today: Feeding the Disassembling of National Territory." *Globalizations* 10, no. 1 (February 2013): 25–46. https://doi.org /10.1080/14747731.2013.760927.

———. "A Savage Sorting of Winners and Losers: Contemporary Versions of Primitive Accumulation." *Globalizations* 7, no. 1–2 (June 2010): 23–50. https://doi.org/10.1080/14747731003593091.

Schipani, Steven. "Ecotourism as an Alternative to Upland Rubber: Cultivation in the Nam Ha National Protected Area, Luang Namtha." *Juth Pakai: New Thought* 8 (2007): 5–17.

Schliesinger, Joachim. *Ethnic Groups of Laos*. Bangkok: White Lotus, 2003.

Schlimmer, Sina. "Negotiating Land Policies to Territorialise State Power." *Revue internationale des études du développement* 238, no. 2 (May 2019): 33–59.

Schönweger, Oliver, Andreas Heinimann, Michael Epprecht, Juliet Lu, and Palikone Thalongsengchanh. *Concessions and Leases in the Lao PDR: Taking Stock of Land Investments*. Centre for Development and Environment (CDE), University of Bern. Bern: Geographica Bernensia, 2012.

Schuettler, Darren. "Laos Faces Thorny Land Issues in Asia's Orchard." Reuters, April 10, 2008.

Scoones, Ian, Ruth Hall, Saturnino M. Borras Jr., Ben White, and Wendy Wolford. "The Politics of Evidence: Methodologies for Understanding the Global Land Rush." *Journal of Peasant Studies* 40, no. 3 (May 2013): 469–83. https://doi.org/10.1080/03066150.2013.801341.

Scott, David. "Colonial Governmentality." *Social Text* 43 (1995): 191–220. https://doi.org/10.2307/466631.

Scott, James C. *The Art of Not Being Governed: An Anarchist History of Upland Southeast Asia.* Yale Agrarian Studies Series. New Haven, CT: Yale University Press, 2009.

———. *Domination and the Arts of Resistance: Hidden Transcripts.* New Haven, CT: Yale University Press, 1990.

———. *Seeing like a State: How Certain Schemes to Improve the Human Condition Have Failed.* New Haven, CT: Yale University Press, 1998.

Scurrah, Natalia, and Philip Hirsch. "Land and Capital across Borders: A Regional Geopolitics." In *Turning Land into Capital: Development and Dispossession in the Mekong Region,* edited by Philip Hirsch, Kevin Woods, Natalia Scurrah, and Michael B. Dwyer, 3–28. Seattle: University of Washington Press, 2022.

SEI and ADB. "Strategic Environmental Framework for the Greater Mekong Subregion: Integrating Development and Environment in the Transport and Water Resource Sectors (vol. 4): Case Study Reports." Stockholm and Manila: Stockholm Environmental Institute and Asian Development Bank, 2002.

Sen, Gita, and Caren Grown. *Development, Crises and Alternative Visions: Third World Women's Perspectives.* London: Earthscan, 1988.

Shackley, Theodore, and Richard A Finney. *Spymaster: My Life in the CIA.* Dulles, VA: Brassey's, 2005.

Shattuck, Annie. "Risky Subjects: Embodiment and Partial Knowledges in the Safe Use of Pesticide." *Geoforum* 123 (July 2021): 153–61. https://doi.org/10.1016/j.geoforum.2019.04.029.

Shi, Weiyi. "Rubber Boom in Luang Namtha: A Transnational Perspective." Vientiane: German Technical Cooperation (GTZ), 2008.

———. "Rubber Boom in Luang Namtha: Seven Years Later." Field notes, April 27, 2015. http://laofab.org/document/view/2608.

———. "Summary and Analysis: Plan for Industrial Economic Development and Cooperation in Northern Lao PDR (The Northern Plan)." Vientiane: German Technical Cooperation (GTZ), 2009.

Shoemaker, Bruce, and William Robichaud. *Dead in the Water: Global Lessons from the World Bank's Model Hydropower Project in Laos.* Madison: University of Wisconsin Press, 2018.

Sikor, Thomas. "Tree Plantations, Politics of Possession and the Absence of Land Grabs in Vietnam." *Journal of Peasant Studies* 39, no. 3–4 (July 2012): 1077–1101. https://doi.org/10.1080/03066150.2012.674943.

Sikor, Thomas, and Christian Lund. "Access and Property: A Question of Power and Authority." *Development and Change* 40, no. 1 (January 2009): 1–22. https://doi.org/10.1111/j.1467-7660.2009.01503.x.

Singh, Sarinda. *Natural Potency and Political Power: Forests and State Authority in Contemporary Laos.* Honolulu: University of Hawai'i Press, 2012.

Siphavanh, Phonesack, Vongxay Sivilay, Khamnouan Souvannasouk, Vongpheth Oudomlith, Singthong Phuaphom, and Bounkhong Vannasith. "Main Causes of High Repetition Rate in Namfa and Donmai Villages, Viengphoukha District, Luangnamtha Province." Translated by Dr. Khamphay Sisavanh. Vientiane: Lao Ministry of Education, n.d. http://www.moe .gov.la/benc/data/downloads/Publication/Report_Viengfukha.Eng.pdf.

Sneddon, Chris, and Coleen Fox. "Rethinking Transboundary Waters: A Critical Hydropolitics of the Mekong Basin." *Political Geography* 25, no. 2 (February 2006): 181–202. https://doi.org/10.1016/j.polgeo.2005.11.002.

Stern, Laurence. "Deeper CIA Role in Laos Revealed." *Washington Post,* August 8, 1971.

Stoler, Ann Laura, ed. *Imperial Debris: On Ruins and Ruination.* Durham, NC: Duke University Press, 2013.

Stuart-Fox, Martin. "The French in Laos, 1887–1945." *Modern Asian Studies* 29, no. 1 (February 1995): 111–39. https://doi.org/10.1017/S0026749 X00012646.

———. *A History of Laos.* Cambridge: Cambridge University Press, 1997.

———. "Laos: The Chinese Connection." *Southeast Asian Affairs* (2009): 141–69.

———. "On the Writing of Lao History: Continuities and Discontinuities." In *Breaking New Ground in Lao History: Essays on the Seventh to Twentieth Centuries,* edited by Mayoury Ngaosrivathana and Kennon Breazeale, 1–24. Chiang Mai, Thailand: Silkworm Books, 2002.

———. "The Political Culture of Corruption in the Lao PDR." *Asian Studies Review* 30, no. 1 (March 2006): 59–75. https://doi.org/10.1080 /10357820500537054.

Sturgeon, Janet C. "Governing Minorities and Development in Xishuangbanna, China: Akha and Dai Rubber Farmers as Entrepreneurs." *Geoforum,* Themed Issue: Mobilizing Policy, 41, no. 2 (March 2010): 318–28. https://doi.org/10.1016/j.geoforum.2009.10.010.

Sturgeon, Janet C., Nicholas K. Menzies, Yayoi Fujita Lagerqvist, David Thomas, Benchaphun Ekasingh, Louis Lebel, Khamla Phanvilay, and Sithong Thongmanivong. "Enclosing Ethnic Minorities and Forests in the Golden Economic Quadrangle." *Development and Change* 44, no. 1 (January 2013): 53–79. https://doi.org/10.1111/dech.12006.

Su, Xiaobo. "Nontraditional Security and China's Transnational Narcotics Control in Northern Laos and Myanmar." *Political Geography* 48 (September 2015): 72–82. https://doi.org/10.1016/j.polgeo.2015.06.005.

———. "Rescaling the Chinese State and Regionalization in the Great Mekong Subregion." *Review of International Political Economy* 19, no. 3 (August 2012): 501–27. https://doi.org/10.1080/09692290.2011.561129.

Suhardiman, Diana, Mark Giordano, Oulavanh Keovilignavong, and Touleelor Sotoukee. "Revealing the Hidden Effects of Land Grabbing through Better Understanding of Farmers' Strategies in Dealing with Land Loss." *Land Use Policy* 49 (December 2015): 195–202. https://doi.org/10.1016/j.landusepol.2015.08.014.

Sutton, Keith. "Agribusiness on a Grand Scale: Felda's Sahabat Complex in East Malaysia." *Singapore Journal of Tropical Geography* 22, no. 1 (2001): 90–105. https://doi.org/10.1111/1467-9493.00095.

Than, Mya, and Loong-Hoe Tan, eds. *Laos' Dilemmas and Options: The Challenge of Economic Transition in the 1990s.* New York, Singapore: St. Martin's, Institute of Southeast Asian Studies, 1997.

Thongmanivong, Sithong, Kaisone Phengsopha, Houngphet Chanthavong, Michael Dwyer, and Robert Oberndorf. "Concession or Cooperation? Impacts of Recent Rubber Investment on Land Tenure and Livelihoods: A Case Study from Oudomxai Province, Lao PDR." LaoFAB Document Repository, 2009. http://laofab.org/document/view/477.

Thongphachanh and Birgegard, L. "Muong Paksane Regional Development Study (vol. 1): Main Characteristics of Muong Paksane, Proposed Long-Term Development Strategy, Proposals for Action." Vientiane: Lao-Swedish Forestry Project, 1982.

Trankell, Ing-Britt. *On the Road in Laos: An Anthropological Study of Road Construction and Rural Communities.* Bangkok: White Lotus, Uppsala University, 1999.

Trinquier, Roger. *Modern Warfare: A French View of Counterinsurgency.* New York: Praeger, 1964.

Tsing, Anna Lowenhaupt. *Friction: An Ethnography of Global Connection.* Princeton, NJ: Princeton University Press, 2005.

———. *In the Realm of the Diamond Queen: Marginality in an Out-of-the-Way Place.* Princeton, NJ: Princeton University Press, 1993.

Tuffin, William. "Letter Re: Shawn Crispin's 'The Limits of Chinese Expansionism.'" *Asia Times Online*, January 3, 2011.

Turnbull, David. *Maps Are Territories: Science Is an Atlas.* Chicago: University of Chicago Press, 1989.

Turner, Sarah, ed. *Red Stamps and Gold Stars: Fieldwork Dilemmas in Upland Socialist Asia.* Copenhagen: NIAS, 2014.

UNDP. "National Human Development Report Lao PDR 2001: Advancing Rural Development." Vientiane: United Nations Development Program, 2001.

UNODC. "Laos Opium Survey." Vientiane: United Nations Office on Drugs and Crime and Lao National Commission for Drug Control and Supervision, 2005.

———. "Southeast Asia Opium Survey: Lao PDR, Myanmar." United Nations Office on Drugs and Crime, Myanmar Central Committee for Drug Abuse Control, and Lao National Commission for Drug Control and Supervision, 2013.

US Army. "Army Service Forces Manual, Civil Affairs Handbook, French Indochina Section 6: Natural Resources." 1944.

USAID. "Termination Report, Laos." Washington, DC: United States Agency for International Development, 1976.

Vandergeest, Peter. "Land to Some Tillers: Development-Induced Displacement in Laos." *International Social Science Journal* 55, no. 175 (2003a): 47–56.

———. "Racialization and Citizenship in Thai Forest Politics." *Society & Natural Resources* 16, no. 1 (2003b): 19–37.

Vandergeest, Peter, and Nancy Lee Peluso. "Territorialization and State Power in Thailand." *Theory and Society* 24, no. 3 (1995): 385–426.

"Vietnam's Rebellious 'Colony.'" *Far Eastern Economic Review*, August 18, 1978.

Voladet, Saykham. "Sustainable Development in the Plantation Industry in Laos: An Examination of the Role of the Ministry of Planning and Investment." Winnipeg: International Institute for Sustainable Development (IISD), 2009.

Vongkhamor, Simone, Khanchana Phimmasen, Silapeth Bounao, Bounthavy Xayxomphou, and Erik Petterson. "Key Issues in Smallholder Rubber Planting in Oudomxai and Luang Prabang Provinces, Lao PDR." Vientiane: National Agriculture and Forestry Research Institute, Upland Research Development Program, 2007.

Vongvisouk, Thoumthone, and Michael Dwyer. "After the Boom: Responding to Falling Rubber Prices in Northern Laos." Vientiane: Mekong Region Land Governance Project (MRLG), 2017.

Wakin, Eric. *Anthropology Goes to War: Professional Ethics and Counterinsurgency in Thailand*. Madison: University of Wisconsin, Center for Southeast Asian Studies, 1992.

Walker, Andrew. *The Legend of the Golden Boat: Regulation, Trade and Traders in the Borderlands of Laos, Thailand, China and Burma*. Honolulu: University of Hawai'i Press, 1999.

———. "Regional Trade in Northwestern Laos: An Initial Assessment of the Economic Quadrangle." In *Where China Meets Southeast Asia: Social and*

Cultural Change in the Border Regions, edited by Grant Evans, Christopher Hutton, and Kuah Khun Eng, 122–44. Singapore: Institute of Southeast Asian Studies, 2000. https://doi.org/10.1007/978-1-137-11123-4_7.

Walker, Kathy Le Mons. "From Covert to Overt: Everyday Peasant Politics in China and the Implications for Transnational Agrarian Movements." *Journal of Agrarian Change* 8, no. 2–3 (April 2008): 462–88. https://doi.org/10.1111/j.1471-0366.2008.00177.x.

Warner, Roger. *Shooting at the Moon: The Story of America's Clandestine War in Laos*. South Royalton, VT: Steerforth, 1996.

Watts, Michael. "Resource Curse? Governmentality, Oil and Power in the Niger Delta, Nigeria." *Geopolitics* 9, no. 1 (March 2004): 50–80. https://doi.org/10.1080/14650040412331307832.

Wellmann, Dominik. "Discussion Paper on the Legal Framework of State Land Leases and Concessions in the Lao PDR." Vientiane: Integrated Rural Development in Poverty Regions of Laos (IRDP) under the Northern Upland Development Programme (NUDP), 2012.

West, Paige. "We Are Here to Build Your Capacity." In *Dispossession and the Environment: Rhetoric and Inequality in Papua New Guinea*, 63–86. New York: Columbia University Press, 2016.

White, Ben, Saturnino M. Borras, Ruth Hall, Ian Scoones, and Wendy Wolford. "The New Enclosures: Critical Perspectives on Corporate Land Deals." *Journal of Peasant Studies* 39, no. 3–4 (July 2012): 619–47. https://doi.org/10.1080/03066150.2012.691879.

Whitington, Jerome. *Anthropogenic Rivers: The Production of Uncertainty in Lao Hydropower*. Ithaca, NY: Cornell University Press, 2019.

———. "Beleaguered Village Leader." In *Figures of Southeast Asian Modernity*, edited by Joshua Barker, Erik Harms, and Johan Lindquist, 104–6, 2014.

Winichakul, Thongchai. "The Others Within: Travel and Ethno-Spatial Differentiation of Siamese Subjects, 1885–1910." In *Civility and Savagery: Social Identity in Tai States*, edited by Andrew Turton, 38–62. Richmond, Surrey, UK: Curzon, 2000.

———. *Siam Mapped: A History of the Geo-Body of a Nation*. Honolulu: University of Hawai'i Press, 1994.

Wolford, Wendy, Saturnino M. Borras, Ruth Hall, Ian Scoones, and Ben White. "Governing Global Land Deals: The Role of the State in the Rush for Land." *Development and Change* 44, no. 2 (March 2013): 189–210. https://doi.org/10.1111/dech.12017.

Wong, Eleanor. "In the Space between Words and Meaning: Reflections from Translating Lao Laws to English." *Singapore Journal of Legal Studies* (2006): 439–58.

Wood, Denis, John Fels, and John Krygier. *Rethinking the Power of Maps*. New York: Guilford, 2010.

Woods, Kevin. "Ceasefire Capitalism: Military–Private Partnerships, Resource Concessions and Military–State Building in the Burma–China Borderlands." *Journal of Peasant Studies* 38, no. 4 (October 2011): 747–70. https://doi.org/10.1080/03066150.2011.607699.

Work, Courtney. "'There Was So Much': Violence, Sovereignty, and States of Extraction in Cambodia." *Journal of Religion and Violence* 6, no. 1 (May 2018): 52–72. https://doi.org/10.5840/jrv201851451.

World Bank. "Operation Manual on OP 4.12—Involuntary Resettlement." 2001. https://policies.worldbank.org/sites/ppf3/PPFDocuments /090224b0822 f89db.pdf.

———. "Rising Global Interest in Farmland: Can It Yield Sustainable and Equitable Benefits?" Washington, DC: World Bank, 2010.

Xu, Jianchu. "The Political, Social, and Ecological Transformation of a Landscape." *Mountain Research and Development* 26, no. 3 (August 2006): 254–62. https://doi.org/10.1659/0276-4741(2006)26[254:TPSAET]2.0.CO;2.

Young, Gordon. "The Hill Tribes of Northern Thailand: A Socio-Ethnological Report." Bangkok: Siam Society, 1966.

Zhai, Qiang. "1959: Preventing Peaceful Evolution." *China Heritage Quarterly* 18 (2009). http://www.chinaheritagequarterly.org/features.php?searchterm =018_1959preventingpeace.inc&issue=018.

Zoomers, Annelies. "Globalisation and the Foreignisation of Space: Seven Processes Driving the Current Global Land Grab." *Journal of Peasant Studies* 37, no. 2 (April 2010): 429–47. https://doi.org/10.1080 /03066151003595325.

INDEX

Page numbers in *italic* refer to illustrations.

business models of rubber plantations (*continued*) contract farming, 8, 43, 45–46, 103–5, 119–20; "4+1" (quasi-concession) variant, 22, *22–23*, 45, *46*, 49, 101, 103, 119, 124, 127, 155; "4+1" areas (Bolisat Ltd.), 34, 45, 105–7, 109, 118–23, 141–42, 145, 146; independent smallholding, 8, 26, 106, 169n93; slippage between "3+2" policy and "4+1" variant, 45, 49, 103, 105; "3+2" (contract farming) policy, 21–24, 26, 43–45, 49, 101, 103, 118–20, 124, 127; "3+2" areas (Bolisat Ltd.), 105, 106, 110–11, 120, 128, 141–42. *See also* managed enclosure

Cambodia, 24, 28, 29, 30, 76, 152
cartography. *See* maps
Central Intelligence Agency (CIA), 17, 50, 53, 56–59, 63, 67–71; Nam Nyu, 52; Phillips, 65, 70; STOL airplanes and sites, 57, 58, 63, 112; US congressional investigation, 68
Chao La, 61, 62
Chao Mai, 61
China, 3, 4, 5, 16; in Africa, 7, 15; "Beijing Consensus," 16, 155; Belt and Road Initiative (BRI), 15, 24, 27, 29, 30, 150; Bo Yibo, 126–27; Burma relations, 58–59; Cold War, 24–25; Deng Xiaoping, 132; development assistance, 16, 23–24, 27, *148*; "Going Out" policy, 6, 26, 33, 48; Lahu, 62; Mao Zedong, 126–27; Nyíri, 6–7; opium replacement policy, 47–48, *148*; People's Liberation Army, 59, 62; roadbuilding, 66–68; Soviet relations, 75; US relations, 69; Vietnam relations, 75–76. *See also* Yunnan
Chinese Nationalist Party. *See* Kuomintang (KMT)
Chinese rubber projects, 1, 5, 8, 13, 15, 16, 20–49, 102–29, 150–51. *See also* Bolisat Ltd. (pseudonym); Sino-Lao Rubber Company; Yunnan Rubber Company
CIA. *See* Central Intelligence Agency (CIA)
Cohen, Paul, 160n22
Cold War, 11, 13, 26, 29–30, 49–73, 100–101, 115, 127, 151; China, 24–25
Committee for Land Management and Land-Forest Allocation, 137
concessions, xi, 8, 15, 136, 152; inventorying, 48, 145, 151, 152; logging, 128–29, 131; Lao national moratorium, 43, 143; taxation, 146. *See also* business models of rubber plantations; natural resource rents
contract farming, 8, 21, 33, 45, 105, 116, 120. *See also* business models of rubber plantations
corruption, 5, 55, 131, 156, 160n22
corvée labor, 29, 61
counterinsurgency, 56, 64, 65, 72, 73, 77, 87, 89, 93
coups, 51, 55, 56

dams, 16, 138
deforestation, 129, 136
Deitchman, Seymour, 72
denationalization, 50–73, 77, 101
De Soto, Hernando: *Mystery of Capital*, 157
development assistance, 2–9, 37–38, 153–57; German, 187n26, 188–89n45; neoliberalism and,

3, 6, 30, 48, 132, 153–54; Swedish, 17–18, 79–82, 84. *See also* Asian Development Bank (ADB); China; Lao-Swedish Forestry Project (LSFP); state development banks (Lao); US Agency for International Development (USAID); World Bank

Diouf, Jacques, 3–4, 7, 9

disappeared people, 125–26

displacement and resettlement, 90, 91–92, 99, 109, 111–16, 118–20, 123; map, *110*

Dommen, Arthur, 70, 174n97

Dulles, John Foster, 126

economic corridors, 30, *31*, 48. *See also* Northern Economic Corridor (NEC)

ecotourism, 125

Edelman, Marc, 152

Eisenhower, Dwight, 55, 56, 126

Elden, Stuart, 127

enclosure. *See* managed enclosure

ethnic groups. *See* indigenous peoples

eucalyptus, 27, 39

Evans, Grant, 70, 72, 178n45

Evrard, Olivier, 111, 112

exports: rubber, 32, 117; timber, 79, 133–34

Fall, Bernard, 70, 174n97

farming. *See* agriculture

Ferguson, James, 7, 154

First Indochina War, 54, 55, 62, 71

focal sites (focal development sites), 77, 91, *92*, 93–95, 96, 114, 116, 119; New Economic Mechanism, 132. *See also* Khet Nam Fa

Food and Agriculture Organization (FAO). *See* UN Food and Agriculture Organization (FAO)

food security, 2, 3, 82, 84, 114, 124

forest regeneration. *See* reforestation

forestry, 76, 78–85, 91, 92, 94–95, 99–100, 108, 132; colonial practices, 77, 78–79; maps, *81*, 139. *See also* Land and Forest Allocation (LFA) program; logging; Ministry of Agriculture and Forestry; sawmills

formal geography, ix, 1, 17, 129, 132, 134–47, *140*, 153, 157. *See also* maps; property formalization; territorialization; zoning

Foucault, Michel, 95, 102; governmentality, 84, 95; micropolitics, 102; *Security, Territory, Population*, 84–85

French colonialism, 24, 25, 28–29, 30, 53, 54, 56; Blaufarb and, 65; forestry, 78–79; *montagnard* program, 61–62; opium, 61; roads, 68; "unblocking," 29, 132; William Young and, 59

French war with Indochina. *See* First Indochina War

Garnier, Francis, 28, 29

Geneva Accords (1954), 171n23

Geneva Accords on Laos (1962), 56, 58, 59

geography, formal. *See* formal geography

global land rush, vii–viii, 2–10, 14, 48–49, 153–54. *See also* land grabbing

Golden Quadrangle, 27, 30

Golden Triangle, 21, 59, 146

Goudineau, Yves, 111, 112

GRAIN (organization), 3, 4, 14

Greater Mekong Subregion (GMS), 30, 32; map, *31*

Long Cheng, 58, 63, 64, 65, 173n63
LSFP. *See* Lao-Swedish Forestry Project (LSFP)
Luang Namtha (city and province), 7–8, 25, 32, 33, 43, 44, 45, 57; maps, *46*, *110*; provincial museum, 98–99, 180n1; roads and roadbuilding, 67, 68, 69; rubber, 150
Luang Prabang (city and province), 28, 29, 59, 63, 70, 103; map, *46*

Malaya, 24, 54
Malaysia, 48
managed enclosure, 6–9, 12–13, 33, 45, 77, 89, 90, 105–7, 116–18, 153, 157; LFA, 141; partial, 12, 120, 121; socially uneven distribution of enclosure, 9, 13, 107–25, 127, 155
Mao Zedong, 126–27
maps, 17, 26, 41, 60, 108, 111, 112–13, 129–32; Bolisat Ltd., 1–2, *104*, 129, 138–39, *140*; cartographic genealogy, 138–39, *140*; economic corridors, *31*; forestry, *81*, 139; French, 99; large Chinese rubber plantations, *46*; LFA zoning, 107, 108, 113, 129, *130*, 137–41, *140*, 143; Luang Namtha provincial museum, 98, *99*, 119; state forest enterprises, 80, *81*; STOL sites, 63, 112; "then make land maps," 137, 153; US, 112; Vieng Phouka, *130*. *See also* formal geography; property formalization
maquis (militias), 56, 57, 59, 61, 64, 75, 76, 85, 113
Marx, Karl, 12, 102, 127, 181n10; primitive accumulation, 7, 9, 12, 84
McCoy, Alfred, 61–62, 63
Mekong River, 28, 29, 69
micro-geopolitics, 11–13, 98–127

Mien people. *See* Iu Mien (Yao) people
migration, 77, 93. *See also* displacement and resettlement; refugees
Ministry of Agriculture and Forestry, 34–37, 134, 145
Mon-Khmer groups, 61, 62
Mountainous Areas Development Company (BPKP), 133, 134
muang (region/territory), 10, 116
Muang Houng, 18, 80, 91, 92–95, 119; map, *81*
Muser people. *See* Lahu (Muser; Kui) people
Myanmar, 47, 124; Northern Economic Corridor, 27–28, 30. *See also* Burma
The Mystery of Capital (De Soto), 157

Na Le (district), 102, 109, 111, 112, 114; map, *110*
Nam Ha National Protected Area, 109
Nam Nyu, 17, 52–53, 58–59, 61–67, 69, 113, 173n63; map, *110*; Nam Nyu special zone, 52, 107, 115
Namtha, Battle of. *See* Battle of Namtha
Nathan Associates, 38–39
National Agriculture and Forestry Research Institute, 43
National Forestry Conference, May 1989, 134–35
National Land Management Authority (NLMA), 16–17, 110, 144
national security. *See* security (military and economic)
natural resource rents, 14, 144–46, 153, 155–57. *See also* concessions
NEC. *See* Northern Economic Corridor (NEC)
Neutralists, 51, 55, 58, 64, 66, 68. *See also* non-alignment

Sino-Lao Rubber Company; Yunnan
Rubber Company

sampathan (concession), 121, 136

sawmills, 80, 128–29, 133

Saysomboun special zone, 52, 85;
map, *81*

Schlesinger, Arthur, Jr., 70

Scott, James, 10, 52

"secret war." *See* United States:
"unconventional"/secret war in
Laos

security (military and economic),
17–18, 74–97; Foucault on, 84;
insurgency, 75, 85, 90, 91, 100, 108,
113; uplands and, 52, 76. *See also*
counterinsurgency; food security

SFEs. *See* state forest enterprises
(SFEs)

Shan people, 58, 62

Shan state, 30, 62, 63

sharecropping of rubber. *See* business
models of rubber plantations

shifting cultivation, 52, 81, 82, 83, 89,
118; replacement of, 129. *See also*
rice cultivation: dryland shifting
("upland")

Siam, 28, 29

Sing (district), 28, 98, 99, 114–15

Sino-Lao Rubber Company, 32, 35–37,
42, 45, 103, *104*, 105, 114, 128;
collapse, 129

"Sixteen Musketeers," 63

Smith, Adam, 12

Sombath Somphone, 125

Sompawn Khantisouk, 125–26

songserm ("promotion"), 2, 43, 105, 121,
168n88

Soto, Hernando de. *See* De Soto,
Hernando

Souvanna Phouma, 69

sovereignty, 6, 127, 150, 151, 153

Soviet Union, 54, 55, 67, 75, 80, 126,
132

state development banks (Lao),
26, 27

state forest enterprises (SFEs), 80–86,
81, 88–95, 133, 135

state-owned enterprises, 89, 133

STOL (short takeoff and landing)
airplanes and airstrips, 57, 58, 63, 85,
112, 113; map, *81*

Stoler, Ann, 152

Stuart-Fox, Martin, 53, 78–79, 147

surveying of land, 41, 103, 137

Sweden, 84

Swedish-Lao Forestry Project. *See*
Lao-Swedish Forestry Project
(LSFP)

taxation, 6, 27, 42, 61, 141, 144–46,
183n55; land tax, 39, 42, 117, 137.
See also property formalization

territorialization, 53, 123, 131

territorial sovereignty. *See*
sovereignty

Thailand, 30, 69, 75, 76; Battle of
Namtha and, 58; domestic logging
ban, 133; French colonial era, 28,
30; KMT, 58, 71; Lahu, 62; map,
31; Northern Economic Corridor,
27–28, 30, 32, 59, 67, 68; Paru, 56–57,
63; rubber, 16, 24; state enterprises,
48; United States and, 54, 56–57, 58,
62, 63, 71; Xayaboury war, 75. *See
also* Siam

Thongphachanh, 82–95

timber cutting. *See* logging

Touby Li Fung, 61

Trankell, Ing-Britt, 90–91, 95

CULTURE, PLACE, AND NATURE
Studies in Anthropology and Environment

Upland Geopolitics: Postwar Laos and the Global Land Rush, by Michael B. Dwyer

Turning Land into Capital: Development and Dispossession in the Mekong Region, edited by Philip Hirsch, Kevin Woods, Natalia Scurrah, and Michael B. Dwyer

Spawning Modern Fish: Transnational Comparison in the Making of Japanese Salmon, by Heather Anne Swanson

Misreading the Bengal Delta: Climate Change, Development, and Livelihoods in Coastal Bangladesh, by Camelia Dewan

Ordering the Myriad Things: From Traditional Knowledge to Scientific Botany in China, by Nicholas K. Menzies

Timber and Forestry in Qing China: Sustaining the Market, by Meng Zhang

Consuming Ivory: Mercantile Legacies of East Africa and New England, by Alexandra C. Kelly

Mapping Water in Dominica: Enslavement and Environment under Colonialism, by Mark W. Hauser

Mountains of Blame: Climate and Culpability in the Philippine Uplands, by Will Smith

Sacred Cows and Chicken Manchurian: The Everyday Politics of Eating Meat in India, by James Staples

Gardens of Gold: Place-Making in Papua New Guinea, by Jamon Alex Halvaksz

Shifting Livelihoods: Gold Mining and Subsistence in the Chocó, Colombia, by Daniel Tubb

Disturbed Forests, Fragmented Memories: Jarai and Other Lives in the Cambodian Highlands, by Jonathan Padwe

The Snow Leopard and the Goat: Politics of Conservation in the Western Himalayas, by Shafqat Hussain

Roses from Kenya: Labor, Environment, and the Global Trade in Cut Flowers, by Megan A. Styles

Working with the Ancestors: Mana and Place in the Marquesas Islands, by Emily C. Donaldson

Living with Oil and Coal: Resource Politics and Militarization in Northeast India, by Dolly Kikon

Caring for Glaciers: Land, Animals, and Humanity in the Himalayas, by Karine Gagné

Organic Sovereignties: Struggles over Farming in an Age of Free Trade, by Guntra A. Aistara

The Nature of Whiteness: Race, Animals, and Nation in Zimbabwe, by Yuka Suzuki

Forests Are Gold: Trees, People, and Environmental Rule in Vietnam, by Pamela D. McElwee

Conjuring Property: Speculation and Environmental Futures in the Brazilian Amazon, by Jeremy M. Campbell

Andean Waterways: Resource Politics in Highland Peru, by Mattias Borg Rasmussen

Puer Tea: Ancient Caravans and Urban Chic, by Jinghong Zhang

Enclosed: Conservation, Cattle, and Commerce among the Q'eqchi' Maya Lowlanders, by Liza Grandia

Forests of Identity: Society, Ethnicity, and Stereotypes in the Congo River Basin, by Stephanie Rupp

Tahiti Beyond the Postcard: Power, Place, and Everyday Life, by Miriam Kahn

Wild Sardinia: Indigeneity and the Global Dreamtimes of Environmentalism, by Tracey Heatherington

Nature Protests: The End of Ecology in Slovakia, by Edward Snajdr

Forest Guardians, Forest Destroyers: The Politics of Environmental

Knowledge in Northern Thailand, by Tim Forsyth and Andrew Walker

Being and Place among the Tlingit, by Thomas F. Thornton

Tropics and the Traveling Gaze: India, Landscape, and Science, 1800–1856, by David Arnold

Ecological Nationalisms: Nature, Livelihood, and Identities in South Asia, edited by Gunnel Cederlöf and K. Sivaramakrishnan

From Enslavement to Environmentalism: Politics on a Southern African Frontier, by David McDermott Hughes

Border Landscapes: The Politics of Akha Land Use in China and Thailand, by Janet C. Sturgeon

Property and Politics in Sabah, Malaysia: Native Struggles over Land Rights, by Amity A. Doolittle

The Earth's Blanket: Traditional Teachings for Sustainable Living, by Nancy Turner

The Kuhls of Kangra: Community-Managed Irrigation in the Western Himalaya, by Mark Baker

CPSIA information can be obtained
at www.ICGtesting.com
Printed in the USA
BVHW040638251022
650116BV00024B/45